# Tell Me Africa

AN APPROACH TO
AFRICAN LITERATURE

Le XXe siècle restera celui de la découverte de la Civilisation négro-africaine.—*Léopold Sédar Senghor*

Autobiography is the highest and most instructive form in which the understanding of life confronts us. Here is the outward, phenomenal course of a life which forms the basis for understanding what has produced it within a certain environment. The man who understands it is the same who created it. — *Wilhelm Dilthey*

After all, what makes any event important, unless by its observation we become better and wiser, and learn "to do justly, to love mercy, and to walk humbly before God"? To those who are possessed of this spirit there is scarcely any book of incident so trifling that does not afford some profit, while to others the experience of ages seems of no use; and even to pour out to them the treasures of wisdom is throwing the jewels of instruction away.—*Olaudah Equiano*

The white man . . . may teach me how to make a shirt or to read and write, but my forebears and I could teach him a thing or two if only he would listen and allow himself time to feel. Africa is no more for the white man who comes to teach and to control her human and material forces and not to learn.— *Ezekiel Mphahlele*

BY JAMES OLNEY

# Tell Me Africa

*An Approach to African Literature*

PRINCETON UNIVERSITY
PRESS

LCC: 72-1211
ISBN: 0-691-06254-4 (clothbound edition)
ISBN: 0-691-01310-1 (paperback edition)

Library of Congress Cataloging in Publication data will
be found on the last printed page of this book

Publication of this book has been aided by the Andrew W.
Mellon Publication Fund of Princeton University Press

This book has been composed in Linotype Caledonia

Printed in the United States of America
by Princeton University Press, Princeton, New Jersey

*For Judith,*

WHO  SHARED  IT  ALL,
WITH  LOVE

# Preface

I DO NOT PRETEND to speak in this book as an authority on Africa: I am not African; neither am I what is called an "Africanist" or an "African Studies" expert. I consider this latter fact, however, rather a claim to virtue than a confession of weakness. My "approach to African literature" is addressed primarily to a non-African and a non-specialist audience and while it presumes, on the part of the reader, an interest in things African and especially in African literature—an interest, that is to say, both in the quality of life in Africa and in the literature that grows out of that life—it does not require any specialized knowledge and it certainly expects no expertise in the technical jargon of Africanists. Autobiography, which is the "approach to African literature" proposed by this book, and analyzed in the first two chapters, is, as I argue below, a non-specialist literature; that is what makes it of unique and inestimable value as an access to a culture and to writing undoubtedly different from our own. If African thought and African literature were so inaccessible or so obscure that only the initiate could claim a right to speak and only an inner circle could hope to understand the cryptic words spoken, then Africa would be unlike any known civilization and, being so private, would—to put it bluntly—not be worth the effort of understanding. Of course, however, it is nothing like so private an affair as that. On the other hand, African literature is unquestionably different from the literature of the Western world, primarily because the mode of cultural consciousness that it expresses is a different one, and it therefore requires and rewards an "approach"—a way of getting into it and of feeling out its special qualities.

In an earlier book (*Metaphors of Self*) I formulated a rather elaborate theory about autobiographical literature, maintaining that any autobiography constitutes a psychological-philosophical imitation of the autobiographer's personality. That theory still seems to me to provide the most rewarding general way of thinking about writing that is autobiographical in source, in impulse, and in final form. The present book, however, though it takes its initial bearings in autobiographical literature, looks at the subject in a somewhat different perspective. Specifically, it considers autobiography from Africa less as an individual phenomenon than as a social one. There are two good reasons for this: first, the life that provides the subject for African autobiography is much less individually determined, much more socially oriented, than the life recounted in Western (European and American) autobiography; and, second, whether or not people from various cultural backgrounds differ basically as individual human beings, societies certainly differ. Coming, as one does, to African society and literature from without, one has first of all to give some attention to the difference in social and cultural context by which the individual has, in part, been shaped. "When you are criticising the philosophy of an epoch, do not chiefly direct your attention to those intellectual positions which its exponents feel it necessary explicitly to defend. There will be fundamental assumptions which adherents of all the various systems within the epoch unconsciously presuppose." Thus A. N. Whitehead, on approaching a philosophy that is temporally and culturally removed from us as readers. Likewise, there are, I think, "fundamental assumptions" that any creative writer will "unconsciously presuppose," and his work will be partly determined by these cultural myths and philosophical presuppositions that are so basic and so commonly shared that they are unquestioned by the writer and his reader alike—unquestioned, that is, except when the reader is of another culture and so participates in different myths and holds other philosophical presuppositions. Then, as we do with African literature, the reader will naturally question them and must do so to understand them and make the literature somehow his own. It is precisely here, in the approach to African literature—though not in criticism of it, for that is a separate and subsequent act—that autobiography from Africa is of great value.

Though I willingly disclaim any specialized authority that would allow me to pronounce oracularly and confidently on the vast subject of Africa, this does not at all mean that I admit the scholarship of this book to be either thin or careless. Indeed, the logic of the case, I believe, is quite the contrary: *because* the book claims no private, unavailable, inside knowledge, *therefore* the reading and research in available sources—I mean available to the Western reader in the Western world—demands to be done with particular thoroughness and sensitivity. No doubt some of the insights expressed in this book are the result of the two years that I lived in West Africa; nevertheless, what I have tried to show is how a Western reader can approach the literature of Africa with nothing more remote or technical than a general critical sense, a sensitivity to literary modes and cultural expressions, and an interest in the African experience. The kind of authority that this book does claim depends simply on an extensive, sympathetic, and close critical reading of that body of literature which describes, in one form or another, the writer's experience in living as an African. Because the research for this book has been almost entirely library work rather than field work, I owe an extraordinary debt to libraries, librarians, and others who have provided me with the materials for study: the James E. Shepard Library of North Carolina Central University; the Perkins Library of Duke University; the Library of Congress (and in particular Mrs. Milly Balima of the African Section); the British Museum; the New York Public Library; and Mr. Bill French of the University Place Book Store in New York City, who supplied me not only with books but with some especially valuable bibliographical information. Many friends have contributed much to my understanding in writing this book: African students and friends first of all, both in the United States and in Africa—Miss Susan Nah of Liberia; Mr. Zachariah Memoh, Mr. Atogho Enyih-Paul, Mr. Sammy Nyambi, and Mr. Vincent Feko of the Cameroons; Mr. Ifeanyi C. Emma Okeke, Mr. Godwin Mbachu, Mr. Alex Dillibe, Mr. Peter Iniodu, Mr. Cyril Nwosu, and Mr. Ndubisi Egemonye of Nigeria; Mr. Aloysius Hansen of Sierra Leone; and Mr. Gershon Fiawoo of Ghana. In addition to these I owe a debt of gratitude to Dr. Horace G. Dawson, Jr., who began conversations with me in Africa on the subjects of this book and who has generously continued them in this country; Dr. Charles A. Ray, who has likewise provided me with many and varied insights in conversation; Mr. Ernest Mason, whose theories about black American literature have given me an increased understanding of black African literature; and Mr. Ralph Manheim, whose correspondence gave me some most timely information for Chapter V. A much shorter version of Chapter IV appeared in *South Atlantic Quarterly*. Miss Miriam Brokaw and Mrs. Joanna Hitchcock of Princeton University Press have been unfailingly intelligent, sympathetic, and helpful in preparing this book for publication, and I am grateful for that tact they have always shown which is composed of equal parts of editorial wisdom and human sensitivity. The greatest debt incurred in the writing of this book—and in living while writing it—is recorded in the dedication.

# Table of Contents

# Tell Me Africa

## AN APPROACH TO
## AFRICAN LITERATURE

# Introduction and Methodology

THE MAGISTRATE who heard the case of *Regina* v. *Kenyatta and others* was no doubt speaking the simple truth when, in exasperation with the African defendants and in a tone of fellow feeling with the British prosecutor, he muttered, "I cannot follow the African mind." That was most assuredly not the first time the remark had been made by a European, probably not even the first time by that particular judge; and neither—again most assuredly—was it to be the last time that someone from the Western world would express similar sentiments. But here a curious paradox insinuates itself into the African-European confrontation, for one can have no doubt, after a careful reading of Montagu Slater's interesting and revealing book, *The Trial of Jomo Kenyatta*,[1] that both the magistrate and the prosecutor, in another context, would have been among those who claim to "know" the African very well indeed: to know his simple thoughts and his primitive motives, to know, in a paternal but often irascible manner, what is and what is not good for him. Fifteen years before the time of his trial, but referring to a type very like the magistrate and the prosecutor, Jomo Kenyatta himself had occasion to ask rhetorically, "How often have we not heard such people saying: 'We have lived in Africa for a number of years and we know the African mind well'?"[2] After all, the prosecutor, who was the crown counsel in Kenya, and the magistrate, who was retired from the Supreme Court bench of Kenya, had for years been freely administering justice to the colony and especially to its very large majority of Africans. How could they possibly *not* know the people with whom they were dealing, and had

[1] *The Trial of Jomo Kenyatta* (London: Mercury Books, 1965); the magistrate's remark is reported on p. 192.
[2] *Facing Mount Kenya* (New York: Vintage, n.d.), p. 148.

been dealing for years, almost as gods—even if they could not quite "follow the African mind"?

Indeed, this same magistrate, when he came to pronounce judgment on Kenyatta (possessed unquestionably of an eminently "African mind"), appears to have been sufficiently confident: "You have protested that your object," he said, has been thus and so. "I do not believe you. . . . You commenced to organise this Mau Mau society. . . . I am satisfied that the master mind behind this plan was yours." And then, having fixed Kenyatta's mind, the magistrate proceeded to the general character of Kenyatta's people: "I also believe that the methods to be employed were worked out by you and that you have taken the fullest advantage of the power and influence which you have over your people and also of the primitive instincts you know lie deep down in their characters" (Slater, p. 242). No one but a man who knows the Gikuyu character deeply and thoroughly would dare to pronounce so confidently; or so one would say if Westerners had not been making confident pronouncements about the African mind and character for these past one hundred and fifty years. That this particular magistrate, on the evidence of Slater's book and others,[3] seems to have been a pathetic and wretched specimen, in that special way that only the British in their colonies succeed in being, does not make him the less representative—unfortunately, quite the contrary.

This minor incident in the encounter of Africa with the West is trivial enough and in a sense outdated, and therefore may seem insignificant, especially in these days when the Queen of England (the same Queen who was "against Kenyatta and others" in the trial at Kapenguria) visits Kenya not as the sovereign of that colony but as the official

[3] For example, D. N. Pritt, *The Autobiography of D. N. Pritt*, 3 vols. (London: Lawrence & Wishart, 1965-1966); Jomo Kenyatta, *Suffering Without Bitterness* (Nairobi: East African Publishing House, 1968); and Jeremy Murray-Brown, *Kenyatta* (London: George Allen & Unwin, 1972). See note 19 in Chapter II below.

guest of Jomo Kenyatta, President of the Republic of Kenya. But Africa and the West go on meeting one another all the time and at all sorts of contact points—political, cultural, economic, educational, literary—and, as many people have observed, they go on not understanding one another very well. Or at least—to speak only where one has authority—the West knows very little, and understands less, about Africa and Africans. Chinua Achebe was unquestionably right, both in his estimate of the situation and in his analysis of the underlying causes, when he recently wrote, "The African intellectual's knowledge of the West (and he knows a lot more about the West than the Western intellectual knows about Africa) comes to him not from literature but from personal contact."[4] For a variety of reasons, as Achebe demonstrates, the African intellectual, who reads comparatively little, has on the other hand had considerably personal-social contact with the West; the Western intellectual, who has probably read a great deal, ordinarily cannot claim anything like the same intimate, firsthand knowledge of Africa. This is incontestably the case at the present and will remain so for the indefinite future; and if, as Léopold Senghor claims, this is to be the century of the discovery of black Africa, Western intellectuals and Western readers would do well, in order to "follow the African mind," to apply themselves to that literature which gives, with all possible inwardness, an accurate image of Africa and a faithful reflection of the African mind. "If you want to know what we believe in," an African has written, "watch how we live."[5] Exactly—but not many Westerners have the oppor-

---

[4] "What Do African Intellectuals Read?" *Times Literary Supplement*, 12 May 1972, p. 547.

[5] Stephen U. O. Anyaibe, from a MS. quoted by Adda B. Bozeman in *The Future of Law in a Multicultural World* (Princeton: Princeton Univ. Press, 1971), p. 94. Professor Bozeman holds much the same view as I do of the integrity and distinctiveness of cultural expressions, though she discusses the subject from a broader perspective (including the cultures of Islam, sub-Saharan Africa, India, and China) than I can claim to command.

5

tunity to watch how the Ibo live in Eastern Nigeria or how the Gikuyu live "facing Mount Kenya," how the Malinké live in villages in West Africa or how the urbanized and "detribalized" South African lives in Johannesburg; so it is to literature that the Western reader turns for the picture that he seeks of how Africans live and hence for an understanding of what they "believe in" and think. Autobiography, which is the literary mode just described (how an individual or a group live, as recorded from within) is thus seen to provide, according to the logic of the remark quoted above, the most direct narrative enactment and immediate manifestation of the ways, the motives, and the beliefs of a culture foreign to the reader. The picture derived will be more comprehensively valid if we take "autobiography" to include "autobiographical" writings—"autobiographical" fiction, "autobiographical" ethnography, "autobiographical" sociology and philosophy—as well as books that bear the title *An Autobiography*.

Wilhelm Dilthey, speaking as a philosopher of history, has had some especially insightful things to say about the significance and the uses of autobiography, among which aperçus is the observation that autobiography, being the product of a conscious awareness shaped by and operating at the center of a total environmental situation, affords a unique means of access to that situation for someone culturally or historically outside it. When the South African writer Lewis Nkosi says, "Certainly the picture of the Sophiatown ghetto in Bloke Modisane's book *Blame Me On History*, or passages in Ezekiel Mphahlele's autobiographical essay *Down Second Avenue* are far superior to anything these writers have attempted in creative fiction,"[6] one would not only agree with this specific estimate of Modisane's and Mphahlele's books and with Nkosi's judgment of South African themes and performances more generally, but one would go further, to claim that autobiography can

[6] "Fiction by Black South Africans," in *Introduction to African Literature*, ed. Ulli Beier (London: Longmans, 1967), p. 213.

legitimately be assigned a primary role in approaching African literature generally, and this on three counts: first, for the non-African reader, autobiography offers a way of getting inside a world that is inevitably very different from his own in its assumptions and values, in its attitudes and beliefs, in its practices and observances; second, as Nkosi suggests is true for South Africa, much of the best literature from Africa generally is—in a strict as well as in a loose sense of the word—autobiographical; third, through autobiography one can, in many instances, approach fiction or whatever other literature with considerably greater assurance and validity (*Radiance of the King*, for example, yields a much richer meaning with a prior reading of *Dark Child*). When Peter Abrahams, on the penultimate page of *Tell Freedom*, says, "With my eyes on the stars, I took stock and searched for the meaning of life in terms of the life I had known in this land for nearly twenty-one years,"[7] he offers us both a clue and an example—a clue for reading African literature and an example in his practice of autobiography and fiction. The best way we can have of understanding what an African feels about human existence is to read his own account of "the life I had known" as he seeks "the meaning of life" itself; a reading of *Tell Freedom* (which many observers have claimed is Abrahams' best book) will unquestionably help us in an understanding not only of Abrahams' own fiction but of other South African fiction or drama or poetry as well.

The political environment in South Africa is different, of course, from what is to be found in most other parts of Africa, and we must consider where an autobiography comes from before reading its lessons into literature from elsewhere in Africa. With this proviso, autobiography offers, I think, a uniquely clear and persuasive testimony about African life that comes from the very heart of African experience, from the central consciousness that participates in and

[7] *Tell Freedom: Memories of Africa* (New York: Alfred A. Knopf, 1954), p. 369.

7

registers the experience. "Yet," Chief Albert Luthuli says in his autobiography, speaking of the black South African's situation and his suffering from the evils of apartheid, "confronted with all the evidence, many white would-be sympathisers tell us uneasily: 'Oh, come along, *surely* it's not as bad as you make out. It can't be *all* negative!'" To which Luthuli responds, and all other black South African writers agree, "It is worse than they seem able to imagine."[8] The cumulative evidence of a dozen or fourteen lived and living documents from that unhappy land—all telling very much the same story of oppression, violence, and inhumanity, and telling it from the point of view of the tyrannized, brutalized victim—composes testimony too eloquent to deny or to avoid. The lesson that South African autobiographies teach is a political and social one; elsewhere it is different, and in other cases the lesson will be cultural, psychological, philosophical, anthropological. The point is that if we attend closely to the performances in autobiographies from Africa, and especially if we take together a number of autobiographies from a single social, cultural, or political context, we can hope, given enough human sympathy and imagination, to understand that other environment which was originally foreign and incomprehensible. Then, in a subsequent act, we may hope to exercise a necessary awareness of cultural assumptions in our criticism of the imaginative literature that gives conscious expression to that culture out of which it grows.

An important fact about autobiography—it becomes doubly important in a consideration of Africa and African literature—is that in it the whole man speaks in a way that he may not in certain other kinds of writing. Scratch the surface of a specialist and you will find a man, unspecialized and professionally unlimited, beneath. When the specialist, be he politician or priest, doctor or lawyer, economist, chief, or soldier (we have autobiographies from Africa by

---

[8] *Let My People Go* (New York: McGraw-Hill, 1962), p. 52.

all these specialists and more), comes to write his autobiography, he expresses not merely his political or religious or other sensibilities but his totality as a man. Of course it may be true that his totality is a limited or partial one, but such as it is it will all be there in his autobiography, consciously or unconsciously, in statement, in structure, in style and in tone. Moreover, scratch the surface of (for example) an African politician and you will find not only a man generally but a specifically African man, not only homo sapiens but homo Africanus. And, finally, scratch the surface of a number of Africans of various professions and classes (as Diedrich Westermann does in his excellent and fascinating anthology)[9] and you will come up with a number of perspectives on and expressions of the one experiential fact: what it has been like and what it is like to be an African. A

[9] Diedrich Westermann, ed., *Autobiographies d'Africains: onze autobiographies d'indigènes originaires de diverses régions de l'Afrique et représentant des métiers et des degrés de culture différents* (Paris: Payot, 1943). The eleven autobiographers, with their chapter titles, demonstrate the geographical, cultural, and professional diversity of the collection: Xkoou-Goa-Xob, un Bochiman du Sud-Ouest Africain; Boniface Foli de Glidyi, Togo; Samba, un Mendé de Sierra Léone, paysan et soldat; Événements de la vie d'un Zoulou Mazwimabi Nyandéni, dit Salomon; La vie d'Igbinokpoguié Amadasou de Benin, Nigéria Méridionale; Biographie de Christophe Mtiva du Kenya en Afrique Orientale; Fritz Gabousou, chef et instituteur du Togo; Madame Marthe Aféwélé Kwami du Togo; Samuel Edward Kgouné Mqhayi un poète Sud Africain; Benjamin Akiga de la Nigéria Septentrionale, auteur d'une histoire de son peuple; Martin Akou, de Lomé au Togo actuellement étudiant en médecine à Bâle.

In his introduction Westermann provides the rationale for his anthology—and for the present study: "L'Africain est trop souvent une victime de notre esprit de généralisation. Nous voyons l'extérieur . . . et nous prenons trop rarement le temps et la peine de chercher à comprendre ce qui se passe à l'intérieur ou ce qui s'y introduit lentement. C'est l'indigène lui-même qui peut le mieux nous donner des renseignements sur tout cela . . ." (p. 8).

The anthology compiled by Margery Perham, *Ten Africans: A Collection of Life Stories*, 2d ed. (London: Faber & Faber, 1963), is similar to Westermann's both in its intention and in the variety of autobiographers included.

9

number of anthropologists have remarked—Jomo Kenyatta, writing anthropology from within the African experience, is perhaps the most pertinent example—that the dominant characteristic of the African world, in contrast to the Western world, is its unity, its indivisible coherence and singleness, its non-compartmentalized texture. To look at one aspect of Gikuyu life, as Kenyatta emphasizes—and this seems to be true of other African cultures as well (excepting, probably, South Africa)—is to look at the whole: the whole is concentrated in every part and each part fully embodies the whole. The Ghanaian philosopher W. E. Abraham points to this unified existence when he says, "According to such a view [as the Akan hold], therefore, the true metaphysics must be a deductive system. And morality, politics, medicine, are all made to flow from metaphysics."[10] It is both natural and necessary, given what autobiography is, that this total, unified, integrated view will be the informing spirit in accounts written by Africans of their own lives. Such accounts possess unity and integrity from the personality of the writer who, as an autobiographer and an African, gives a complete rendering of interior, subjective, and African experience: how it feels, as an African, to look out at an African world and to look back over African experiences. He looks with African eyes and records and analyzes with an African mind; this gives to his account an interior integrity that one can never hope for or expect in the alien, if sometimes sympathetic, view of a non-African. Being himself the center and seismograph of the experience he records, the African autobiographer must give, so far as his vision extends, a unified and total view rather than the partial, exterior, objective view of, let us say, anthropology.

"If you look into the bag of an outgoing missionary," Mbonu Ojike says in *My Africa*, "you will find five tools with which he must condemn and evangelize. These are:

[10] *The Mind of Africa* (Chicago: Univ. of Chicago Press, 1962), p. 49. Cf. Mbonu Ojike in *My Africa* (New York: John Day Co., 1946), p. 182: "For us, religion and law are unalterably interdependent."

10

absolute religious dogmas, Western legal thought, Western political ideas, Western social philosophy, and Western economic theories" (p. 195). No doubt the Western literary critic who picks up an African novel will unconsciously be carrying in his overnight bag all the philosophical and psychological assumptions programmed into him as he grew up, as he pursued his studies in the Western tradition, as he read the masterpieces of Western literature. To take an example: the European or American reader, for whom, as Kenyatta says, "Individuality is the ideal of life," cannot hope to read, with full comprehension or imaginative sympathy, the writing of Africans for whom, again according to Kenyatta, "the ideal is the right relations with, and behaviour to, other people" (*Facing Mt. Kenya*, p. 118), unless he first understands that the highest good of the society in which he has had his growth and being is not the highest good in African society, nor, probably, for the African writer. The adjustment required in reading African writing is greater than the adjustment a Protestant or agnostic or atheistic reader of the twentieth century finds necessary in reading Dante or Homer, because Western thought and literature have developed directly and consistently from the Greeks through the Renaissance to the present time; all that while African thought was developing in its own and different way on a continent where the effect of the Greco-Roman and Hebraic-Christian traditions was almost nil. This is to say what is perhaps over-simple and obvious: that there are traditions of art and literature in African society, growing directly out of the cultural matrix of that society, and they are different from traditions in the West. I do not intend this as special pleading for African literature, nor do I mean to suggest (as indeed some critics have done) that there should be special standards, lower and more lenient and thus contemptuous, for judging African literature. With the best will in the world, the critic will not find in the written literature of Africa anything that is the equal of *The Odyssey* or *The Divine Comedy*—but where else and how

11

often does one find their equal? On the other hand, in the literature of the past fifteen or twenty years, not many but a few works have come from Africa that can be compared with the best literature produced in the same period in Europe or America. The critic ought, nevertheless, to consider, analyze, and judge African literature with some imaginative understanding of the assumptions that lie behind it and that make it what it is. Autobiography, I suggest, provides a most convenient way to make this overwhelmingly important, primary adjustment from the literary assumptions of the West to the literary and other interrelated assumptions of Africa.

But does "Africa" exist? Is there such a single entity as "an" Africa that would comprehend within its literary boundaries and traditions such diverse and frequently quarrelsome writers as Léopold Senghor, Wole Soyinka, Camara Laye, Chinua Achebe, Yambo Ouologuem, Ezekiel Mphahlele, Mongo Beti, and others? Certainly, these people have been, in a literary sense, at one another's throats often enough to make one hesitant about putting them together within the covers of a book. Chinua Achebe may have been right when, after distinguishing between what he calls "*national* and *ethnic* literatures of Africa," he said of the former: "What we tend to do today is to think of African literature as a new-born infant. But in fact what we have is a whole generation of new-born infants. Of course if you only look cursorily one infant looks very much like another; but each is already set on its own journey."[11] It may be, as Achebe virtually implies, that these infant literatures look alike only because they are presently in a state of infancy and because their skins, if not their souls, are all colored black; and it may further be that their strangeness or their group distinctiveness, as seen from the perspective of the West—their blackness as against a prevailing white skin color in Western literature—causes us to see them as

[11] "English and the African Writer," *Transition*, 4, No. 18 (1965), p. 27.

all basically similar. It could well be the case, in other words, that some of the unity and similarity that Western observers seem to discover in African cultures and literatures is merely a matter of point of view and appearance, for we are essentially outside the cultures in question and initially have few or no interior apprehensions of the beliefs and meanings of those cultures since they have not been educated into our moral bones and sinews as they have with the Africans involved.

Yet in recent times, in spite of Achebe's caveat as regards literature, it has been Africans who have evoked and advocated an "African personality" or (though the notion and phrase were West Indian in origin rather than African) who have theorized about a unified cultural and personal identity determined and vaguely defined by what is called "négritude." One has only to cite the title of Cheikh Anta Diop's *L'unité culturelle de l'Afrique Noire* to demonstrate the tendency. W. E. Abraham, though he sets himself up as an analytic philosopher in the Western tradition, looking at *The Mind of Africa* from a Fellowship at All Souls College, Oxford, still implies a root unity in African cultures when he calls his second chapter "Paradigm of African Society" and when he says, "I am an African, with responsive throbbings in the collective consciousness of Africa" (p. 9). Here, as almost everywhere, Abraham's phrasing is vague enough to mean many different things, but a "collective consciousness of Africa," which calls forth "responsive throbbings" from an exemplary African, implies a psychological unity for the whole continent and all its peoples. Jomo Kenyatta, who is first a spokesman for the Gikuyu and then a symbol of unity for the Kenyan nation, is also committed to an East African federation and beyond that to the ideal of Pan-Africanism. Julius Nyerere, likewise, foresees a day when there will no longer be a Tanzania, and he would like to see the day when East Africa will be replaced by "an *Africa*."[12]

[12] See the conclusion of the three-part "profile" of Nyerere by William Edgett Smith in *The New Yorker*, 30 October 1971, p. 99.

13

Yambo Ouologuem inveighs against all the doctrines of *négritude*, yet in *Le devoir de violence*—or so the techniques of that novel imply—he would compress the entire history of all Africa into a symbolic drama that comprehends the whole continent, and his symbolic compression must logically depend for its validity upon there being some kind of unity in African experience and personality. Ezekiel Mphahlele, who ordinarily insists on the distinction between South African life and life elsewhere on the continent, referred in an interview with Lewis Nkosi to "My African values [which] continue to remain a top, solid thing inside me, the African humanism, this sense of being one . . . wanting to be one of a community which is very African."[13]

Boubou Hama, a writer and political figure from Niger, has presented the diversity and unity of African cultures as clearly as anyone by taking his experience to be representative of all African experience in the autobiography that he calls *Kotia-Nima*.[14] He tells how he gradually moved out in ever-widening circles from his tiny home village, Fonéko, in pursuit of education, to Téra, the next town of any size, to Dori, in Upper Volta, to Ouagadougou, the capital city of Upper Volta, to Gorée, in Sénégal, and finally to France as an elected representative in parliament, then back to Africa and to Niger with the fruits of his experiences and observations. What Boubou Hama, the representative, archetypical African (as he would be taken to be), learned about Africa is put very neatly in his two-fold vision in Ouagadougou (the writer goes under the name "Kotia-Nima" in his autobiography): "Kotia-Nima y [in Ouagadougou] rencontra des enfants d'autres pays, y entendit des dialectes nombreux. Il finit de se convaincre de la diversité de l'Afrique" (i, 105). But two pages later Boubou Hama develops the other parallel and contrary thematic thread of his African autobiography: "A Ouagadougou,

[13] "Conversation with Ezekiel Mphahlele," *Africa Report*, 9, No. 7 (July 1964), p. 8.
[14] *Kotia-Nima*, 3 vols. (Paris: Présence Africaine, 1968-1969).

14

cependant, Kotia-Nima eut une nette vision de l'unité du continent africain, de l'uniticité du fond mystique de ses croyances" (I, 107). When Boubou Hama, with his vision of unity-in-diversity, answers our question about Africa— "Nous prétendons au Niger que l'Afrique existe, que l'homme africain—frère de tous les autres—a son cachet particulier, sa civilisation spéciale" (II, 188)—he echoes Mbonu Ojike, who finally, despite qualifications and paradoxes and hesitations, says in *My Africa*, "There is an African culture" (p. 85). One comes to this conclusion about the essential unity or basic consistency of different African cultures (which Basil Davidson in his *Africa in History* compares to an *Ursprache* for all the various African languages): whatever its source and explanation, if we discover a unity of approach to experience, or a similarity of attitude toward what constitutes existence, in the autobiographical and personal-historical writings of geographically various Africans, there is little need to worry over the historical causes or to dispute the metaphysical sources of this unity. The symptom or manifestation in literature is of interest rather than root causes, since what is proposed is not an essay in history or in anthropology or in philosophy but an approach to and a study of a body of literature produced by Africans, from sub-Saharan Africa, reflecting on the nature of their own experience both individual and communal.

The assumption of unity, however, that is implied by the very fact of a study of "African" literature, should not provide an excuse for disregarding cultural diversity where it exists or for failing to notice the uniqueness of the achievements of various writers: to demonstrate such individual coherence and uniqueness is unquestionably one of the primary intentions of the critical act. A work of literature—if culture is going to be brought in at all, and I think it must be in discussing African literature—should be considered in terms of the specific culture from which it comes and not in terms of some other, even if related, culture. Further, a

15

work of literature should be talked about in its own internal terms of genre, structure, and theme. It would be both wrongheaded and sterile, though not uncommon, to approach Ezekiel Mphahlele, Chinua Achebe, Camara Laye, and Yambo Ouologuem without taking note of the different cultural premises informing their fiction; and it would be vicious to attack Ezekiel Mphahlele for not being Léopold Senghor (or vice versa), or to censure Camara Laye for not writing Mongo Beti's novel. It would also be an obvious mistake, and quite unrewarding, to read *A Child of Two Worlds* or *My Africa* as novels or to imagine that *No Longer at Ease* or *Bound to Violence* are literal autobiographies. Consequently, each of the following chapters, except for Chapter I, which is given over to general questions of the African ethos, takes up the "autobiographical" literature (as I have freely characterized it) of a specific group, whether that group be determined ethnically (the Gikuyu, the Malinké, the Ibo), nationally (Kenya, Nigeria, South Africa), or linguistically (French as contrasted with English). "The Children of Gikuyu and Mumbi" (centering on Jomo Kenyatta and *Facing Mount Kenya*) presents a sort of "profile" of the Gikuyu people who represent a centripetal, coherent, traditional community—a "paradigm of African society," to borrow the phrase that Abraham applies to the Akan of Ghana.

At this point I then assume that the general approach to African literature has been demonstrated and that thereafter what is appropriate is an approach to and treatment of specific works of literature as literature—a treatment, that is, as expressions of both a personal vision and a permeating cultural reality. "Ces pays lointains," which is mostly devoted to Camara Laye's autobiographies and fiction, shows how his art reenacts the breakup and separation of the traditional (Malinké) community, as that breakup was experienced by the individual now painfully separated from the coherent body. "Love, Sex, and Procreation" demonstrates the different attitudes toward the titular subjects

16

typically displayed by Africa and the West; it deals with the traditional (Ibo) community in change as seen from the comprehensive, fictional point of view of three generations. In Achebe's fiction, I have argued, we are given something like a supra-personal, multi-generational autobiography of the Ibo people. Yambo Ouologuem's historical revision of the African image, achieved in an epic and symbolic drama covering many generations and several centuries, constitutes the matter of "Pornography, Philosophy, and African History." In addition to contrasting the characteristic features of French-African literature and English-African literature in this chapter, I have suggested that what Ouologuem attempts to present in *Le devoir de violence* can be figuratively seen as a symbolic autobiography of the entire continent and community of Africa. "Politics, Creativity, and Exile" looks at the completely divided community of black South Africa—"detribalized," urbanized, alienated, often driven into exile—a community, as we see especially in Ezekiel Mphahlele's writings, defined only negatively by opposition to the oppressive policies of apartheid.

Because of the premises of this study, I have not been shy about quoting with great frequency, though, again because of the premises, the quotations are often short (to get as many perspectives as possible) and nearly always from primary sources. Victor Uchendu, an Ibo anthropologist who in the course of ethnography dips into the well of autobiography for confirmation and authority, says that when he began to read anthropology, "I observed that the culture-bearer's point of view was (and is) absent from this literature. . . . To 'live' a culture demands more than a knowledge of its events' system and institutions; it requires growing up with these events and being emotionally involved with cultural values and biases."[15] It is, of course, in autobiography

---

[15] *The Igbo of Southeast Nigeria* (New York: Holt, Rinehart & Winston, 1966), p. 9. Though it reads strangely, "events' system" is correct; whether it represents some strange anthropologist's jargon or a typographical error—an apostrophe for a comma—I do not know.

that one gets, more immediately than anywhere else, the "culture-bearer's point of view," or, one might say, the life-bearer's point of view: the African point of view in African autobiography. If it is going to be the "culture-bearer's point of view," it should as well be in the "culture-bearer's" own words.

There has been a continuing and, I think, unfortunate tendency in academic criticism of African literature to base an understanding of African philosophy or of an African world-view on the observations of foreign writers. Thus, a great deal of the criticism of African literature has taken its bearings from Father Placide Tempels' *Bantu Philosophy*, most often, however, not going directly to Tempels but receiving his already secondhand understanding as it is filtered through Janheinz Jahn's *Muntu*. Writers who practice this sort of philosophical-cum-cultural criticism bring to African literature a philosophical framework, too often resembling Procrustes' bed, derived from Tempels and Jahn, and "apply" it instead of (*if* a philosophical picture be necessary or desirable at all) finding the picture in the assumptions and actions, in the statement and tone and manner of the literature. *Bantu Philosophy* and *Muntu* are both no doubt valuable works, but neither of them, though they both profess to present the African philosophical world-picture to a foreign audience (the one is a systematic explication, the other a popularization of that systematic treatment), is by an African, a "culture-bearer." Sympathetic the two writers undoubtedly are—but one wonders if they are the best sources in whom to seek an understanding of these matters. Surely John Mbiti, being African born, raised, and educated and therefore, presumably, African in assumptions, attitudes, and philosophy, is a more logical source for an understanding of what and how an African thinks (in contrast to what and how a European thinks). But yet better than Mbiti—and doubly better than Tempels, triply better than Jahn—if one wants to see how Africans view experience, what they feel and understand about their ex-

perience, and how they draw on this feeling and understanding in writing fiction, poetry, and drama, would be to
go directly to writers who describe, re-create, and analyze
their experience. In reading African autobiographies, one
does not have philosophical schematizing about African
experience, nor a guided tour around such a neat scheme,
but an actual record, taken from within and so shaped in its
ultimate form, of the living of African experience. This is
the reason and the justification for quoting so copiously: so
that understanding will not be distorted by filtering
through a foreign medium, or by being forced to a precon-
ceived pattern or philosophical scheme. Another, and purely practical, reason is that one cannot assume a universal
acquaintance with the subject matter of this study. It would
be a very misguided fancy to imagine that all the works dis-
cussed here are easily available or commonly known—
some, indeed, are entirely unknown and virtually impossible to find. Yet, as Olaudah Equiano says, the capable reader will find something of value (sometimes not much, it is
true, but something) in each of the books, no matter how
obscure. Consequently, if one is going to have available, as
one desires, the very voice of African recollection and reflection, it will often be necessary—without, however,
resorting to anthology—to reproduce it right on the page.

The criterion of accessibility has led me to deal only with
works in English or French, though a few of the autobiographies touched on (e.g., *Baba of Karo, Akiga's Story*, and
those in the Westermann anthology) were not written originally in English or French but have been translated into
the one or the other from various African languages.[16]
Moreover, on the same grounds, where adequate English

[16] The best critical comments available about the use of English by
African writers are to be found in Gerald Moore's *The Chosen Tongue*
(London: Longmans, Green, & Co., 1969). Elsewhere Moore has
urged that the bodies of literature in English and French from Africa
should be drawn together, and in *Seven African Writers* and in various articles he has provided the critical example.

translations exist of works originally written in French, I have chosen to quote in English (except when verbal or stylistic matters are in question). Otherwise, the choice of materials for this study has been determined by two non-linguistic considerations: those autobiographies to which particular attention is given have been selected for their pertinence in reading other varieties of literature (*Baba of Karo*, for example, charming and interesting as it may be in itself, will yield fewer insights, in many ways and for many reasons, than *Down Second Avenue* or *L'enfant noir* or even *My Africa* when one comes to move from autobiography as such to different literary genres); and, as a genre of literature, fiction has received special emphasis because of its close narrative tie to autobiography and because autobiography and fiction come more or less immediately out of the same social matrix. What I propose, in any case, is to bring autobiography to the service of reading other literature, not vice versa.

Here, however, one must urge a critical caution lest it seem that the reader is being encouraged to confuse two different literary modes or genres to the detriment of the one (fiction) that is ordinarily and no doubt, as a general rule, justifiably considered to have superior claims to being a work of art. It is true, of course—and this is what might sometimes betray a reader into confusing the two modes— that some novels cannot be judged works of art at all, and it is equally true that there are a few books (*Dark Child, Down Second Avenue, Road to Ghana*, for example, in African literature) that must be called works of art while being, nevertheless, autobiographies. One explanation for this, on either side of the line, is that the "artistic" autobiographies are organized like novels while the failed novels adhere all too closely to a chronological, biographical arrangement— which is to say simply that these novels are meaningless because mere chronology, mere serial biography, never does, in itself, possess significance. Events recalled from the past assume such significance only when a pattern has been discerned, achieved, and imposed, out of the author's own internal order, by himself, thus acting as an artist. Mere chronology—"and then . . . and then . . . and then . . ."—achieves no pattern and hence discovers no meaning. The autobiography is no more bound, of necessity, to serial chronology than the novel, and so either can succeed in being a work of art just as either can fail to be one. Moreover, when an autobiography succeeds, it does so, it seems to me, in much the same way as the successful novel: that is, by a significant ordering of recalled experience drawn from the writer's observation and awareness of himself, of his past, and of the entire social and spiritual context in which he has and has had his moral being. An interviewer in Texas put a question to Ezekiel Mphahlele that bears very directly on this matter; the response Mphahlele gave, from his own experience as autobiographer and novelist, points the way to an understanding of the relation between the two modes. "In the mid-fifties," the interviewer said, "it was reported that you were working on a novel while in South Africa. What was this about, and what became of it?" To which Mphahlele responded (and what he said does not indicate a confusion of two literary genres but a way of seeing the artistic possibilities of autobiography and also a way of seeing something of the common material lying behind both): "It was really a novel that had been turning around in my mind which later became *Down Second Avenue*. I decided to chuck the novel altogether and simply write an autobiography." This decision did not, as Mphahlele clearly understood, mean binding himself, hand, foot, and creative imagination, to a chronological and insignificant series of events: "What was your method of composing *Down Second Avenue*? . . . Did you go back and write the interludes later?" "No, I did the interludes at the same time. I would write about my people and the events they were caught up in, and then literally come to a stop and try to think about what these things were doing to me, and found I could not express it in the strict order of biography. So I decided on

21

the method of the interlude."[17] The writer—autobiographer or novelist—casts a net of present awareness back over the past in an attempt to find a significance there that exists, in fact, not in the past itself but in this very effort of present consciousness to order and to organize according to the pattern that has evolved as the artist's own personality, his vision, his moral awareness. Without that vision or that moral awareness, the novelist will fail to produce a work of art and so will the autobiographer; with it, an autobiography can be as much a work of art as a novel. This is not to say, however, that autobiographies and novels are exactly the same, but only that there are autobiographies and autobiographies, there are novels and novels, and that the two modes draw on much the same material.[18]

[17] Bernth Lindfors et al., eds., *Palaver: Interviews with Five African Writers in Texas* (Austin: African and Afro-American Research Institute, 1972), p. 40.

[18] In the same interview quoted above, Mphahlele was asked, "Do you feel that there is a clear distinction between fiction and autobiography or that there is really just a continuum?" To which Mphahlele responded first in general, then in particular: "It's difficult to find a dividing line in one's mind between fiction and autobiography. All I can say is one's own experiences have a lot to do with any kind of fiction—much more to do than you probably would be aware of. . . . I think one could say something is more autobiography than fiction and something is more fiction than autobiography, but the two are never completely separate in the novelist. . . . I would say *The Wanderers* is more fiction than autobiography. It has an autobiographical framework and it has real-life people in it, but it is still more fiction than autobiography. . . . I have a beginning and an ending, as distinct from *Down Second Avenue*" (*Palaver*, p. 41). It is just here that one would disagree with Mphahlele, for *Down Second Avenue* has a structural beginning and end, *The Wanderers* does not (see the discussion in Chapter vi below). This difference of judgment in the case of a particular work, however, in no way suggests that Mphahlele's general observation is anything other than entirely valid.

In a similar vein, one would not have thought of Kofi Awoonor's *This Earth, My Brother* . . . as being particularly autobiographical—except in the figurative sense in which one gives that designation to *Bound to Violence*—yet Kofi Awoonor, in an interview in *Transition*, No. 41 (1972), p. 44, speaks of the hero of his book thus: "All that

There are, of course, African autobiographies (as there are also African novels) that will serve the useful and perhaps pedestrian purpose of mediating between the African world and non-African readers but that no one would think of calling works of art—*Child of Two Worlds, My Africa, The Autobiography of an Unknown South African, Akiga's Story, "Mau Mau" Detainee*, and others. The obvious solution is to take from these works, whether novels or autobiographies, what they have to offer and not to seek in them for more than is there. On the other hand, when one is dealing with a work of art, in whichever mode, then, whether or not one finds it performing a mediatorial role (and surely this is an altogether legitimate, if partial, way of regarding literature), to deal with it also *and primarily* in its own terms as a work of art with its own internal logic, structure, and significance, and not as a document of history (personal or public), or of sociology, or of polemics. Wole Soyinka has said, and very brilliantly, I think, that "the artist has always functioned in African society as the record of the mores and experience of his society *and* as the voice of vision in his own time. It is time for him to respond to this essence of himself."[19] It would be a very great critical error to disregard the "voice of vision" that informs a work of art. It is precisely this "vision," as I have suggested, that is the *sine qua non* of a work of art: by definition there can be no work of art without it. On the other hand, it would be nothing like so serious a mistake to fail to notice that the artist is functioning "in African society as the record of the mores and experience of his society"—nothing like so serious a mistake *and yet*, since the record, according to Soyinka, is in fact there, and since the non-African reader

---

goes into the making of his persona is authentic, historical, autobiographical if you like. Scraps of a life, but they all go to make a total statement." Awoonor is no more confused about the intentions and possibilities of literature than is Mphahlele.

[19] In *The Writer in Modern Africa*, ed. Per Wästberg (Uppsala: Scandinavian Institute of African Studies, 1968), p. 21.

23

requires such a record to get inside the literature and make it somehow his own, it would be a tactical fault, merely because of squeamishness about genres, not to avail ourselves of it or make use of it.

Soyinka's remark implies that African fiction, in his opinion, has tended to be excessively, and in a restrictive sense, autobiographical, or has been too much a mere "record of the mores and experience of his society." In a general way I would agree, though with certain exceptions, qualifications, and explanations. Camara Laye has exhibited all the possible variations—an autobiography that is a work of art, a novel that is too much bound by biography, and another novel that breaks free of those bonds to be a fine work of art. Chinua Achebe has likewise broken free, especially in his last novel. With *A Grain of Wheat* James Ngugi has tried, but in my opinion not altogether successfully, to organize a novel in other than biographical, chronological terms. Ezekiel Mphahlele is an artist in *Down Second Avenue* and not, unfortunately, in *The Wanderers*. I have called Yambo Ouologuem's *Bound to Violence* a symbolic autobiography of the African continent, but this is merely a way of saying that he intends to take the African past and the broad sweep of the continent for his subject, and his art, which is that of the satiric novelist and the pornographer and philosopher, is no way limited by the simplistic chronological scheme, unredeemed by pattern, of the literal-minded biographer or autobiographer. He, like Achebe, whom I have also called, for convenience and in a sort of trope, an "autobiographer"—not as to the organization and arrangement of their novels but as to the nature and scope of their subjects—has written a book that is a work of art, and that is a name that transcends either "novel" or "autobiography." But here one returns to the premise and the title of this book: what is suggested in the first instance is merely an approach to a literature and is so developed in Chapter I and to a certain extent in Chapter II. Thereafter, when the approach has been effected, and when it is a ques-

24

tion of individual books as works of art (or failed works of art)—*Dark Child* and *Radiance of the King* in Chapter III, *Things Fall Apart, No Longer at Ease,* and *A Man of the People* in Chapter IV, *Bound to Violence* in Chapter V, and *Down Second Avenue* and *The Wanderers* in Chapter VI— then the critiques are scrupulously performed as literary analyses and not as potential contributors to a cultural vade mecum. Though we may begin with autobiography, we ought to conclude with works of art. This, I believe, is the best way for a non-African reader to approach, get inside, and respond to African literature.

# CHAPTER I

# African Autobiography and the Non-African Reader

## (A) AFRICAN AUTOBIOGRAPHY . . .

AUTOBIOGRAPHIES from Africa are plentiful in their number, diverse in their motives, revealing in their implicit, inherent psychologies, and (if I may be allowed to define autobiography, as I intend to do in the chapters that follow, in the very general way that I believe African literature demands) very varied in the forms they assume. But they are also, all of them, African. The interesting and, I think, very important paradox about African autobiographical literature is that while it can be extremely diverse in apparent motive and in manifest form, it also displays, especially for the non-African reader, an underlying unity in the way the writers view their own experience and the African experience, in the way they conceive of human existence and human society, and in the way they transform these views and conceptions into works of literature. If we discern a philosophical or psychological unity informing African literature, however, this ought not lead to a neglect of its formal and motivational diversity, nor vice versa. The special task of the critic who approaches African literature from without is to define, simultaneously and equally, both the unity and the diversity, both the essential African one that lies beneath and the formal, cultural many that appear on the surface. Let us (without disregarding the unity) consider first the diversity of motives, points of view, and forms in African autobiographical literature, then (without disregarding the diversity) consider the unity of the African vision of human experience.

Benjamin Franklin—who was hardly an African but who nevertheless provides a model of conscientious clarity in stating the reasons for performing the autobiographical act —enumerates, in his own *Autobiography*, four motives: to satisfy for his descendants the same sort of curiosity he himself had about ancestors; to provide an example or a model for others; to relive an essentially enjoyable life by recreating it in narrative form; and to satisfy his vanity. To these four motives—for each of which one can find relevant examples among African autobiographies—we might add three more that, if not peculiar to African autobiography, are more likely to be found there than in the European or American practice of autobiography: to preserve a disappearing world; to describe the African milieu for outside readers; and, which is often closely related to the previous motive, to describe a representative case of a peculiarly African experience. Obviously, as is true with Franklin's autobiography also, most African autobiographies show, in one degree or another, several different motives; few of the writers had one, and only one, reason for putting on paper the record of their lives. And, to complicate the matter considerably, some of the writers (Ezekiel Mphahlele, for example, see Chapter VI) were temperamentally moved to the act of autobiography by a psychological instinct very much prior to the actual putting of characters on a page. In any case, the reasons a man has for writing about his own life will tell us a good deal about him psychologically, about his environment socially and philosophically, and about his book structurally.

Most books, and this naturally includes autobiographies, are written to an audience, whether clearly or vaguely conceived. Franklin's *Autobiography*, for example, is addressed to his son, who is presumed to have the same curiosity about his father as his father had about his ancestors. Thus Franklin, looking back to his own father and grandfather, is not only an ancestor of natural curiosity to the son but is also the chronological link connecting the son with more distant reaches of the ancestral past. In African autobiography, however, the ancestral-descendant motive is something infinitely deeper than curiosity—which suggests merely viewing a subject with interest but from a certain distance. It is something that points to an entirely un-Western relationship between the individual and his past. Far from being a mere link in serial time between past and future, the present, according to the assumptions of African autobiography, is a ritual repetition, or reincarnation, of the past and a precise rehearsal of the future. It may be, as Pliny reported the Greeks as saying, that there is always something new from Africa; but *within* Africa, and especially within any given African culture, both experience and personality tend to be conceived of as repetitive and unchanging, the same in the past, now, and (it is assumed) forever. Thus, Jomo Kenyatta can perform the unusual feat of writing the biography of Chief Wangombe, a Gikuyu predecessor of one hundred plus years ago, not by consulting any written documents (because there are none), nor by simply following the details of oral tradition (because oral tradition seldom descends to such details), but by looking to his own—Jomo Kenyatta's—life, where, the writer assumes, he will discover not only the same general pattern of a ritualized life but the same details within the pattern as well. For a Gikuyu, the writing of biography is virtually indistinguishable from writing autobiography because Gikuyu life in the present is virtually indistinguishable from Gikuyu life twenty-five years ago or one hundred years ago or five hundred years ago.[1] Likewise, when an Ibo like Dilim Okafor-Omali writes ancestral biography—*A Nigerian Villager in Two Worlds*, ostensibly the biography of his father—he does the portrait of Ibo character equally

---

[1] Whether this notion is historically valid or not is beside the point; in fact, I do not suppose it is, especially because of the disruptions of the past fifty years. Nevertheless, the technique employed by Kenyatta here and elsewhere implies a belief in the absolute continuity of Gikuyu culture.

from himself and from his father. Chinua Achebe, another Ibo, carries the generational merger a step further into fiction that displays Ibo personality as constant and recurrent over a period of three or four generations. The African autobiographer who satisfies his children's curiosity about their father, also tells them—and in a single portrait—about their grandfather, their great-grandfather, and the clan founder and about themselves, the children, as they live the same one life.

Where there exists a spiritual identity between generations, it may be supposed that the autobiographer who offers his own life as an example or a model will do so in a larger, more symbolic sense than the literal way suggested by Franklin to his son. Boubou Hama, always very conscious of his representative status, suggests that his African readers could do much worse than to emulate his own efforts in mediation between Africa and Europe: "Et je propose," he says, "une autre route, celle de la synthèse entre l'Afrique Noire et l'Europe, c'est-à-dire, celle qui découlera de la mentalité de l'humanité la plus attardée techniquement, mais aussi peut-être la plus au centre de la réalité de l'homme vivant en harmonie avec la nature, et, c'est le cas de l'Europe, la plus avancée dans le domaine du progrès matériel."[2] Boubou Hama proceeds to present his own life as typical and his own conclusions as exemplary so that in his marriage, for example—he the évolué, knowledgeable in European ways; his wife, ignorant of the West but closely tied to the harmonies of nature—the desired synthesis of European and African worlds stands both as a symbol and as a model for imitation. Clarence Simpson of Liberia also finds a symbol and a model in marriage, though for him the example worthy of imitation was, significantly, not his own but his parents' union. Simpson's father, an "Americo-Liberian," came to Liberia from the United States with his father, and, when he grew up, married a Vai girl; as Clar-

[2] Boubou Hama, *Kotia-Nima*, I (Paris: Présence Africaine, 1968), p. 74.

ence Simpson points out in his *Memoirs,* "the Liberian tradition is essentially based on a combination or assimilation
of these two elements"—i.e., "new-comers from America . . .
with knowledge and experience of Western civilization"
and "the tribal people" who "had deep-rooted traditions
and customs of their own which they had acquired throughout the ages." Simpson goes on to say, "It can, therefore, be
seen that a marriage like that of my parents was to some
extent symbolic of the pattern of the country itself."[3] As
Simpson saw it, the marriage was not only a small symbol
of the history of Liberia but an indication as well of how
things ought to go in her future: "Born of the unity of the
two elements of our country, I was confronted each day of
my childhood with a living example of how these elements
could work side by side, without conflict, to their mutual
unity and enrichment" (p. 77).

Davidson Nicol, the Sierra Leonean physician, educator,
and writer, has more than once emphasized the significance
of autobiographical literature for the student of African
civilization and writing. "This nostalgic literature," as he
calls writings about childhood, "is most revealing, not only
to the non-African reading public but also to Africans themselves."[4] Nicol's point is that Africans come from many different cultural backgrounds, and if they are to find a pan-
African literary or political unity they must be aware of the
diverse strands that are woven together to form the African
experience—and autobiography, he says, is the way Africans can become aware of their differences and their similarities. The classic instance of "African writing . . . that . . .
describes childhood memories" (*ibid.*) is no doubt Camara

[3] *The Memoirs of C. L. Simpson, Former Liberian Ambassador to
Washington and to the Court of St. James's* (London: Diplomatic
Press & Publishing Co., 1961), p. 68.
[4] *Africa: A Subjective View* (London: Longmans, Green & Co.,
1964), pp. 76-77. Cf. Nicol's "Closing Address" at the Fourah Bay
Conference on African literature, included in *African Literature and
the Universities,* ed. Gerald Moore (Ibadan: Ibadan Univ. Press,
1965), esp. pp. 134-35.

30

Laye's *L'enfant noir*, a book in which the author relives the joys of his childhood by recreating that childhood in narrative form. Indeed, for a number of other African writers who remembered their own childhood experience differently, Camara Laye's account is a little too classic, a little too nostalgic, a little too good to be true. On the other hand, a few African autobiographers share Camara Laye's delight in recalling a time that was better, more coherent and unified, than the present. Robert Wellesley Cole (like Nicol a Sierra Leonean and a physician) concludes his account of an essentially happy, normal childhood—a childhood abnormal only in the social position of the parents, in the psychological balance of the mother and father, and in the extraordinary intelligence of the writer—by saying, "I must bring to an end what after all is a story about a *boy*. As to when I ceased to be a boy, and became a young man, I do not know. . . . All I know is that one day I woke up to find that that cocoon of a boy with which we started at Kossoh Town was gone. When it happened I do not know. But I am glad to have been that boy."[5] Camara Laye would willingly echo Cole's last sentence, as would Joseph Seid, who tells of his happy childhood, youth, and early maturing in *Un enfant du Tchad*;[6] all three would agree with Franklin that no man, no matter how much he wishes it, can have his childhood back, but "that which resembles most living one's life over again, seems to be to recall all the circumstances of it; and, to render this remembrance more durable, to record them in writing." Unable to live their lives again, Camara Laye, Robert Wellesley Cole, and Joseph Seid do the next best thing in recalling the circumstances of life in Kouroussa, Freetown, and Fort Lamy and recording them in writing.

No doubt the very act of writing an autobiography im-

[5] *Kossoh Town Boy* (Cambridge: Cambridge Univ. Press, 1960), p. 191.

[6] Joseph Brahim Seid, *Un enfant du Tchad* (Paris: Sagerep L'Afrique Actuelle, 1967).

plies a certain vanity on the author's part, but there is one variety of African autobiography—viz., political autobiography—in which the author's high opinion of himself and his achievements is not merely implicit or discreetly veiled but is spread broadcast across the page in accounts of heroic martyrdom and marvellous accomplishments, in stirring descriptions of lonely grandeur, faulty friends, and villainous opponents. No one, I imagine, would confuse Kwame Nkrumah (or "Osagyefo," as he liked to be called) with a shrinking violet in *Ghana: The Autobiography of Kwame Nkrumah* and in *Dark Days in Ghana*; indeed, in the titles and in the attitudes of both those books, Nkrumah seems rather to fail to distinguish between himself and his fate and Ghana and her fate, and many of Nkrumah's critics maintained that his ego was capable of devouring not only the whole of Ghana but all of Africa as well. If he was vain, however, Nkrumah had no corner on that special human quality, not even within the struggle for political power in Ghana. In *Dark Days in Ghana* Nkrumah almost disdains to speak of a certain military leader, instrumental in the coup of 1966, whom the Osagyefo, one gathers, considered to be a snot-nosed brat unworthy of his lofty attention from exile in Guinée. Ironically one has only to read *The Ghana Coup* by Colonel Afrifa (the military man in question)[7] to see that Nkrumah was pretty much right in his estimate of Afrifa if not, perhaps, in his estimate of himself. Or to take the several cases of politicians in Nigeria, we get fascinating but (to say the least) contradictory estimates of personal worth in a number of autobiographies, all of which are more or less vainglorious and each of which manages to savage one or more of the others: the Sardauna of Sokoto's *My Life*, Chief Anthony Enahoro's *Fugitive Offender*, Chief Obafemi Awolowo's *Awo*, and Nnamdi Azikiwe's *My Odyssey*. Even Aderogba Ajao, who would seem to have little political authority to pronounce but consider-

[7] Akwasi Amankwa Afrifa, *The Ghana Coup, 24th February 1966*, preface by K. A. Busia (London: Cass, 1966).

32

able daring and vanity, hazards a few firm opinions about Nigerian politics in *On the Tiger's Back*. If we skip over to Kenya, we see that few people would accuse Jomo Kenyatta of undue reticence in proclaiming his own virtues, but even fewer readers of *Not Yet Uhuru* would make that mistake about Kenyatta's erstwhile friend and sometime enemy Oginga Odinga.[8] Seldom has so much been done by so few —and with so little gratitude to show for it as a reward— as in these political autobiographies. Even the politically feckless Kabaka of Buganda—Mutesa II to his subjects, "King Freddie" to his chums in England—hapless and unfortunate as his kabakaship eventually proved to be, is not, in his autobiography,[9] given to hiding the light of his elephant-hunting achievements or his man-of-the-world accomplishments under a basket; and he treats his opponents, whether English or Ugandan, with a regal contempt. African politics, as African political autobiographies demonstrate, is not the ground on which to cultivate humility. Speculating on the larger implications of this fact, one might imagine that the special egocentricity of political autobiographies is very likely an accurate reflection of the personality that naturally gravitates to politics.

The expressions of concern of African politicians may be no more than lip service, but many of them have emphasized the need to respect and preserve, at least in record, a fast-disappearing past of unique glory. This reverential attitude toward the past, whether it be an individual, an ethnic, or the African past, motivates not only historians and anthropologists but also autobiographers whose work, depending on which past they choose to embrace (some, like Boubou Hama, embrace all three), will issue in personal, cultural, or symbolic autobiography. Bokar N'Diayé,

[8] See Chapter II below on Kenyatta; for Oginga Odinga, *Not Yet Uhuru* (London: Heinemann, 1967). Odinga's title means that "uhuru" (freedom) was "not yet" under Kenyatta's presidency in Kenya.

[9] Mutesa II, Kabaka of Buganda, *Desecration of My Kingdom* (London: Constable, 1967).

33

an anthropologist and historian from Mali, sets the tone in the conclusion to *Les castes au Mali*, which is an exercise in recording and preserving a social structure now passing: "En tout état de cause, devant la transformation profonde que subit l'Afrique, qui, en moins d'un demi siècle, est passé avec une rapidité surprenante de l'état statique à l'état dynamique, il n'est que temps de recueillir tous les renseignements utiles sur son passé auprès des derniers survivants d'une époque qui sera bientôt totalement révolue."[10] This is the motive for African autobiographies, from Camara Laye (whose world is mostly the world of family and village) to Jomo Kenyatta and from Benjamin Akiga to Mbonu Ojike to Joseph Seid. "It is not every elder who is well versed in Tiv lore," Akiga, the anthropological autobiographer, tells us. "Some know, others do not. It is the men of mature years who know best. . . ."[11] Men of mature years, as Akiga goes on to say, will not be available to the inquirer forever, and the knowledge they possess, heretofore transmitted only orally, if not set down in more permanent records, is in danger of being totally lost because of the tremendous social changes current in Africa. Adding social change to the inherent weakness of oral transmission is like the introduction of foreign ideals and techniques in the making of African masks: what humidity and termites have not caused to be lost in the case of masks, or oral transmission in the case of cultural lore, foreign ideals and social change respectively will soon destroy. "Sous l'apport d'idées nouvelles, des chocs de civilisations diverses, du progrès intellectuel et technique, la vieille espérance théologique des ancêtres s'amenuise de jour en jour, devient de moins en moins ferme, appréhensible et cède peu à peu la place à une éthique nouvelle, à un nouveau mode de vie sociale, à une

[10] Bokar N'Diayé, *Les castes au Mali* (Bamako: Éditions Populaires, 1970), p. 126.

[11] *Akiga's Story: The Tiv Tribe as Seen by One of Its Members*, trans. and annotated by Rupert East, 2d ed. (London: Oxford Univ. Press, 1965), p. 2.

34

nouvelle croyance dont on ne sait où elle débouchera. Déclin, catastrophe, régénération, destinée éminemment épanouie et sereine?"[12] Joseph Seid asks his question of the future to which no man has the answer, but, turning to the past, he does what is possible by way of recreation and preservation: "De cette transmutation qui s'accomplit, Abakar [i.e., the autobiographical hero] a pris profondément conscience. Sans vouloir pourtant la déplorer, il voudrait simplement faire revivre ici des temps qui ne sont plus!" (p. 15). From historian to anthropologist to autobiographical romancer, the desire to preserve the times that are no more—to preserve them by recreating, recording, and transmitting them to future generations—is a great and durable motive for going back and bringing forward, for recapitulating the past in a present act of memory, for, in short, writing autobiography.

Making the past live again in the present and for a future that would otherwise know nothing of it is similar to describing the African world for an outsider otherwise altogether ignorant of it. One may surmise that this desire to inform the world outside provides a major motive in African autobiography by the fact that the great majority of the autobiographies were originally written in either English or French, that is, in one of the languages of the outside world. This mediation between two worlds (cf. the title of Mugo Gatheru's autobiography—*Child of Two Worlds*— and Dilim Okafor-Omali's biography of his father—*A Nigerian Villager in Two Worlds*) has provided the African intellectual and writer with his special role and his most common theme in fiction as in autobiography. Also, however, because the African world has been so utterly unknown to the West, the mediatorial and informative function, especially when performed by an unscrupulous or non-intellectual autobiographer, has led to some eminently grotesque results. The autobiography called *Alice Princess*,

[12] Joseph Seid, *Un enfant du Tchad*, pp. 14-15.

for example (introduced and given its prevailing tone of simpering idiocy by Ralph Edwards), describes the great humanitarian act that brought Alice Princess (Msumba) Siwundhla from "primitive," "heathen," "superstitious," "filthy," "ignorant," "tribal" Africa (specifically Nyasaland) to wonderful, warmhearted, generous, Christian, clean, modern America (specifically Los Angeles and Alabama) to appear on "This is Your Life." More wonderful perhaps than Alice Princess' memories, but no less grotesque, are some of the events of African life retailed to an amazed foreign public by Bata Kindai Amgoza ibn LoBagola (whose book, *LoBagola: An African Savage's Own Story*, Jahn and Dressler rudely bibliograph as a forgery). *LoBagola* is a sort of *Gulliver's Travels*, except that it is supposedly written by a "savage," fitted out with some very strange customs indeed, surrounded by such frightening creatures as pygmy cannibals, and capable of throwing in snatches of odd language now and then for the sake of verisimilitude. Lo-Bagola tells how and why he married "Gooma, the Princess" (because she "had saved my life from the wounded man-eating lion, by stopping it in its course with a poisoned assegai"),[13] but he says he was not allowed to consummate the marriage because the clever and courageous but unfortunate Gooma had committed a ritual offence; however, somewhat later—at the age of eleven or twelve—he married five other wives in a single ceremony and by them produced fourteen boys (he neglects to say how many girls) in less than two years from the date of marriage. It is a matter of interesting speculation what the child-wonder Lo-Bagola might have been able to accomplish if he had been allowed his favorite, "Gooma, the Princess," among his other wives. LoBagola comments, more in sorrow and disbelief than in anger, on the extreme skepticism of an Englishman who dared to doubt the story that LoBagola produced regularly on demand for paying audiences: "It is the

[13] *LoBagola: An African Savage's Own Story* (New York: Alfred A. Knopf, 1930), p. 38.

same in the United States today. People all over the country try to show that I am deceiving people in this story of my life. They have told me to my face that I never saw Africa; that I was born somewhere in western Pennsylvania or in some place in the South" (pp. 257-58). Whether he was born in western Pennsylvania, in the South, or in the French Sudan, as he claimed, LoBagola's story, though sometimes entertaining, clearly does not give the reader the secure sense that he gets from the autobiographical writings of Joseph Seid, Jomo Kenyatta, Ezekiel Mphahlele, or Mbonu Ojike of being informed about a real, historical, and existent Africa.

Many of the writers, as I have suggested, choose to inform the outside world about Africa and the African experience by dramatizing their lives and then taking their own case as representative. Joseph Seid does this both in his story and in his title (*Un enfant du Tchad*), and Boubou Hama does it when he speaks, but in his own voice, for all Niger, or when, at a more inclusive level of representativeness, he says, "Kotia-Nima est l'Afrique Noire."[14] André Maurois warns us, however, that we cannot take childhood memories, such as those evoked by Joseph Seid and Boubou Hama, by Camara Laye and Robert Wellesley Cole, for accurate descriptions of the reality of growing up: "Of the vast accession of vocabulary, ideas, and emotions; of our own introduction to the world outside, of the successive pictures of society which are formed in the mental vision of a child —of all this we retain practically nothing; and so an autobiography of childhood is nearly always commonplace and

[14] *Kotia-Nima*, ii, 38. Lamine Gueye does something very similar in *Itinéraire africain* (Paris: Présence Africaine, 1966) when he traces simultaneously his own development and the evolution of a nation. In his life's experience, Gueye sees the developing face of Sénégal, the two going hand in hand, and that double development is further parallel to the liberation in the course of history of all of Africa. Kwame Nkrumah does almost exactly the same thing in his autobiography except that the developing nation is Ghana rather than Sénégal.

untrue, even when the author himself is sincere."[15] What validity can there be, then, in trying to understand a people, a nation, a continent from a typical case that, in its description, "is nearly always commonplace and untrue"? The pointless details from childhood that do remain in memory, according to Maurois, are "not enough to explain the complex individuality which we all acquire by the age of six or seven" (p. 152). If, however, individual lives are not developed by a bias for "complex individuality," but are lived according to a single and general pattern (as it has always been in the past, so also will it be in the present), and if childhood and youth consists in passing through ritual stages observed countless times in countless lives, a tale told a thousand and a million times, then it would be reasonable to imagine that autobiography could be written around this ritualized experience that would be both personal and communal, typical and archetypical—and though it might be "nearly always commonplace," it would not necessarily be therefore "untrue." "Where is the point," T. S. Eliot asks,

> at which the merely individual
> Explosion breaks
> In the path of an action merely typical
> To create the universal, originate a symbol
> Out of the impact?[16]

African autobiography, which imitates African life in universalizing the individual experience, would seem to demonstrate that "the point" is in ritual—in the "rites de passage" that mark individual life with the imprint of general humanity. Robert Wellesley Cole describes the exact ritual ceremony performed at his own birth and says, "What I have described actually happened. I saw it myself"

---

[15] André Maurois, *Aspects of Biography* (New York: D. Appleton & Co., 1929), pp. 152-53.

[16] From "A Note on War Poetry," *Collected Poems 1909-1962* (New York: Harcourt, Brace & World, 1963), p. 215.

(*Kossoh Town Boy*, p. 29)—he saw it in the case of brothers and sisters, repeated step for step the same. "In my mind those events have been telescoped into a symbol," he continues, "a symbol repeated on each occasion, until it did not matter who the central figure was. In this drama the principal actor could be any one of us children, including me. I was the first, that is all." This is what causes descriptions of personal experience in African autobiographies to be so consistent and similar and sometimes repetitive, even from parts of Africa far removed from one another. African life is marked, directed, and regulated by ritual repetition so that the description, like the experience, assumes a communal and archetypal quality. Consequently, we have reason to trust an account of African childhood—not in spite of its being commonplace but because it is commonplace—and reason, further, to take the commonplace as eminently representative.

As there are many possible motives for African autobiography, so also its writers approach the African experience from many different, "specialist" points of view, though, as I have pointed out, the veneer of specialization is generally much thinner (and one can see this in comparing autobiographies) in Africa than in the West. Of the kinds of autobiography, or the points of view from which the writers view their experience, one might mention political, literary, and ethnographic autobiographies. There are also, in addition to these three central varieties, African autobiographies written by students, by travellers (who are frequently also students), by slaves or ex-slaves, and by men of religion. There are finally those autobiographies written from a unique point of view (e.g., the point of view of a twin in a society that either fears or reverences twins) or from no particular point of view at all but only as human address to human readers. One is compelled to recognize, however, that for all this variety of points of view, African autobiography has a distinctively African and noticeably non-

Western quality about it: unity, both in a positive sense (as being African) and in a negative sense (as being non-Western), is there not far beneath the surface of diversity.

I have already mentioned the unique opportunity offered by the autobiographies of Nigerian writers for reading in Nigerian politics and in the modern history of Nigeria. We now have autobiographies from all the major actors in the movement for Nigerian independence: the Sardauna of Sokoto from the Northern Region (leader of NPC, the Northern Peoples Congress); Chief Obafemi Awolowo from the Western Region (leader of the Action Group); and Nnamdi Azikiwe[17] from the Eastern Region (leader of NCNC, the National Council of Nigeria and the Cameroons)—and, thrown in for extra measure, the autobiographies of a few peripheral figures like Chief Anthony Enahoro. With these various autobiographies centered on a single event—Nigerian independence—which was composed naturally of many events, one can, as it were, surround the subject. Reading these autobiographies gives one the sense that Nigerian history happened as it did because these men, singly and together, were as they were; it gives the sense, that is, that history might most fruitfully be read not in terms of documents and dates but as a function of the interplay of personalities. What these books offer us is (to adapt Victor Uchendu's phrase) the history-bearer's point of view. Autobiography, which reveals—sometimes consciously, sometimes unconsciously—the motives and the psychologies of the men who act out history, may tell us more about the sources, the causes, the reasons of history than the formal writing of history itself. Consider a very minor, but repeated, detail from the Sardauna of Sokoto's *My Life*: of Oliver Lyttelton (later Lord Chandos) the

---

[17] Azikiwe's *My Odyssey: An Autobiography* (London: C. Hurst & Co., 1970) carries his story only up to 1947 when he entered politics; another volume is promised that will continue the story of his political career after 1947. One nevertheless gets a good idea of the man behind the politician from *My Odyssey*.

40

Sardauna says, "He is a big man physically, with a comprehensive intelligence. Being a big man myself, I find that I can get on with big men better than I can with small ones. . . ."[18] Later he remarks, "My own Secretary was R. E. Greswell, an officer as tall and as big as I am myself, and one on whose ability and integrity I have always placed the greatest reliance" (p. 167). These remarks, echoed several times elsewhere, do not mean much in themselves, but in his own autobiography and in the autobiographies of others, as well as in histories of the time, the Sardauna comes off as an extremely proud and imperious man; and who can say how much of history does or does not depend on a political leader's manifest attitude toward himself and on his consequent relations with others—both of which, as with the Sardauna, may be determined by the psychology of relative physical size? This same sort of interplay of personalities, issuing in the making of history, can be observed in the autobiographies of Nkrumah and Afrifa in Ghana; in the autobiographies of Jomo Kenyatta, Oginga Odinga, Tom Mboya, and various "Mau Mau" figures in Kenya; in several autobiographies from South Africa; and in single autobiographies from Liberia (Clarence Simpson); Sénégal (Lamine Gueye); Niger (Boubou Hama); Uganda (the Kabaka of Buganda);[19] Rhodesia (Ndabaningi Sithole);

[18] *My Life* (Cambridge: Cambridge Univ. Press, 1962), p. 159.

[19] Ham Mukasa's *The Story of Ham Mukasa, told by himself* describes the Kabaka's court around the turn of the century and the same author's *Uganda's Katikiro in England* contains the impressions of a Muganda on tour in England.

Though Simon Mpondo, in an article in *Présence Africaine* (NS No. 78, p. 131), calls Akiki K. Nyabongo's *Africa Answers Back* (in America, *The Story of an African Chief*) an "autobiography," it is not that at all but rather poor historical fiction about the Kingdom of Buganda beginning with Stanley's penetration of Buganda in the time of Mutesa I. Mutesa II, the great-grandson of the first Mutesa and the thirty-sixth Kabaka of Buganda, gives a very interesting and revealing account of his ancestor's meeting with Stanley in *Desecration of My Kingdom*, which *is* an autobiography. (As Mutesa II describes it, the craft and guile that the old rogue practiced to maintain rule is remark-

Zambia (Kenneth Kaunda); and, no doubt, other nations besides. There are, one gathers from these political autobiographies from Africa, many Africans who would understand, as W. B. Yeats refused to do, Thomas Mann's pronouncement on the twentieth century: "In our time the destiny of man presents its meaning in political terms."

The political conditions of South Africa have been uniquely terrible in our time. An odd consequence, which no one could have foreseen, is that South Africa has been especially prolific in literary (as well as other) autobiographies. Caught, and in various degrees mangled, in the wheels of political oppression, a number of South African writers have responded with personal documents testifying to what it is to be black and to be a creative artist in twentieth-century South Africa. Oppressed by politics, they have written, nevertheless, not political manifestoes but literary autobiographies. Ezekiel Mphahlele, Peter Abrahams, Arthur Hutchinson, Bloke Modisane, Dugmore Boetie, and, in a rather different sense, Noni Jabavu, Todd Matshikiza, and Gerard Sekoto have all produced accounts of their experience in South Africa that take their bearings in the politics of that nation—in the fact that South Africa is a police state—but that thematically and structurally play off against this political reality the literary or artistic (Matshikiza was a musician, Sekoto is a painter) creativity of the autobiographer at the heart of his work. For all these writers, the question that insists on being answered in their lives and their autobiographies is what or how they can create in a nation divided and oppressed by apartheid. Exile and literary autobiography have been their typical answers. There are, of course, literary autobiographies from else-

---

ably like the political means of the Saifs in Yambo Ouologuem's *Bound to Violence.*) James Rubadiri, in an interesting poem called "Stanley Meets Mutesa" (with echoes of Eliot's "Journey of the Magi" but ironically and from an African point of view) deals with the same momentous penetration of an ancient black African kingdom by the white world.

where in Africa. Many of Chinua Achebe's essays and interviews, for example, could be seen in that light; or there is
Boubou Hama, who cannot for long refrain from verse in
his autobiography; or Mbella Sonne Dipoko, from the Cameroons, who has written about the cultural experience of his
generation in a poem that he calls "Autobiography." But the
paradoxical truth is that, certainly without willing or desir-
ing it, the political machine of South Africa has been the
secondary cause of all of the finest literary autobiographies
from Africa.

Because of the more than intimate relationship in Africa
between individual existence and group existence, personal
literary expression tends very frequently to shade off into
cultural expression (though this is much less true in South
Africa, due to the politicized life there). Mbella Sonne
Dipoko conducts the poem mentioned above—his "Autobiography"—all in the first-person plural and concludes, "our
hearts listen to the voice of days in flight/ Our thoughts
dusting the past." This philosophical and psychological
tendency to merge the singular and the plural of the first
person and to bring together present consciousness with
past experience is what produces the considerable amount
of ethnographic autobiography from Africa—Jomo Kenyatta's *Facing Mount Kenya* and *My People of Kikuyu*;
Mugo Gatheru's *A Child of Two Worlds*; Victor Uchendu's
*The Igbo of Southeast Nigeria* (which moves not only between singular and plural but, like Kenyatta's works,
between first and third person); Prince Modupe's *I Was a
Savage*; Dilim Okafor-Omali's *A Nigerian Villager in Two
Worlds*; Rems Nna Umeasiegbu's *The Way We Lived*;
Mbonu Ojike's *My Africa* and *I Have Two Countries*; Ben-
jamin Akiga's *Akiga's Story*. In the more detached voice of
fiction, Chinua Achebe (particularly in his early novels),
Onuora Nzekwu, and James Ngugi[20] frequently resort to

[20] Though it is not notably successful as a fictional technique,
Ngugi shifts from an omniscient point of view to a first-person plural
point of view in the description of the *Uhuru* celebration in *A Grain*

something that could fairly be called fictionalized ethnography, or the dramatized autobiography of a people. Damien d'Almeida, choosing to leave his round tale unvarnished by the faculty of imagination and seeing clearly to what audience it will therefore appeal, says of his book, "C'est l'expression libre d'une réalité vécue. Rien n'y est artificiel, rien n'y est fantaisie. La réalité ne dépasse-t-elle pas la fiction? L'ethnologue y lira avec quelque intérèt la dualité de deux civilisations, de deux croyances religieuses, comme le public y trouvera l'ambiance toute particulière qui entoure LE JUMEAU dans la Société Sud Dahoméenne."[21] The special experience of a twin in Dahomean society is of potential interest to both the ethnologist and the general public (and to the museum-keeper who has Ibeji figures— i.e., ritual twin figures—in his collection); but of particular interest to the foreign anthropologist, d'Almeida suggests, will be his representative, "child-of-two-worlds" experience as a Christian, educated in Catholic schools, raised, however, by a grandmother who was a priestess of Tchango, an "animist" god. *Le jumeau* has several things to recommend it, not the least of which is its peculiar blend of a more or less unique experience with an experience that is very commonly shared all across West Africa.

One thing that d'Almeida, like almost all his fellow practitioners of autobiography, describes in detail is his Western education. "The most significant feature in all these childhood memories of African writers," Davidson Nicol has remarked, and with reasonable accuracy, "is the enormous desire and striving for education, at home and overseas. . . ."[22] In a number of African autobiographies, this intense desire for education, being much more than a mere

---

*of Wheat*, as if to suggest that that event was a corporate, community affair to be presented in fiction as the experience of the entire group (*A Grain of Wheat* [London: Heinemann, 1968], esp. pp. 244-47).

[21] Damien d'Almeida, *Le jumeau; ou mon enfance à Agoué* (Cotonu: Les Éditions du Bénin, 1966), p. 5.

[22] *Africa*, pp. 77-78.

detail among details, is the chief motive in the writer's life and the controlling structural principle in his book. Legson Kayira's hunger for education, though it was extreme in degree, was not different in kind from the feelings of half a hundred other African autobiographers nor from the desire of millions of his fellow Africans who have not written about themselves. In *I Will Try* Kayira describes his fantastic adventure in education: setting out one morning from his home village in Nyasaland (now Malawi), and carrying food for his lunch, Kayira, with no very clear ideas about geography, started to walk to the United States to go to school. Two years later, and with his lunch long since gone and forgotten, he had walked as far as Khartoum in the Sudan (whence he was flown to his destination in Washington state), which on any map of Africa is a distance of two thousand miles even as the crow would fly it. Paraphrasing *Pilgrim's Progress*, Kayira says (and he speaks for many others), "I had already started my journey and had already gone so far, and there was no reason to turn back. I would go forward. There where I was going I would get an education, incorruptible and undefiled, and one that would not fade away. I was leaving my family, I was leaving all my friends, and I was leaving all that I had at home in order to find that education."[23] Earlier, Kayira, more simply, perhaps more accurately, and certainly, in the eyes of the villagers, more truly, calls this motive to journey a "greediness for learning" (p. 81). Greediness or glorious vision or simple mental hunger, whatever we may call it, this instinct has impelled a great many Africans to do impossible things in order to "learn book" and it has led several of them to write about it autobiographically. We can content ourselves with mentioning three out of many who have thinly veiled the experience with fiction and thus provided it with a thematic structure—Bernard Dadié in *Climbié*, Francis Selormey in *The Narrow Path*, and William Conton in *The*

[23] Legson (Didimu) Kayira, *I Will Try* (Garden City, N.Y.: Doubleday & Co., 1965), p. 109.

*African*—and then pass on to autobiographers whose books combine the point of view of the student with that of the traveller.

The African who writes of his experiences abroad may be imagined to be addressing one of two audiences, or, sometimes, both simultaneously: he may be describing for an African public customs and a place with which they are not familiar; or he may be describing for a foreign public his reactions as an African to that foreign milieu. Aderogba Ajao's *On the Tiger's Back* offers the fruit of his experience —first as a student in Scotland and England and then as a "kidnap" victim subjected to Communist indoctrination in East Germany—to the newly independent nation of Nigeria: his message to Nigeria and West Africa—the wisdom, as Ajao obviously feels, won from days of bitter suffering—is to avoid the wily snares of Communism. Other African students with experience of Communist countries have returned to write the same message into their autobiographies: Emmanuel John Hevi's *An African Student in China*; Andrew Amar's *A Student in Moscow*; and William Anti-Taylor's *Moscow Diary*. On the other ideological hand, there are some rather acute satiric pictures of the United States to be had in John Pepper Clark's *America, Their America* (which, as a piece of literature, is no doubt the best of these travel documents), in Bernard Dadié's *Patron de New York*, and in Lewis Nkosi's *Home and Exile*. The account of Mugo Gatheru's experiences as a student with U. S. immigration authorities during the heyday of Joseph McCarthy—all a result, apparently, of his being from Kenya in the time of "Mau Mau," which was supposed to be Communist-oriented—makes harrowing enough reading, though temperamentally Mugo Gatheru is not much given either to satire or to excessive criticism. Legson Kayira's *I Will Try* (not to mention *Alice Princess*) affords much more comfort to the would-be defender of the United States than Mugo Gatheru's book. Two other books, neither very significant, complete the list: Joseph N. Major's *Forever a*

*Stranger*, which is the narrative of his religious education in Kenya and Uganda and in Rome and then his travels, as a failed priest, throughout Europe; and Olabisi Ajala's *An African Abroad*, an account of his travels around the world (India, Russia, Iran, Israel, Egypt, Australia) on nothing but a motor-scooter and a considerable nerve, the second of which brought him meetings with Nehru, Khrushchev, the Shah of Iran, Golda Meir, Nasser. Ajala threatens that this is the first volume of a trilogy as he continues on his intrepid way.

Narratives of slave life in the United States are currently receiving a good deal of attention from historians and, occasionally, literary critics. A few of these narratives, though unfortunately not the most reliable of them, go back in the author's memory to Africa. From the autobiographies, narratives, brief descriptions, and letters of a number of eighteenth- and nineteenth-century Africans one can get some idea of what slavery was and how it came into the lives of people in sometimes (but by no means always) peaceful and remote villages in Africa. The two best and most reliable accounts are Olaudah Equiano's *Interesting Narrative* and Samuel Crowther's *Narrative of His Early Life* (which exists both in a "first" and a "second" version). The terror, the desperate fear and hopelessness, the sickening wrench from a known life to something unknown and inconceivable are better conveyed in these two remarkably sober and unhysterical accounts by the victims than anywhere else. There are other documents—James Gronniosaw's pietistic *Narrative of the Most Remarkable Particulars*; Venture Smith's Paul Bunyanesque *Narrative of the Life and Adventures*; a number of descriptions of slavery anthologized in Philip Curtin's *Africa Remembered*; and the lively, observant, and shrewd narrative (included in Kirk-Greene's *West African Travels and Adventures*) of Dorugu, who was captured in a slave raid when well under ten, served a number of African masters before going with the explorers Overweg and Barth, travelled with Barth

47

across the Sahara to Tripoli, and from there eventually visited Malta, France, England, and Germany. For a feeling of what it is to commence a life of slavery, however, no account is better than those of Crowther and Equiano.

Crowther, wherever one reads him, whether in his *Narrative* or in his *Journals* describing different expeditions up the Niger River, is always a humane and intelligent writer. He is also—naturally, given his life-story—a deeply Christian writer. Crowther was born in Nigeria, captured in a slave raid as a child, sold quickly to one master after another, marched down to the sea, and sold on board a Portuguese slave-ship that was stopped in Lagos harbor by a British ship doing antislave-trade duty. He was carried on the British ship to Sierra Leone and there placed in a mission and educated; he was sent to England and then went on the 1841 Niger expedition; was ordained, returned to Nigeria as a missionary, and eventually became a bishop of the church. Crowther, like James Gronniosaw, approaches his experience not only from the point of view of an ex-slave but from the point of view of one who is religious and specifically Christian. Thomas Beselow's *From the Darkness of Africa to the Light of America*, otherwise an insignificant book written to please a complacent and (Beselow hoped) patronizing America, combines the student's and the Christian's point of view. It is unlikely, of course, that priests or serious practitioners of traditional religions would write their autobiographies for an outside world. They are, for one thing, frequently illiterate, but also, and more important, publishing secrets to the world is not encouraged—in fact, very much the opposite—in their professional training. Accounts of religious beliefs and ceremonies can be found in many of the autobiographies from Africa, but always by an observer half-removed or more by his own education, beliefs, and attitudes.

Finally, there are autobiographies written from a unique point of view or from no particular point of view at all—

which often comes to much the same thing. I have already mentioned Damien d'Almeida's autobiography, written as a twin, in which he says, explaining why that point of view makes him unusual, "Quant aux jumeaux eux-mêmes, incarnations d'une divinité, ils sont l'objet d'un véritable culte" (*Le jumeau*, p. 45).[24] Unusualness in d'Almeida's case was not something caused by him, but simply came to him concomitant with his birth. N.G.M. (Abdoulaye) Faye, on the other hand, shows us an autobiographical hero in *Le débrouillard* who fought hard for all the extraordinary honors that came to him: the boxing championship of Sénégal and West Africa, a professional boxing career in France, and a starring role in the movie that won the Delluc Prize for the best French film of the year and the first prize in an international film festival in Lucarno. Faye's experiences, as he recounts them in *Le débrouillard* ("Mais croyez-moi, ce n'est pas une histoire gratuite que je vais vous raconter, c'est une réalité, du fait que je l'ai vécue moi-même"),[25] are not so much unusual as unique; his autobiography, consequently, is not really typical of anything African (nor—which is perhaps surprising, given his life—is it very interesting). Charity Waciuma and Baba of Karo have produced autobiographies—the first written in Eng-

24 Other West African peoples adopt an opposite attitude toward twins. Udo Akpabio, of the Anang in Nigeria, tells how his mother was treated: "Unfortunately, she gave birth to twin children and had to leave the town. According to our custom twin children are unnatural and the mother of such children is considered unclean. She is banished to a lonely part of the forest called the Ikot Iban Ekpo [Bush of the Women Devils. It is believed that one of the twin children is the result of association with an evil spirit] and the children are killed. Sometimes they were put into water-pots and left in the bush; other times they were placed in white-ant hills" (*Ten Africans*, pp. 43-44).

In the brief autobiographical sketch by Madame Marthe Aféwélé Kwami of Togo we are presented with the story of another twin, but she says little about the consequences of that special birth circumstance. See *Autobiographies d'Africains*, pp. 236-45 (esp. pp. 236-37).

25 N.G.M. Faye, *Le débrouillard* (Paris: Gallimard, 1964), p. 7.

lish, the second delivered orally in Hausa to Mary F. Smith —that give some idea of the point of view of the African woman. It says something about African social and sexual ideas and, probably, African educational practices that these two books, together with Noni Jabavu's two books and items in the Westermann and Perham anthologies, constitute the whole literature of autobiography from the woman's point of view.[26] Particularly prominent in Baba's version of the woman's point of view—and it is significant and natural that it should be so—is her concern with the complex, protracted, and precise rituals observed at childbirth and at betrothal and marriage (see *Baba of Karo*, esp. pp. 85ff., 126, and 138-47). Antera Duke's diary, published as a part of Daryll Forde's *Efik Traders of Old Calabar*, is written from his unique point of view as a particular man and from no special professional point of view (though he dealt in slave-trading). It is difficult to say what the significance of Naiwu Osahon's *The Climate of Darkness* and Nii Kwabena Bonne III's *Milestones in the History of the Gold Coast* might be; one can say, however, that each of them, though in ways quite different, is entirely pointless, a shambles both structurally and logically.

[26] Charity Waciuma, *Daughter of Mumbi* (Nairobi: East African Publishing House, 1969); *Baba of Karo* (New York: Philosophical Library, 1955); Noni Jabavu, *Drawn in Colour* (London: John Murray, 1960) and *The Ochre People* (New York: St. Martin's Press, 1963); Madame Marthe Aféwélé Kwami in *Autobiographies d'Africains*; and Nosente and Kofoworola Aina Moore in *Ten Africans*.

There is also, of course, the rather bad joke called *Alice Princess*, which can be safely disregarded. In *Black Background* John Blacking transcribes the autobiography of a girl who is known only under the pseudonym of Dora Thizwilondi Magidi, but this, like *Baba of Karo*, is more an anthropologist's fieldwork than it is African autobiography. Likewise, the autobiographical sketches in Lorene K. Fox's *East African Childhood*, one of which is by a girl, were written as school exercises, not as autobiography per se. The only autobiography, in a pure sense of the word, written by an African woman is Charity Waciuma's *Daughter of Mumbi*.

The formal variety of African autobiography is more quickly dealt with. At one extreme there is the factual and chronological record of a certain part of a life, with no attempt to impose a thematic pattern or to discover any significance in what happened: Antera Duke's diary provides one kind of example, Equiano's *Narrative* and Cole's *Kossoh Town Boy* another. A step removed from this, and perhaps the most common variety of autobiography from Africa (or anywhere), is the factual but "plotted," or thematically arranged, narrative: for example, Mugo Gatheru's *Child of Two Worlds*, Alfred Hutchinson's *Road to Ghana*, Boubou Hama's *Kotia-Nima*. Cultural autobiography takes advantage of the fact that the life of the individual African is so closely related to the life of those around him; it describes a community existence in conjunction with a personal narrative: Kenyatta's *Facing Mount Kenya*, for example, or *Akiga's Story* or Mbonu Ojike's *My Africa*. The autobiographical novel—say Mphahlele's *The Wanderers* or Dadié's *Climbié* or Selormey's *The Narrow Path*—transfers the personal experience of the writer more or less directly into the material of fiction. In a larger body of fictional work, taking a longer, multi-generational view of his experience, a writer like Chinua Achebe dramatizes the cultural autobiography of his people. The last step in this circle of expanding significance, which begins in individual autobiographical experience and moves outward to a fictional embrace of family, clan, culture, and Africa, is taken in a novel like Yambo Ouologuem's *Bound to Violence*, where the person whose "autobiography" is attempted is no less than the symbolic African and the content of the autobiographical presentation is no less than the whole of African history. Though they need not detain us, one should mention those "autobiographical" books in which not only the events are imaginary rather than historical but the authors are a fiction as well—that is, those works which purport to be written by Africans but which either

51

certainly were not or probably were not: "Akosua Abbs," *Ashanti Boy* (by M. E. Nockolds); "Georges Diallo," *La nuit du destin* (by le Révérend Père Georges Janssens); and, of course, "LoBagola," *LoBagola* (by God knows whom).

### (B) ... AND THE NON-AFRICAN READER

Despite the superficial diversity to be discovered in the motives, in the specialized points of view, and in the forms of African autobiographies, the writers, nevertheless, as human beings and as conscious speculators on their own lives, share (and this is no doubt especially true as the matter is viewed by a non-African reader) attitudes about the nature of human existence, assumptions about individual personality and its relation to communal life, and premises about perception and expression that are characteristically African and that therefore shape the autobiographies into a distinctively African configuration. The shape of an African autobiography—because any autobiography is in one sense a psychological and philosophical imitation of the writer's personality—is determined by the especial Africanness of the writer. This intimacy between culture and book is presumably present in Western autobiography as well, but I imagine that we think less often of such work as distinctively "Western" simply because we share in the outlines of thought that determine its form. Do we often think of John Stuart Mill as peculiarly Western? Surely not. Yet, the African reader would undoubtedly find him so, and if we consider Mill in relation to African autobiographers, he is in fact very Western, even excessively Western. What, on the other hand, makes *Kotia-Nima*, for example, so intensely and thoroughly African is not the fact that its events are located in Niger, in Upper Volta, and in Sénégal (Isak Dinesen's *Out of Africa* is not at all African, though it is set in Kenya) but that Boubou Hama is very consciously African and African through and through. One could logically trace the relationship between personality and completed work in African autobiography in either direction: from psychological tendencies and philosophical assumptions to finished form; or from finished form to psychological tendencies and philosophical assumptions. What is, however, available to most non-African observers is only the finished work, so one had better move in the direction that takes that for a starting point.

Anyway, though there is a typical unity about African autobiographies, there fortunately exist, as the bibliography to this study will demonstrate, many examples of the species and through these many examples one might hope to move inductively to the formal premises and philosophical attitudes that make them African. I have suggested earlier that it is a tactical mistake to take over a Western-derived world-view, to label it African, and then to force it on the individual work of literature. No doubt, as W. E. Abraham says, African metaphysics "must be a deductive system," but not being African and without that deductive system in our bones, in our blood, in our very moral being, we would make a very serious (but, I think, rather common) mistake if we tried to perform a deductive literary criticism. Moreover, though they may live the system, Africans are not great systematizers, and they show little interest in the bare outlines and abstractions of schematic philosophy. If we have access to no system or scheme, however, we do, on the other hand, have a fair number of lived documents and from them we may well expect to discover the source and the nature of the unity that informs these many and in some ways various autobiographies.

African life (and here again the sharp contrast with Western life serves to emphasize the fact), as I have already pointed out, has about it an extraordinary unity and cohesion. There is a single principle lying behind the practice of African politics and economics, African education and literature, African religion and ritual, whether the ritual be daily, seasonal, or generational; there is a single, comprehensive premise that determines African ancestral reverence or worship and that leads to what is called African socialism and African humanism and the African extended family. This single principle or premise is to be found, whether as conscious statement or as unconscious reflection of moral personality, in all African autobiography. In his poem called "Autobiography" Mbella Sonne Dipoko says, referring to a personal and historic time before the apparent disappearance of unity,

> We crawled and cried and laughed
> Without hope
> Without despair.
> We grew up
> Fenced in by the forest.

Samuel Crowther, a century earlier, after he had returned as a Christian missionary to Nigeria, spoke of the Brassmen as "a people who know no heaven, fear no hell, and who are *strangers from the covenant of promise, having no hope, and without God in the world.*"[27] There is a certain apparent connection between these two statements, but what is not at all apparent, yet no less real, is the connection between the observations of Dipoko and Crowther and the half-joking but also half-serious remark of the Kabaka of Buganda about his studies: "In the last algebra paper before School Certificate I received a very low mark, as my mind failed to grasp the significance of the unknown" (*Desecration of My Kingdom*, p. 78). It seems like a paradox to say that the Africans of these three comments— Dipoko and his contemporaries, the Brassmen, and the Kabaka—fail "to grasp the significance of the unknown," since there is no question but that an African feels the presence of spirits much more nearly and more numerously than a Westerner would. But this is precisely the point: those spirits, far from being unknown or mysterious or in-

[27] *Journals of the Rev. James Frederick Schön and Samuel Crowther . . .* , 2d ed. (London: Frank Cass & Co., 1970), p. 277.

comprehensible, are very intimately and familiarly known to the African. The truly unknown and the experientially unreal (as the spirits are not)—heaven or hell, the symbol *x* in algebra or mathematics in general (as Martin Akou says), abstract schematizing and zoological classifications (as Kenyatta argues), hope of the future and despair for the past—these do not touch him, do not determine his very existence, as present and immediate spirits do.

When Boubou Hama refers to "un tout collectif et religieux où l'homme n'est jamais seul" (*Kotia-Nima*, II, 15); when Kenyatta says that a father "is the proper means of communication and fellowship with his ancestors" (*Facing Mount Kenya*, p. 110); when Robert Wellesley Cole describes his home as "a nest, characterised by warmth, cosiness, loving parents, grandparents, aunts, uncles, cousins, foster brothers, held together as one large family" (*Kossoh Town Boy*, p. 32); when Noni Jabavu refers to her mother's people as "those of the umbilical cord" with "certain functions to perform" (*Ochre People*, p. 93), speaks of children as "symbols of continuity" (*Drawn in Colour*, p. 207), and declares that "in all things, human relationships with us rank supreme" (*ibid.*, p. 33); when Victor Uchendu tells us that "Igbo is a society which has no concept of celibacy" (*The Igbo*, p. 86) and Kwame Nkrumah maintains that "the worst thing that can befall" an African woman is sterility (*Ghana*, p. 3); when Julius Nyerere writes a collection of essays called *Ujamaa* about the extended family, African Socialism, and Pan-Africanism; and when Victor Uchendu says that at his birth it was determined that he was the reincarnation of his uncle and Birago Diop declares that "The dead are not dead" but are constantly, in the wind and in all of nature, breathing

> The heavy pact which ties us to life,
> The heavy law which binds us to acts—

they are not talking about ten different, distinct, or separable things: about religion, ancestor worship, extended family, parental relations, social structure, celibacy, sterility, politics, reincarnation, and the existence of spirits. Not at all: they are talking, all of them, and so are Dipoko, Crowther, and the Kabaka, about (in Hopkins' phrase) "one thing and the same." It would be easy enough to produce Jomo Kenyatta on education, Mbonu Ojike on economics, Onuora Nzekwu on sexual mores, Léopold Sédar Senghor on literature and art, Yambo Ouologuem on pornography, and Igbinokpoguié Amadasou or John Mbiti or Mugo wa Gatheru or Martin Akou[28] on religion to demonstrate that the case is the same with all those other areas, aspects, and interests of human life or in all those other disciplines that the Western world might separate from one another. It comes down to the belief that in Africa, or at least in African autobiographies, is less a belief than a certainty: human life, here and now, lived in the present moment and on a known, very precise piece of land, is the summary and the necessary conclusion of family and ancestral experience, the climax of all history, the focus of all spiritual being, both human and extra-human. This certainty determines the shape of autobiography and the mode of fiction from Africa as surely as it decides the nature of African politics, education, economics, and religion.

Whatever hazards this attitude toward human existence may portend—and no doubt there are hazards, especially as regards the free and full development of the extraordinary individual—the African runs little danger of what E. M. Forster describes in *Howards End* as the great and characteristic shortcoming of Western life: the failure to live in the present moment and in relation to immediate

[28] I shall not resist the temptation to quote Martin Akou on religion —he can fairly be taken to speak for the others: "Nous, Africains, nous sommes profondément religieux, c'est notre force. Notre religion est l'élément essentiel de notre être, *la base de notre communauté ethnique et de notre vie en commun.* Nous ne comprenons le sens de la vie qu'en partant d'elle" (*Autobiographies d'Africains*, p. 326). Italics are mine.

surroundings. In Africa, human history (which is really the only history conceivable according to African assumptions) does not look forward to any apocalypse or to any Second Coming ("Without hope," in Dipoko's phrase), nor does it look back with regret to a fall from grace ("Without despair"). This again may seem paradoxical since Africans, so much more than Westerners, are involved with ancestors and descendants and presumably, therefore, with the past and the future. However, they are connected with the past not as past but as present and with the ancestors not as dead but as very much living in their current embodiment, in their present descendant; likewise, the necessity to produce children is not to populate some unknown and distant future but is to continue life *as it is at this moment* in a timeless state. The ancestors, though individually long dead, have not been shunted off to heaven or hell: they are right there in the soil, in the air, in the life of the present descendants no matter how many generations removed; and there too exist the children and grandchildren who have yet to achieve physical embodiment. This attitude toward past and future, or, more properly, this attitude toward present time and present circumstance as the only reality, has tremendous consequences for individual life and for all other lives to which it may relate.

Virtually every African autobiography implies by its nature and displays in its performance a communality of existence that is unknown in the Western world.[29] In *Dark Child* Camara Laye speaks of all the reapers in the field as being humanly and mystically one in their work, "as if the same

[29] To be more specific: this communality of existence is unknown, or virtually so, in autobiographies of white writers of the West. There is an intriguing similarity often traceable between the autobiographies of Africans and such black American autobiographies as Frederick Douglass' *Life and Times* (and other slave narratives), Richard Wright's *Black Boy*, W.E.B. DuBois' *Dusk of Dawn*, and *The Autobiography of Malcolm X*. The similarity turns on the communality of experience and the consequent representativeness of the author's voice.

soul bound them,"[30] and this spiritual community, which is a much deeper thing, as Camara Laye describes it, than simply sharing a single task, often makes the line between individual personality and group personality a very difficult one to draw both in *Dark Child* and in other African autobiographies. True, Camara Laye did separate his own being from the being of the family and the group when he went to France, but he never fails to describe that separation as a terrible tearing apart, a rending of the communal soul, a sort of death for that which could only exist as a vital unity. In *Kotia-Nima*, Boubou Hama, the particularized, autobiographic case, begins in first-person but then becomes the third-person Kotia-Nima, the typical and representative case, the spokesman of Niger and the essence of Africa. "L'unité," according to the first-person Boubou Hama and his third-person representative case Kotia-Nima, "c'est, d'abord, chez nous, avec nos vastes horizons, 'un cas': l' 'individu,' tout un univers à discipliner pour qu'il prenne corps avec la famille, le village,—quand il existe—le groupe ou la tribu, la race et le peuple, l'ensemble fédéré qui se réalise *en unité compacte, nationale*" (*Kotia-Nima*, III, 175). Thus Boubou Hama, because there is a soul real and binding at each remove, progresses from himself to his family, his village, his village group, his people (Sonraï), his nation, finally to African unity: "Kotia-Nima est l'Afrique" (III, 193). Indeed, he proceeds eventually to a human and mystical unity, schematized on pages 153 and 155 of vol. III, leading from the individual through the family, the "corps social," the state and the nation, the earth and the universe, right up to "Dieu ou"—as he rather more cautiously rephrases it—"quelque chose." The focus of this great expanding circle is the being, simultaneously both personal and communal, of Kotia-Nima *né* Boubou Hama.

The unity of life and the communality of existence, as African autobiographies display it, might be described as

[30] *Dark Child* (New York: Noonday Press, 1954), p. 61.

both lateral or social and as vertical or ancestral. These two varieties of unity, far from being exclusive of one another, could not exist independently: the same idea of human life determines both. Lateral unity is a social phenomenon in which the individual is taken as essentially identical with the group and the group as identical with the individual, and it is a fact of African autobiography that one might describe as social, philosophic, and literary synecdoche. "According to the African tradition," Ndabaningi Sithole says (though, as a strong Christian, he had come to deplore the African tradition), "the individual counted in so far as he was part and parcel of the group"[31]—part and parcel that could stand for the whole group as the whole group can also be a personification from or a figure of speech for the part and parcel. "All authority flowed from the Kabaka," according to the thirty-sixth in that line of kings. "Just as he was the personification of the Baganda, so he and his actions were beyond judgement or question" (*Desecration of My Kingdom*, p. 31). Mutesa II goes on to explain that an action did not become right in the eyes of the Baganda merely because it had been performed and thus validated by their Kabaka, for that would almost imply questioning and judgment; the identification of the people and their personification—of the Baganda and their Kabaka —took priority over any such moral dilemma or decision. The Baganda accepted and welcomed any of the Kabaka's actions (and some of Mutesa I's deeds could have been endured and explained only in this way) as their own corporate and necessary act performed out of their deepest and most essential being. This notion that a people's spirit may be personified in a part or a parcel, and personified especially in a man whose acts in every area are their acts, has obvious and endless religious, political, social, even literary

---

[31] Ndabaningi Sithole, *African Nationalism*, 2d ed. (London: Oxford Univ. Press, 1968), p. 85. The first part of Sithole's book is his autobiography.

consequences, the most immediate of which, for our purposes, being that the Kabaka's autobiography is not his alone but the autobiography of the Baganda: the history of his people by way of being an account of his (and their) family, his (and their) ancestors, his (and their) trials, martyrdom, and exile, and his (and their) eventual foreseen glorious triumph and restoration. It is true that recent history seems to have proved this last element in their story, as told by Mutesa II, to be erroneous, yet the belief of the Baganda in the continued life of their Kabaka-personification no doubt remains undiminished in spite of the death in exile in England of Mutesa II.

Onuora Nzekwu, whose *Wand of Noble Wood*, ostensibly a novel, contains as much anthropological explanation as any reader could desire and considerably more than the plot can sustain, has one of his characters say this of "*chi*," which is. an important element in Ibo thought and a recurrent presence in Ibo fiction: "*Chi*, according to our traditional religious doctrines, was a genius, a spiritual double connected with every individual's personality. Every individual had a *chi*, a guardian angel, on whom his success or failure in life depended, for fortune was the result of the application of one's *chi* to God."[32] The last remark is explained in Victor Uchendu's discussion of *chi* when he says that it is *chi* which reincarnates in the family line and that *chi* bargains with God between embodiments for the condi-

[32] Onuora Nzekwu, *Wand of Noble Wood* (New York: New American Library, 1963), p. 96. The concept of *chi* is apparently similar to a Krio belief described by Robert Wellesley Cole in *Kossoh Town Boy*: "Sierra Leoneans have a belief that each child brings into this world its own destiny. Its own 'luck,' they call it. It is this, they say, which in the long run guides and shapes its future, and not the chance accidents that occur from day to day" (p. 155). That the Krios—who, as Cole describes them, are a synthetic, urban amalgamation of various peoples—should hold a belief so similar to the Ibos and other basically rural peoples demonstrates a certain consistency and unity in African thought.

tions of the upcoming incarnation. This is complicated enough, but in Chinua Achebe's *Arrow of God*, when the village of Umuaro seems to be going against the will of their chief deity *Ulu*, it is said that "Umuaro is today challenging its *chi*."[33] Thus one must suppose that there is a *chi* for the village ("a spiritual double connected with [its] personality") which would be the exact counterpart, embodied in the village, of individual *chi*. And when Dilim Okafor-Omali (in *A Nigerian Villager*, p. 32) draws the expanding circles of being in Iboland—individual, family, extended family, village, village-group, Ibo people—we are given to understand that each of these has its *chi* proper to itself and that they are all the same as one another while all being distinct from one another. When Mbonu Ojike declares stoutly that "The African thinks in terms of his family, not individuals; of his village not family; of his town not village; of his nation not his clan; of his race not nation; of mankind, not his race" (*My Africa*, p. 138), he may, toward the end, get rather carried away by his rhetoric into the mists of the United Nations; but what he begins with is indisputably true and what he goes on to say of the extended family— that uniquely African tie that binds all the way from the individual to the great continent itself—is equally important and irrefutable: "A family is not just husband, wife, and children. To us, it is a number of households. Perhaps two thousand persons make a family."[34] This extensive, delicate, and complex reticulation of relationships—so overwhelmingly important and omnipresent in Africa, so nearly

[33] *Arrow of God* (London: Heinemann, 1964), p. 32.

[34] *Ibid.* The Tiv, as we learn in *Akiga's Story*, "regard themselves almost literally as one huge family. . . . Every one of this family of half a million members can trace his descent to the common ancestor, and so can in theory tell his relationship to any other member. This is made possible by the fact that every kinship group, from the smallest unit up to the main divisions of the tribe, is called after its common parent" (p. 17). Cf. Chapter II below on the Gikuyu, where the articulation of social elements is point for point the same.

absent and virtually incomprehensible in the Western world—is to be observed autobiographically in descriptions of social responsibilities, ritual observances, forms of address ("brother" for "cousin"), and in accounts of the benefits accruing to the individual with such an immense and obligated family behind him.

African unity, moreover, is not only lateral and social; it is vertical and ancestral as well and comprehends, in the living present, as the dedication to *Facing Mt. Kenya* makes clear, both the past (but still existent) and the future (but potentially existent): Kenyatta's book, he says, is "for perpetuation of communion with ancestral spirits through the fight for African Freedom, and in the firm faith that the dead, the living, and the unborn will unite to rebuild the destroyed shrines." Those three elements drawn into unity, which one finds echoed in any number of places in African writing, are neither as vague nor as idle as they may sound since both the dead and the unborn have a real existence in the living, the contact point that unites the trinity as a single spiritual entity. "This book," Akiga says to his readers in Tivland, alluding to the notion of ancestral reincarnation, "fulfils a father's duty to all Tiv who have a care for that which concerns their own tribe. You, then, my Tiv brothers of the new generation that can read, read it and tell others, who cannot, of the things of our ancestors. . . . Let us take heart. The old mushroom rots, another springs up, but the mushroom tribe lives on" (*Akiga's Story*, p. 4). This explains, of course, why celibacy is inconceivable in African society and why sterility is the greatest misfortune for the African woman; it explains too the great anxiety of Victor Uchendu's parents until he was born to continue the ancestral line and the family name and the intense concern of Naboth Mokgatle's parents when, as a child, he was sick—concern for him individually no doubt, but concern more relevantly "that I should grow into a young man who would perpetuate my father's name and, if possible, have sons of my own who in their turn would perpetuate it until the end of time."[35] Living in a society that has little of the African sense of the present as the spiritual nexus between revered ancestors and reincarnate children and that therefore becomes ever more "liberal" about contraception and abortion, we may well have difficulty in understanding what Mbonu Ojike means when he says that the contraceptive is the greatest evil introduced to Africa by the West and in understanding the horror attached to the abortion performed in Chinua Achebe's *No Longer at Ease*.[36] It is little wonder that Noni Jabavu, back among her people after a number of years in England, "felt 'baffled with repletion' . . . by the emotions aroused by gazing into the mirror of ancestral conditions and 'umbilical' attitudes" (*Ochre People*, p. 177). Her expression describes very nicely what Western readers must often feel when they immerse themselves in those conditions and attitudes in reading African autobiographies and African fiction.

Naboth Mokgatle, a Mosotho of South Africa, says that

[35] Naboth Mokgatle, *The Autobiography of an Unknown South African* (Berkeley and Los Angeles: Univ. of California Press, 1971), p. 89. Cf. Mokgatle's earlier remark: "At that time my parents' children were all girls, and the chance of ever having a male child was beginning to fade away. The most worried person was my father, because he knew that if there was to be no male child born into the family his name would eventually disappear" (p. 2).

[36] See Chapter IV below for both of these and cf. the mordantly ironic observation in Achebe's "Girls at War," a short story concerned with events during the Biafran war: "One of the ingenious economies taught by the war was that a rubber condom could be used over and over again. All you had to do was to wash it out, dry it and shake a lot of talcum powder over it to prevent its sticking; and it was as good as new. It had to be the real British thing, though, not some of the cheap stuff they brought in from Lisbon which was about as strong as a dry cocoyam leaf in the harmattan" (*Girls at War* [London: Heinemann, 1972], p. 113).

Similarly, when Peter, the narrator of Onuora Nzekwu's *Wand of Noble Wood*, mentions the possibility that he may marry a nurse, one of his uncle's three wives gives him a thorough scolding and concludes by saying, "What is hideous about these nurses is that no week passes without a number of abortions standing to their credit" (p. 65).

his people worshipped a god whom they called *"modimo"* and they "imagined that *modimo* was Mosotho like themselves but beyond their reach and therefore that between them and *modimo*, whom they could not see and talk to, were their dead forefathers, whom they called *badimo"* (*Autobiography of an Unknown South African*, p. 35). The *badimo* (which is simply the plural of *modimo*) they could see and talk to all the time in their own lives, and so they became intercessory spirits to *modimo*. What is particularly interesting about the *badimo* is their reincarnational activity and the naming traditions that followed as a consequence of their perpetual rebirth: "They also believed in the second coming of their *badimo* in new forms. When a male baby was born it was imagined that his dead grandfather had come back to life, and so the child was given dead grandfather's name. The same thing applied to female children, in relation to their dead grandmothers" (*ibid.*, p. 36). A very fine and very short myth from Madagascar explains the origin of this atavistic return which is a common belief, according to autobiographies, across Africa: to the first man and the first woman God gave the choice of two kinds of death—"that of the moon or that of the banana"; and God explained to them that "the banana puts forth shoots which take its place and the moon itself comes back to life."[37] In the choice of deaths, the couple was offered, in effect, an immortality that was personal and cyclical (the moon) or an immortality that was ancestral and linear (the banana). They chose, of course, the children, the "shoots," that come with and perpetuate the second, group immortality; that is why there is no heaven and no hell, no hereafter but only the here and now, according to traditional African belief.

"For a long time, in the night," Cheikh Hamidou Kane says of Samba Diallo, the autobiographical hero of *Ambiguous Adventure*, "his voice was that of the voiceless phan-

[37] Susan Feldmann, ed., *African Myths and Tales*, new ed. (New York: Dell Publishing Co., 1970), pp. 114-15.

toms of his ancestors, whom he had raised up. With them, he wept their death; but also, in long cadence, they sang his birth."[38] Samba Diallo is singing the Koran to his father, and the merger of birth and death, of the living and the dead, in his song is evidence of the mystic union of Islam, but it is also testimony to a belief in ancestral unity that is more than Muslim in the extent of its occurrence. The changing of a child's name to placate a restless and trouble-some ancestral spirit,[39] like the giving of a name to indicate the reincarnation of such a spirit, demonstrates the fluidity, the flexibility, the communality of selfhood and individual personality in African culture; it suggests the extent to which the individual participates in the existence of others and they in his existence—and the others typically includes the dead as well as, perhaps more than, the living. Noni Jabavu mentions, as also do the Gikuyu autobiographers and Camara Laye and various others, the special "link which is felt to exist between the very old and the very young," and she explains this convincingly as the ancestral extremes joining hands or joining spiritual being over the middle: "the 'world of ancestors' to which the old are about to depart, having worked their way up the social hierarchy; and from which the young have newly come, to be trained upwards in order eventually to re-enter that 'ideal state'; life on earth being, as it were, temporal and therefore ar-ranged so that those 'ancestors, *amawetu*' should ap-prove . . ." (*Ochre People*, p. 239). As Noni Jabavu has already made clear earlier—and her books, in their feeling for form and tone, in their stylistic grace, are eloquent wit-ness to this sense of things—life, under such conditions of belief as these, is a ritual performance, a ceremonial ob-servance, a continual drawing and redrawing of the

[38] *Ambiguous Adventure* (New York: Collier-Macmillan, 1969), p. 67.

[39] See, for example, Blacking, *The Black Background: The Child-hood of a South African Girl* (New York: Abelard-Schuman, 1964), p. 19.

delicate network of human relationships out of which individual existence gradually defines itself.

The compelling power of the rituals that mark the major stages of life in a society that is communal and ritualistic at base is to be felt in various accounts of living those ceremonies, accounts of submitting to and growing up through those *rites de passage*. The force of "that which has always been done" in a society that would join the future to the past in a present ceremony of timeless age and quality, is to be seen, for example, in the deflection of Gikuyu history over the matter of female circumcision (see Chapter II); or in "the unconscious way in which" Noni Jabavu's ancient aunt "seemed to observe the conventions" in speaking to a very young child; or in the mystical, overwhelmingly powerful tie of lateral kinship binding those who are initiated into manhood together (as Birago Diop describes it in one of the *Nouveaux Contes d'Amadou Koumba*):

"Plus forte que l'amour fraternel, plus tyrannique que l'amour paternel, la fraternité de 'case' soumet l'homme digne du nom à des règles, à des obligations, à des lois qu'il ne peut transgresser sans déchoir aux yeux de tous. Avoir mêlé à l'âge de douze ans, le sang de votre sexe au sang d'un autre garçon sur un vieux mortier couché sur le sol, par une aubre [sic] fraîche, avoir chanté avec lui les mêmes chants initiatiques, reçu les mêmes coups, avoir mangé, dans les mêmes calebasses que lui, les mêmes mets délicieux or infects; bref! avoir été fait homme en même temps que lui dans la même case, dans la même m'bar, cela fait de vous, toute votre vie durant, l'esclave de ses désirs, le serviteur de ses besoins, le captif de ses soucis, envers et contre tout et tous: père et mère, oncles et frères."[40]

[40] Birago Diop, *Les nouveaux contes d'Amadou Koumba* (Paris: Présence Africaine, 1958), pp. 27-28. Cf. Prince Modupe: "A child learns in the Bondo Bush that his strength and security come from being a part of his tribe. Before one enters the bush school he is a member of his family. . . . During the time one is in cult training, his concept of family is extended to include all of the tribe. The boys

To have been reborn together in a deliberate, symbolic, and ageless ceremony out of the same house ("case") and into the one extended family ("m'bar") makes of the boys now become men something closer even than ordinary brothers, makes them literally blood brothers and a generation of twins, the children now, as Kenyatta would say, not of their mere parents but of the entire group. This, as various people tell us, is the effect of such communal ritual throughout Africa: to merge individual identity with group identity so that the part represents the whole, the whole is embodied and personified in the part, and the linear immortality of either is assured in the birth, reincarnation, and perpetuation of the common spirit.

Listening to her uncles talk about the age of a man as it is traditionally counted from the time of his circumcision and thinking of how this patterns life by the rituals that mark changes in state of being and in personal relationships, Noni Jabavu remarks to herself and her reader in *Ochre People*, "Maybe it is atavistic to be in sympathy with the pagan idea that changes in personal status should be marked, as they are when dramatized by ceremony and ritual" (p. 49). At the end of the same book, however, she tells of her father's death while she was in Europe and of her stepmother's letter that described it "in such a way that I could appropriately 'partake' although far away, in the event which marked his change of status, as we called it" (p. 260). In the great pattern established by ritual, death takes its place with birth, circumcision, marriage, parenthood, and eldership as something "behovely," as another change of status, as the necessary final element without which the pattern itself would not exist. Mourning for the death of her young brother—the last male heir of the Jabavu line—in *Drawn in Colour*, Noni Jabavu describes

---

of his age-group who are trained with him become like actual brothers. A strong lifelong bond of brotherhood is felt among them. The group circumcision ceremony is a physical symbol of their spiritual oneness" (*I Was a Savage* [London: Museum Press, 1958], p. 24).

how the remaining Jabavus, powerless now to perpetuate ancestral spirits, had first to go into seclusion according to custom and then be ritually cleansed before others could "face the bereaved without embarrassment, without pangs; for a new leaf would then be turned over, the tragedy consigned to forefathers and ancestors, the injury healed" (p. 19). This consignment of grief to those who can bear it, sharing it out over the ancestral line rather than allowing it to be concentrated entirely on the single individual, is the effect of custom, of *isiko*, of ritual, of traditional observance, and it is the only way, Noni Jabavu implies, that such personal relief could be accomplished. Though this extinction of the family line is the ultimate tragedy for forefathers and ancestors, yet drawing them into participation in the event through *isiko* relieves the present embodiment of the line, for in an especially poignant way it makes them part of a supra-personal pattern: the last element in the pattern, but to be the last element, no matter how tragic, is nevertheless to be in the pattern.

Prince Modupe, describing a part of his initiation that sent him into the forest to meet a wild animal and so prove his manhood, says, "Part of the terror was that of being alone. Africans conduct most of their activities in groups. We are not a solitary people. Our strength is in our togetherness" (*I Was a Savage*, p. 36). In somewhat more literary phrasing, and speaking not of the Soussou of Guinée but of the Xosa and Zulu some four or five thousand miles away in South Africa, Noni Jabavu says, "I thought how with my people, you are not often left to be merely your private self; you represent others, or others represent you, so that you are ever conscious of relative status, classification, interdependent relationships" (*Drawn in Colour*, p. 51). In *Ochre People* the same participant in and observer of the same people thinks, "I was thankful that we were each brought up to feel ourselves a symbol, 'a representative of a group' not of a family only, and not as a private person. '*Umntu ngumntu ngabantu*. A person is a person (is what he is) because of and through other people.' Otherwise success too often leads to conceit and failure to humiliation that would be an intolerably lonely burden. As it was, the sharing gave a sense of proportion."[41] *The Lonely African* is the title that Colin Turnbull gives to his very moving book that provides a quasi-autobiographical outlet for the story of the African caught and confused between two civilizations, between the foreign European and the traditional African modes of life; but, as Noni Jabavu and numerous other witnesses have pointed out, the African who lives a traditional, ritual pattern is anything but lonely, enveloped in his person as he is vertically with the ancestral dead and laterally with the coherent centripetal society around him.

This complex ancestral and social unity that makes for internal and cultural strength, however, has often, in the history of modern Africa, led to external, inter-cultural, or political chaos. The problem that faces virtually every national leader in Africa is how a nation can possibly be formed out of various and differently structured cultural groups. "Another key characteristic of tribal man," Peter Abrahams has said, "is that his society is exclusive and not, like western society, inclusive. The lines are drawn very clearly, very sharply. Anybody not an 'insider' is an enemy, actually or potentially—someone to distrust, someone to fear, someone to keep at bay. There is no choice, no volition

---

[41] *Ochre People*, p. 69. John Mbiti uses remarkably similar language to describe scarification among the Sonjo: "All the Sonjo must wear a tribal mark, *ntemi*, on their left shoulder. . . . These are marks of identification, incorporation, membership and full rights; they are the indelible scars that 'I am because we are, and since we are, therefore I am.' The individual is united with the rest of his community, both the living and the dead, and humanly speaking nothing can separate him from this corporate society" (*African Religions and Philosophy* [Garden City, N.Y.: Doubleday & Co. 1970], p. 152). The similarity of phrasing and thought in the Xosa and Sonjo expressions is ironically fitting since the Sonjo are "Intralacustrine Bantu"—culturally, that is, they are of the general group whose customs and beliefs Noni Jabavu found so repellent and so utterly different from her own Xosa moral upbringing in *Drawn in Colour*.

about this. It is something ordained by the ancestral dead."[42] The ancestral dead of one people are not, nor can they ever be made, the ancestral dead of another people. Jomo Kenyatta, writing in the 1930's, remarked that the average European observer "thinks of the tribe as if it must be analogous to the European Sovereign State. . . . In doing so he makes a huge mistake, which makes it impossible for him to enter into intelligible relations with the Gikuyu people. They simply do not know where he gets his ideas from, since to them the family rather than the larger unit is the primary reality on which power is based" (*Facing Mt. Kenya*, p. 298). But in the 1960's Kenyatta, as the head of a sovereign state, found himself caught in the toils of his own argument; for one of the major points of *Facing Mt. Kenya* is that the Gikuyu form a huge extended family tracing precise lines back through the nine nominal clans to the nine daughters of Gikuyu and Mumbi, but the sovereign state of Kenya, as Oginga Odinga has been quick to point out, has other clans than the nine, other peoples than the Gikuyu, and it cannot be ruled by the one father of all since there are at least several fathers and several families. As the President of Kenya, Kenyatta has attempted, not altogether logically, to invoke the Gikuyu notion of a proliferating family to include not only the Gikuyu themselves but also the Luo (like Oginga Odinga), the Masai, the Akamba, and all the other peoples of Kenya. "I firmly believe," Kenyatta declared in a speech as prime minister of Kenya, "that, if this country of ours is to prosper, we must create a sense of togetherness, of national familyhood. In Swahili, we express this by the word 'ujamaa,' which can also be roughly translated as socialism."[43] The inexorable logic of cultural in-

[42] Peter Abrahams, "The Blacks," *Holiday*, 25 (April 1959), p. 122.
[43] *Harambee! The Prime Minister of Kenya's Speeches 1963-1964* (Nairobi: Oxford Univ. Press, 1964), p. 8. Tom Mboya, in a chapter of *Freedom and After* that he calls "African Socialism," says, "Most African tribes have a communal approach to life. A person is an individual only to the extent that he is a member of a clan, a com-

tegrity and autonomy, however, which is a great source of strength in other ways, has not been so easily put aside as Kenyatta's optimistic expression would seem to expect.

Kwame Nkrumah, faced with the same problem in Ghana, perhaps in an even more potent form than that troubling Kenyatta, employed rather a different (and historically less successful) strategy. "I had," Nkrumah wrote, after the coup that sent him into exile, "to combat not only tribalism but the African tradition that a man's first duty was to his family group and that therefore nepotism was the highest of all virtues. While I believe we had largely eliminated tribalism as an active force, its by-products and those of the family system were still with us."[44] Instead of trying to turn "the family system" to his advantage, Nkrumah attempted to destroy it—and he failed. As a nationalist and a Pan-Africanist, as an exponent of the African Personality as against the Ashanti or Gikuyu or Ibo personality, Nkrumah's intention was perfectly clear and his method logical; but for the African whose existence is defined by family and kin, the state is a distant, abstract, unreal thing that does not—*cannot*, because it is an entity formed of peoples whose present being is traced back in differing, if parallel, lines—speak in the voice, or with the force and living authority, of the ancestors. The Akan, the Ashanti, and the Ewe have not found in the modern state of Ghana the voice of their past because each traces a different line back through a different past eventually to a different source. The Ashanti ancestors, for example, are real in a way that a conglomerate state can never be because the modern African state is an abstract entity formed, in nearly every case,

---

munity or a family" (*Freedom and After* [Boston: Little, Brown & Co., 1963], p. 166). He goes on to quote admiringly from Julius Nyerere's *Ujamaa: The Basis of African Socialism* and concludes his book with an impassioned call for Pan-African unity: "Our road is a classless socialism, based on Ujamaa, the extended family" (p. 262).

[44] Kwame Nkrumah, *Dark Days in Ghana* (New York: International Publishers, 1968), p. 66.

not by cultural logic but by accidents of history and by the European partitioning of Africa. Nkrumah again, describing the efforts against his life made while he was in exile in Guinée, says, "In March 1967, the 'N.L.C.' [i.e., the leaders of the forces that had overthrown him], panic-stricken at the mounting opposition, went to the length of sending 12 Ewes, all of them illiterate criminals taken from the jails of Ghana, to kidnap me and bring me to Ghana 'dead or alive'" (*Dark Days in Ghana*, p. 131). Why Ewes? and, the reader may wonder, why specify anyway? The answer is obvious: while Nkrumah might profess something as vague as the African Personality and while he might propose to lead the movement to Pan-African Union as a symbolic representative and an embodiment of the abstract African past, he did not, being himself an Akan, speak to the Ashanti in *their* communal voice nor to the Ewe in the language of *their* ancestral dead. Nkrumah might have been the symbol of African unity; he could not be an Ashanti forefather or an Ewe ancestor.

K. A. Busia, who was himself temporarily president of Ghana a few years after Nkrumah's downfall, has described "The African World-View," with its characteristic focus on the living matrix, on the geographical here and the chronological now, in these words: "The African view of man in society in general lays more emphasis on his membership of a group than on his individuality. The membership of the group continues beyond death into the life beyond. The dead, the living, and the yet unborn [that African three-in-one] form an unbroken family, and this concept is given emphasis in institutions and ritual."[45] A world-view like this —assuming that it exists, and the experience, the expression, and the assumptions of African autobiographers demonstrate that for them it unquestionably does—which grows out of and informs not simply a single area or aspect of life

[45] K. A. Busia, "The African World-View," in *African Heritage*, ed. Jacob Drachler (New York: Collier-Macmillan, 1964), p. 150.

but the total moral being of the individual and his society, affects the practice not only of politics and nation-building but of religion, education, and literature as well. In *Daughter of Mumbi*, Charity Waciuma tells of a perplexing conversation with her uncle about the effects of Christianity and the spiritual condition of A-Gikuyu who died before receiving the message of Christianity: "I asked him," she says, "whether the old men who had died before the missionaries came would have gone to heaven." Her uncle's answer, setting Charity Waciuma right on the existence of a hereafter, goes to the heart of Gikuyu and African belief about the real focus of human life, and it suggests, incidentally, that she had been too long in mission schools: "My child, who told you such things, that there is heaven and hell? If they really existed God would have sent a message to tell his children of them long, long ago."[46] As far as the Gikuyu are concerned, what "really" exists is not heaven and hell or anything else unknown, because if such things did exist they would not be unknown; the message would have come down to the children—certainly to the Children of Gikuyu and Mumbi (see Chapter II)—through the traditions of the ancestors and in the knowledge of the elders. The ancestors live; their life, however, is not in the eternal bliss of heaven or in the infinite torments of hell but in the here and now

[46] Charity Waciuma, *Daughter of Mumbi*, p. 87. The Ewe, who live across Africa from Kenya on the border of Ghana and Togo, have no belief in heaven and hell either and no concept of repentance. Their treatment of a dead body is highly revealing: in the casket of the ordinary dead they put clothes, objects of wealth, and food and drink, as if to say, "We would welcome your return"; in the case of a mature woman who has failed to produce children, however, instead of honoring her and encouraging her reincarnational return with signs of respect, they beat the corpse to show their feeling about her failure to fulfill her role and function, stop up the sexual organs in a sort of Dantesque, *Inferno*-like consequence appropriate to the "crime," and bury the body with no trappings of wealth or sustaining food, with the intention of discouraging her rebirth ever again in the line of posterity.

of Charity Waciuma's life and the life of the children.[47] "The white man seems always to be worrying about the future," Joseph Major observes in *Forever a Stranger*, "and does everything in his power to prepare for himself a happy future. He lives more in the future than in the present or the past. . . . The black man, on the other hand, tends to live more in the present than in the future. Actually the past is . . . more close to him than the future."[48] Though Major does not point this out, the way in which the past is closer than the future to the African, as a number of other autobiographers make clear, is that the future is only potential while the past is a real and known and continuing component of present being, the most important element, indeed, in present existence.

The idea that life is not in abstractions from the past nor in predictions of the future but in the concrete and active present thus determines African belief about the nature of existence after physical death; it also determines educational modes in African society. Martin Akou, after remarking that mathematics and its abstractions are not for everyone and are especially foreign to the practical methods of traditional African education, goes on to comment on Western approaches to natural science: "Il y a lieu de mentionner l'histoire naturelle. A mon avis on la faisait assez maladroitement. On s'arrêtait trop peu sur la zoologie et sur l'homme, ce qui nous aurait alors beaucoup intéressés, et on s'étendait trop sur des conceptions générales."[49] The signifi-

---

[47] In *This Earth, My Brother. . .* , Kofi Awoonor echoes the notion expressed by Charity Waciuma's uncle: "The concept of angels is a total fiction for they and devils—evil ones—are one and the same" (*This Earth, My Brother . . .* [Garden City, N.Y.: Doubleday & Co., 1971], p. 207). Angels, in the African view here expressed, do not live in a heavenly paradise, nor devils in an infernal hell; both exist, as one and the same spirit, insofar as they exert influence on present lives and actions.

[48] Joseph N. Major, *Forever a Stranger* (New York: Carlton Press, 1969), p. 294.

[49] *Autobiographies d'Africains*, p. 296.

cance and appeal of abstract learning, or of "conceptions générales," is, for the African, pale and weak in contrast to the living animal and human world. As Jomo Kenyatta points out, "In all tribal education the emphasis lies on a particular act of behaviour in a concrete situation" (*Facing Mt. Kenya*, p. 102). Moral conduct, like any other aspect of education, is taught to the African child, according to Kenyatta, not as abstract principle and not as a science but as a part of the immediate context of living experience: "In the Gikuyu system of education . . . the instruction is always applied to an individual concrete situation; behaviour is taught in relation to some particular person. Whereas in Europe and America schools provide courses in moral instruction or citizenship, the African is taught how to behave to father or mother, grandparents, and to other members of the kinship group, paternal or maternal" (*ibid.*, p. 116). Education is concentrated in the present moment for the African; it is not diffused, not drawn out into abstractions and general conceptions. Existence, likewise, judging by African autobiographies, is intensive rather than extensive; it is not stretched out into a future that pulls consciousness away from the present, nor is it spread out over places geographically remote and unreal. T. S. Eliot's Christian-mystic words appear, in this regard, to be more accurate for the African of traditional attitudes than for the ordinary Western Christian: "And all is always now."

Autobiographies produced by Africans—at least when directed to the experiences of childhood, of family, and of clan—have very frequently a quality about them that may raise suspicions in the fact-reverencing, history-conscious, and literal-minded reader of the Western world. In Prince Modupe's *I Was a Savage*, for example—and it is an example that could easily be multiplied elsewhere—the record of particular events from an individual life shades off into an imaginative recreation that, in turn, shades off into a fictionalized creation and into fabulous adventures; nor is there any clear line that would let the reader know where

he is or which is which. The explanation for this, in Prince
Modupe, in Camara Laye, or in Igbinokpoguié Amadasou,
is considerably more interesting than the fact itself. Individual experience—if it should be called that, for in this case
it is the reverse of "individualized"—is a very different
thing for the African who has grown up with ritual traditions from what it is for the ordinary Westerner. "While I
remained kneeling," Prince Modupe says of the time when
he was preparing to be tested as a man, "Lamina [his teach-
er] repeated many things I had heard over and over previously—how a man has life only in so far as he lives in his
people, how birth, circumcision, the test of manhood, death,
are all parts of a great endless cycle" (p. 31). What to the
Westerner would be an isolated, unique, and individual experience, to the African is a shared, common, and group
experience; far from being something he alone has known,
as would be the case with events described in the ordinary
Western autobiography, the significant events that one finds
in African autobiography are those known a thousand and
a thousand thousand times. What Prince Modupe describes
is to be found, more or less, *mutatis mutandis*, in Camara
Laye and Mugo Gatheru and Jomo Kenyatta, in Naboth
Mokgatle and Boubou Hama and Charity Waciuma. As
the experiences were communal and ritual, as they were
archetypal, so also are the descriptions that are as if seen
and recalled in a mist of great significance where the
individual is scarcely distinguished from the group and his
experience is only real and interesting because it is a typical
recreation of the entire racial experience. This accounts for
the typicality and archetypicality of African stories and
tales: told thousands of times in thousands of places, they
become rounded and smoothed, like stones on the beach,
into the representative contours, the fitting shapes, the necessary curves of the human story.

The principle of social structure drawn from African autobiographies and outlined above extends, naturally, to
apply to art and literature. The human reference in a mask,
in a statue, or in a tale is not to an individual, or not to an

individual as such, but to a corporate entity; individual traces exist in these various works only under the aspect of mythology or legend or ritual history. The rhetorical principle of synecdoche applies equally to the organization, the reference, and the significance of African society, African art, and African literature. "The Kikuyu people," according to Jomo Kenyatta, "have no written records, and all we know of their early history is told in legends and traditions. There is no sharp line to mark where legend ends and history begins. . . ."[50] Kenyatta goes on to argue that there is no reason to doubt these traditions: "But, of course, we must make some allowance for the story-teller's way of expressing himself, which sometimes puts the truth into a mythological disguise" (*ibid.*). The story-teller could hardly fail to do so, since life, under the effect of ritual, frequently puts itself into a "mythological disguise." In James Ngugi's novels the story is never a personal one but the story of a people who are living history and legend, and whose lives, richly informed with their own traditional past, are the stuff of mythology. They are, as Ngugi emphasizes repeatedly, the Israelites, the Chosen People of God, the Children of Gikuyu and Mumbi, Ngai's People of Destiny. Because African life is ritualized, the quotidian, both in life and in literature (and here autobiography is the obvious link), assumes the dimensions of the mythic, and characters in fiction, embodying the personality and the experience of a people, take on mythic significance. African fiction, following in the steps of African autobiography, tends naturally to the mythic (e.g., James Ngugi), the fabulous (e.g., Camara Laye), and the proverbial (e.g., Chinua Achebe) because these qualities represent the patterns observed in life and the distilled wisdom passed down from the ancestors. African literature (being thus like African life everywhere) is an incarnational literature.

The novelist in the Western world, living as he does within a different set of assumptions about the nature of human existence, creates character in a different way and in a dif-

[50] *My People of Kikuyu* (Nairobi: Oxford Univ. Press, 1966), p. 1.

ferent light from the African novelist. Paul Morel, for example, in *Sons and Lovers*, is intimately identified with his
creator—but only with his creator, not with the character
of the family and extended family and clan: he is not a cultural summary. Lawrence's figure assumes the character of
being himself, a unique individual, and of being generally
human, but nothing in between by way of expanding circles
of being. When Lawrence said, "All art is *au fond* symbolic," he had in mind that art rehearses the patterns of
human existence and that every individual acts out the
drama of all mankind. But between the two poles of himself
and humanity there is no intervening group identity, no living group existence. The case is quite the contrary with
African fiction, which, in this sense, in Lawrence's definition, is more representative than symbolic. The character
in African fiction is (in Noni Jabavu's words) "not often left
to be merely [his] private self"; rather, he subsumes in his
being and in his actions—he *typifies*—the family, the extended family, the clan, the culture; only incidentally is he
himself or humanity. The character in African fiction holds
in himself the typicality demonstrated in the lineage scheme
of Dilim Okafor-Omali that goes back to the ancestral Ibo
spirit—but not beyond. The African poem ("j'appelle
*poème* toute oeuvre d'art"), according to Léopold Senghor,
"est fait par tous et pour tous."[51] "Tous," of course, comprehends only the members of a specific culture or, at most, the
world that Senghor calls "négro-africaine"; specifically
"tous" does not, as Senghor emphasizes, include the Westerner. African art and literature, like African autobiography, grow out of general African assumptions; consequently the art and literature reflect simultaneously that
particular culture which gave them shape (Ibo, Gikuyu,
whatever) while being also generally African and distinctly
non-Western.

[51] Léopold Senghor, *Liberté I* (Paris: Éditions du Seuil, 1964), p.
207.

CHAPTER II

# Children of Gikuyu and Mumbi

> They sang of Jomo (he came, like a fiery spear among us),
> his stay in England (Moses sojourned in the land of Pharaoh)
> and his return (he came riding on a cloud of fire and smoke)
> to save his children. He was arrested, sent to Lodwar, and on
> the third day came home from Maralal. He came riding a
> chariot home. The gates of hell could not withhold him.
> Now angels trembled before him.—Description of the *Uhuru*
> celebration in *A Grain of Wheat*

FEW PEOPLE in the Western world, although everyone has
no doubt heard of Adam and Eve, can confidently trace
their ancestry back, as the Gikuyu do, in an unbroken line
to the first man and the first woman: Gikuyu and Mumbi.
Described geographically and linguistically as "Kenya
Highland Bantu," the Gikuyu[1] are a people who know
where they have been and have come from, a people who
are secure in their ancestry because it is kept alive in their
legends, preserved in their land, revitalized through successive incarnations, and embodied in their traditional way of
naming; and, if the ancient prophecies of seers prove valid,
along with the Gikuyu mythic reading of history, they are
also a people with a manifest destiny and a clear promise
of where they are going. "It was before Agu [i.e., before
time]; in the beginning of things," Chege tells Waiyaki,

---

[1] In the preface to *Facing Mount Kenya*, Kenyatta explains the spelling of the name: "The usual European way of spelling this word is
Kikuyu, which is incorrect; it should be Gikuyu, or in strict phonetic
spelling Gekoyo. This form refers only to the country itself. A Gikuyu
person is Mu-Gikuyu, plural, A-Gikuyu" (*Facing Mount Kenya: The
Tribal Life of the Gikuyu* [New York: Random House-Vintage, n.d.],
p. xv). Cf. the headnote to James Ngugi's *The River Between* (London: Heinemann, 1965): "In *The River Between* the form of Gikuyu
is used correctly for the people and language of the Kikuyu area."

79

after bringing his son to the sacred grove high up on the mountain so he can see the ancestral land stretched out below in *The River Between*, by the Gikuyu novelist James Ngugi. "Murungu brought the man and woman here and again showed them the whole vastness of the land. He gave the country to them and their children and the children of the children, *tene na tene*, world without end" (p. 21). But as Waiyaki comes to realize, and indeed as every Gikuyu writer of the Thirties, Forties, and Fifties of this century has emphasized, "the children of the children" were alienated from the "whole vastness of the land" given by Murungu, the Creator, to Gikuyu and Mumbi and to their children forever and ever. Only a new savior, a "Black Moses" or an "African Messiah," a leader of the dispossessed, could restore his children, the children of Gikuyu and Mumbi, to their rightful inheritance. "I am the leader of Mumbi," Jomo Kenyatta declared oracularly to a mass meeting in 1952 as he tried to quiet the Gikuyu crowd so that all could hear the important, even divine, words he had to say to them: "I am the leader of Mumbi and I ask you yet again to keep quiet. What God has told me to say to you today I will now say. . . . You are the earth and the earth is ours so listen to me. . . ."[2] The enthusiastic crowd, thus addressed by their leader, their Moses, their Messiah, did finally submit to his will and become quiet.

One of the almost endless ironies about Jomo Kenyatta is that—many years before he became president of the Republic of Kenya, even many years before he was accused (in 1952) and convicted of leading the "Mau Mau" and was imprisoned for a period going on a decade by the British Kenyan government—he should have written a book that in the opinion of some is the single most authoritative, the one essential and indispensable work in African anthropology. *Facing Mount Kenya* is a classic in the anthropolog-

---

[2] Quoted by George Delf in *Jomo Kenyatta: Towards Truth about "The Light of Kenya"* (Garden City, N.Y.: Doubleday & Co., 1961), p. 166.

ical literature of Africa; what makes it that is, paradoxically but undoubtedly, the distinctive voice of Kenyatta himself continually breaking through the decorous scientific surface of the book to assert the rather larger-than-life-size presence of the man behind it. It is a voice that is simultaneously both private to Kenyatta yet speaking for his people, a voice now angry and bitter, now ironic and scornful, now humorous and bantering, a voice seldom pedantic and never dull, always alive and robust and everywhere intensely personal; and that being so, *Facing Mt. Kenya* is a very odd and special item in any bibliography of African studies. Consider also for oddness the picture that has become so familiar to readers of Kenyatta's monograph: it is unusual, to say the least, for the author of an authoritative and sober ethnographic survey to provide, as Kenyatta has done, a dramatic, albeit handsome, photograph of himself dressed in animal skins and hypnotically fingering the point of a spear as advertising appeal on the front cover of his book. Both the voice and the photograph point up the unique nature of *Facing Mt. Kenya*: it is both ethnography and autobiography, the story of a people and of a person, the life of the children of Gikuyu told by the man who is their proclaimed leader and their own symbolic embodiment, the personification of their spiritual being. Hence it matters little whether the reader is aware that Kenyatta himself posed for the photograph, for it is clearly an image of Gikuyu man, and it is a portrait of that figure, both in general outline and in particular detail, that Kenyatta presents so compellingly in *Facing Mt. Kenya*.

"In the present work I have tried my best to record facts as I know them, mainly through a lifetime of personal experience," Kenyatta says in the preface to *Mt. Kenya* (p. xvii). The book that follows is spotted with such invocations to the authority of personal experience. Contradicting, for example, the "irresponsible statements" of Europeans opposed to female circumcision, Kenyatta argues, as everywhere else, from his own case: "The theory that 'every

81

first child dies as a result of the operation' has no foundation at all. There are hundreds of first-born children among
the Gikuyu who are still living, and the writer is one of
them" (p. 147). When it is a question of what Gikuyu seers
are like or what they do, "My grandfather was a 'seer,'
*morathi,* or 'wise man,'" and Kenyatta had the opportunity
to observe not only how his grandfather performed his divine function but also what happened to his father at the
hands of the British government when he inherited the im-
plements of the seer's profession from the grandfather
(p. 294)

Likewise, in another book (*My People of Kikuyu*), the
first half of which is a description of Gikuyu traditions and
the second a biography of Chief Wangombe, who lived
something over a hundred years earlier, Kenyatta freely
mixes legend with a knowledge, gained of personal experience, of what is always done in Gikuyu land, to produce a
biographical portrait of the chief whose memory has been
preserved heretofore only in oral tradition. As a herdboy
(and Kenyatta was also an ex-herdboy), the young Wangombe went out very early to the pasture lands. "Occasionally, before they left the kraal, several sheep were tapped
on the jugular vein, and the running hot blood, which was
caught in a calabash half full of milk," was drunk for break-
fast. "Besides this they ate the sheep's fat tail, roasted in the
fire. From my personal experience I know that this food and
drink is very refreshing and stimulating and that it helps to
build up the body."[3] It is impossible to say if the Chief
Wangombe of Kenyatta's portrait ever existed in anything

[3] *My People of Kikuyu* (Nairobi: Oxford Univ. Press, 1966), p. 29.
The logic of B. Mareka Gecaga's *Home Life in Kikuyu-Land, or Kariuki and Muthoni* (Nairobi: The Eagle Press, 1949) is the same as
that behind *My People of Kikuyu*: that since their experience is communal and ritually repetitive, the life of the Gikuyu can be accurately
and validly conveyed in the story of one representative, embodying
personification. Gecaga's subtitle tells the same story, with Kariuki as
fully representative of male Gikuyu experience and Muthoni of female
Gikuyu experience.

like the way described, but what is sure is that the figure in
"The Life of Chief Wangombe" possesses such vitality as
it has because it serves as an alter ego of the author. The
biography of Chief Wangombe, like the description of
Gikuyu life in *Facing Mt. Kenya*, is composed in part of
Gikuyu legend, in part of anthropological observation, and
in part of Kenyatta's autobiography; it is, in short, a description of life as myth. In neither book is Kenyatta, like
the ordinary anthropologist or the common biographer, an
interested alien, whether sympathetic or condescending,
who studies, analyzes, describes, and defines a curious and
quaint people or an interesting man. He is, instead, the man
himself, evoking and recreating his own experience and
writing, through what he has known, has been and is, the
autobiography of a people. "I can therefore," Kenyatta says,
summing up all the central roles he has played in Gikuyu
life—herdboy and schoolboy, second-birth and age-group
leader, warrior and elder—"speak as a representative of my
people, with personal experience of many different aspects
of their life" (*Mt. Kenya*, p. xx).

It may well seem nothing more than natural—Kenyatta
being the flamboyant, somewhat ostentatious, perhaps ego-
centric man that he is—that he should write what one might
call cultural autobiography with himself as the centrally
representative figure. After all, when "a rabbit turned
poacher" (as Kenyatta rather archly describes his role as
Gikuyu anthropologist in *Facing Mt. Kenya*) takes to recording the findings of his poaching, what else would he
draw on but his own experience as a big rabbit among all
the lesser rabbits? But this does not at all explain a phenomenon in Gikuyu autobiography that is in some ways the
reverse of this one, in other ways identical to it. Why do
such Gikuyu autobiographers as Charity Waciuma
(*Daughter of Mumbi*), Mugo Gatheru (*Child of Two
Worlds*), and Muga Gicaru (*Land of Sunshine*), and even
such writers as Josiah Mwangi Kariuki (*"Mau Mau" Detainee*), Waruhiu Itote (*"Mau Mau" General*), and Karari

83

Njama (*Mau Mau from Within*), who are presumably concerned only with their parts in the very circumscribed history of "Mau Mau"—why do they all tell much the same story as one another and the same story as Kenyatta tells, beginning with Gikuyu and Mumbi, when each claims to be recounting his own, and only his own, private experiences? Why should it be, when one naturally expects only the personal voice, that one gets simultaneously the communal voice of Kenyatta-esque ethnography sounding as a sort of reverberation and expansion of the personal voice? The same is true of autobiographical fiction produced by a Gikuyu: except that they are not generally written in the first-person, the novels of James Ngugi tell quite the same story, often in quite the same way—dramatization of group belief and community history—as *Facing Mt. Kenya* and *My People of Kikuyu, Daughter of Mumbi* and *Child of Two Worlds, Land of Sunshine* and *"Mau Mau" Detainee*.

In a consideration of Gikuyu ideas of the nature of human existence, it is clearly of primary significance that in all these books about the writers' lives, individual experience merges with group history, so that the two become indistinguishably one. For a Gikuyu, the relationship between the individual's experience and his people's experience is nothing like what it would be for a Western autobiographer (think, for example, by way of contrast, of the uniqueness or the non-communality of experiences described by Thoreau or John Stuart Mill, by Freud or Benjamin Franklin). When Charity Waciuma calls her book *Daughter of Mumbi*—and the title is perfect for the book's contents— she thereby places it and her notion of self-existence in a very different world from the world occupied by Western autobiography. It is, of course, true that an autobiography written by a Western woman might conceivably be called *Daughter of Eve*—but how totally different are the connotations of feminine frailty and individual waywardness contained in that title from the connotations of ancestral strength and group unity implied in Charity Waciuma's

84

title. The connotations, in fact, are as different as are African ancestral lines from Western ancestral lines, as different as African social organization from Western social organization. As for *Daughter of Mumbi* and the society from which it comes, except that others might not have its author's abilities in writing, any Gikuyu woman could take, as a description of her own life and identity, the title of Charity Waciuma's book. On the other hand, however, one might legitimately expect from any autobiography called *Daughter of Eve* a description of experiences not shared by sisters in a family, in a clan, or in any other kinship group. (They would probably be shared only by sisters in one of the older professions.) For Charity Waciuma—though she is a Christian (or was one during the time described in *Daughter of Mumbi*) and thus was never "reborn" as a member of the group through traditional initiation—there is no writing about herself except as she is the present representative of the whole people; indeed, her description of Gikuyu customs implies that there is no existence except as the individual is the present embodiment of the ancestral spirit. Consequently (and this is true for the other writers as well, from Kenyatta to Ngugi and Mwangi Kariuki), the autobiography of a Gikuyu individual (Mu-Gikuyu) is virtually co-terminous—identical in event, in pattern, and in significance—with the "autobiography" of the Gikuyu people (A-Gikuyu).

In *Facing Mt. Kenya* Kenyatta tells how, after circumcision and ritual rebirth, boys and girls acquire an age-group identity and new forms of address signifying new relationships to the group: the initiates call their sponsors (an elder and his wife) "my tribal father" and "my tribal mother" as the sponsors call them "my tribal son" and "my tribal daughter," because, as Kenyatta points out, it is considered that "the children have now been born again, not as the children of an individual, but of the whole tribe" (p. 145). Where birth, or rebirth, means coming into the world as children of the entire group, as children of Gikuyu and

Mumbi and their symbolic representatives, the elder and his wife, no line can be drawn between individual identity and communal identity, between Mu-Gikuyu and A-Gikuyu. During the painful trial of initiation, according to Kenyatta, the sponsors sing encouraging songs to the initiates with reference to their own joy at coming through the ordeal and what they gained from it. "These songs," he says, "have a great psychological effect on the minds of the initiates, for they strongly believe that what has happened to their predecessors will also happen to them" (*Mt. Kenya*, pp. 142-43). There is really, for the Gikuyu, nothing new under the sun, and one must observe that in fact, as in theory—because the Gikuyu child goes through the same ritual experiences with the same expectations as his ancestors have always known—A-Gikuyu autobiography and Mu-Gikuyu autobiography are the same thing. To put the matter another way, in the Gikuyu practice of autobiography, the "bio-" or "bios" must be taken as referring to a communal life embracing both the living and the dead, and the self of "auto" is virtually synonymous with, and could be replaced by, "Gikuyu."

The story that Gikuyu autobiography tells has an infinitely extended perspective into the past, and it has found, at least momentarily, a dramatic resolution in the present in the representative person of "Mzee"[4] Jomo Kenyatta (with the confrontation of the Kenyatta-led Kenya African Union

[4] Though he has other titles by which he could be known, Kenyatta apparently prefers to be addressed as "Mzee"—"Old Man." As the African uses it, this title is filled with respect and dignity, almost with reverence, suggesting a great wealth of experience transformed by maturity and age and the proper observation of all the ritual stages of life into wisdom and authority. "The Old Man" (President Tubman of Liberia was always known by this title, Julius Nyerere of Tanzania is known as "Mzee," and no doubt other African leaders as well choose the one or the other), being so old in the experience of the people, speaks for them all and not only for the living but for the dead too, the two being joined together through him—Elder, Father, Mzee, Old Man.

86

and the Kenyan colonial government; the violent chaos of "Mau Mau"; the trial and detention of Kenyatta as leader of the Gikuyu; Kenyatta's release and election as prime minister of a self-governing Kenya and eventually as president of the Republic of Kenya). All this tells us much about what one might take as a particular, perhaps characteristic, African culture and about the relationship within that culture of the individual to his society. It also tells us sadly much, incidentally and in contrast, about the European world, with its entirely alien ideas about human existence and human society, which came to "civilize the savages" and stayed to witness and participate in, if not in fact to cause, a terrible human tragedy. If the African seems to view his own life and all experience as repetitive, recurrent, and archetypal, he has been pretty much right in regard to his experience of the white man, for the actions of Western man in Kenya and throughout Africa have been monotonously repetitious and only too archetypical. Ironically and without his knowing it, the white man, as one can discover in Kenyatta, in Charity Waciuma, and in James Ngugi, was only playing a part in the mythic history of the Gikuyu people and fulfilling the prophetic vision of Mugo wa Kibiro, a Gikuyu seer. Rather than being, as he supposed, the chief actor in his own drama and on the stage of the world, the white man was all the while only a player, with a minor if despised role, in the providential destiny of the Gikuyu people and in the story that unfolds to become that destiny.

The Gikuyu elders, we can judge from all the books mentioned and more, tell the Gikuyu story to their young people, and the story they tell is simply the one they have themselves already lived. They tell the young people the legendary and mythical story and tell them to remember it and to repeat it in their turn when they, the children who will grow up through the outlines of the tale, have lived the story and made it, by their lives, more real than legend and more immediate than myth. This "history shading into legend" (as Kenyatta calls it in *My People of Kikuyu*, p. 5)

87

that the elders have always told, this story and myth that the children are now transforming into autobiography, invariably begins with Gikuyu, the first man, and Mwene-Nyaga (or Ngai or Mogai or Murungu: the Creator), his god. Gikuyu was not the son of human parents, nor was Mumbi, his wife, the daughter of man; both were the children and the living creation of Mwene-Nyaga. At the same time that he created Gikuyu, or before time itself began, Mwene-Nyaga pushed up a great mountain which is called "mountain of brightness" or Kere-Nyaga (Mt. Kenya),[5] and at the foot of this mountain he caused a sacred fig tree to grow: "This tree had *Life*. . . . This was Mukuyu, God's tree."[6] To the top of the mountain Mwene-Nyaga took Gikuyu and, indicating all the lands in view, he gave them to Gikuyu and his children, "*tene na tene*," forever and ever. "But he had shown them all the land—yes, children, God showed Gikuyu and Mumbi all the land and told them,

> 'This land I hand over to you. O Man and woman
> It's yours to rule and till in serenity sacrificing
> Only to me, your God, under my sacred tree. . . .' "
> (*Weep Not, Child*, p. 46)

Mwene-Nyaga then pointed to the sacred fig tree growing below and told Gikuyu that in that holy place, called Mukurweini-wa-Gathanga, he should make his home, and with Mumbi, created by Mwene-Nyaga to be Gikuyu's wife, he should reproduce and through children and grandchildren make for himself an abundant, living immortality.

[5] Karari Njama explains how Kere-Nyaga became Mount Kenya: "The correct name of Mt. Kenya is *Kirinyaga*. The Akamba people have neither the letter r nor g standing alone in their language and therefore their pronunciation for *Kirinyaga* is *Kiinyaa*, out of which the Europeans, being unable to pronounce it, created Kenya" (Donald Barnett and Karari Njama, *Mau Mau from Within: Autobiography and Analysis of Kenya's Peasant Revolt* [New York: Monthly Review Press, 1966], p. 53).

[6] James Ngugi, *Weep Not, Child* (New York: Collier-Macmillan, 1969), p. 46.

88

Gikuyu and Mumbi, the elders say, produced nine children, all daughters: "Waithira, the beautiful, Wanjiku, the
gossip, Njeri, the devoted, Wanjiru, the generous, Wairimu,
the dullard, Wangui, the clever, Wambui, the talker, Wangari, the farmer, Wamuyu, the hardworking."[7] Some say
that the last daughter was not Wamuyu but Warigia (or
Mwetagha), and still others say that there were really more
than nine daughters but that to name and number them
exactly would bring evil on all the Gikuyu ("Although the
clans of Gikuyu are 'Kenda muiyuru'—the nine that fills,
there are really ten. But no one can say that plainly because
this would mean the end of our people").[8] Gikuyu, remembering that Mwene-Nyaga had promised the land to all his
generations and realizing that "If a man dies without a male
child his family group comes to an end" (*Mt. Kenya*, p. 15),
sought out Mwene-Nyaga and asked his aid in solving the
dilemma. At Mwene-Nyaga's command, Gikuyu sacrificed
a ram under the great fig tree and returned home to find
nine handsome young men who, as Mwene-Nyaga had
promised, were "willing to marry your daughters under any
condition that will please you and your family" (*Mt. Kenya*,
p. 6). And so Gikuyu gave his daughters to the men to be
their wives on the single condition "that the women should
be the heads of the households and . . . all of the sisters,
their husbands, and their children would live together in
one village" (Mugo Gatheru, pp. 4-5). From the very beginning, then, from the hand of Mwene-Nyaga, was estab-

[7] Charity Waciuma, *Daughter of Mumbi* (Nairobi: East African
Publishing House, 1969), p. 12. Mugo Gatheru in *Child of Two
Worlds* (London: Routledge & Kegan Paul, 1964), p. 5, and Kenyatta
in *Mt. Kenya*, p. 7, and in *My People of Kikuyu*, p. 4, give the alter-
nate names mentioned for the ninth daughter.

[8] *Daughter of Mumbi*, p. 18. Chapter X of Josiah Mwangi Kariuki's
*"Mau Mau" Detainee: The Account by a Kenya African of His Expe-
riences in Detention Camps 1953-1960* (London: Oxford Univ. Press,
1963) is called "Kenda Muiyuru," which is explained in a footnote:
"This is a Kikuyu expression. After naming the nine clans, people refer
to the tenth as *Kenda muiyuru*" (p. 162).

lished the prototype of the *mbari*, the family group, settled on its *shamba*, its "acre" or homestead. Radiating out from the primordial family group and from its village came all the Gikuyu clans yet in existence today. "The nine daughters were married to nine men who were sent by the god of Kirinyaga. Each of the girls then moved a few yards away to her new home to live with her new family. The families grew into clans and Gikuyu named the clans after his daughters who had founded them. Thus the tribe expanded and dispersed."[9]

This matriarchy, joined together under the inclusive name of *mbari ya Mumbi*, i.e., Mumbi's family group, worked well for a number of generations; it worked well, that is, until the women—forgetting that, in spite of the matrilineal clan names, Gikuyu came before Mumbi—became tyrannical and overbearing. Then there was nothing for the sons of Gikuyu to do but to assert themselves, and so, by the ingenious device of getting all the female leaders and many of their women followers pregnant, thus rendering them ineffective in battle, the Gikuyu men, some six months after conceiving their plan, managed to defeat the daughters of Mumbi and throw off their rule. "When most of the women were heavy with child the men took over the government."[10] Moreover, once they were dominant in the political sphere, the men set about putting things right in their social and sexual life as well: "Immediately steps were taken to abolish the system of polyandry and to establish the system of polygamy" (*Mt. Kenya*, p. 9). The sons of Gikuyu were able to get away with that change,

[9] Charity Waciuma, pp. 12-13. The story of the origins of the Gikuyu and their clans is told by Kenyatta in *Facing Mt. Kenya*, pp. 5-10 and in *My People of Kikuyu*, pp. 2-4; by Mugo Gatheru in *Child of Two Worlds*, pp. 3-7; by James Ngugi in *Weep Not, Child*, pp. 45-48, and in *The River Between*, pp. 2, 18-19, and 20-25; and by Josiah Mwangi Kariuki in *"Mau Mau" Detainee*, pp. 2-3.

[10] *"Mau Mau" Detainee*, p. 3. The same traditional story is recounted in James Ngugi's *A Grain of Wheat* (London: Heinemann, 1968), p. 14.

90

and have maintained their polygynous luxury to this day, but when the men foolishly decided to meddle with clan names, the women, who had had more than enough of male nonsense, turned on them with the direst threat known in Gikuyu land: "if they dared to eliminate the names which stood as recognition that women were the original founders of the clan system, the women would refuse to bear any more children. And to start with, they would kill all the male children who were born as a result of the treacherous plan of the revolt" (*Mt. Kenya*, p. 9). In face of this threat to the immortality promised them by Mwene-Nyaga, the men relented and agreed to retain the matrilineal clan names, but by the success of the revolt, each man was now head of his house and his *mbari*.

Gikuyu ancestry is thus traced through the father's line—the men are the heads of household and the rulers—and this patrilineal ancestry is emphasized by the given name, but clan groups continue to be known by the nine (or ten) names of the daughters of Gikuyu and Mumbi. Mugo Gatheru, for example (more properly, Mugo wa Gatheru, or Mugo-son-of-Gatheru), derives his name and his ancestry from his father (Gatheru wa Mugo, or Gatheru-son-of-Mugo), but his clan is nevertheless the clan of Ethaga, after Mwethaga, one of the daughters of Gikuyu and Mumbi. Each clan and sub-clan embodies not only the general Gikuyu spirit but its own personality as well and each clan also has its appropriate totem. "We do not worship these animals, but we do not eat them. My own totem, that of Ethaga clan, is 'all wild game'" (Mugo Gatheru, p. 5). Perhaps through oversight, Mugo Gatheru neglects to mention the distinctive personality that is, according to Charity Waciuma, associated with the clan of Ethaga. "Some of the clans," she says, "are despised by others because of certain old, old traditions about them. Ethaga . . . are said to be poisoners and thieves" (p. 19). Though his father, as Mugo Gatheru points out, was "what American Indians call a 'medicine-man' and what we call a 'mundumugo'" (p. 1),

91

he was undoubtedly an exception to the rule of clan character; Mugo Gatheru, at any rate, tells only of his father's making good medicine, not bad, and he never mentions thievery at all.

Describing himself and his clan, Karari Njama (Karari-son-of-Njama) says, "I was the first born of Njama Karari [i.e., Njama wa Karari] and Wanjiru Wamioro. My father and grandfather belonged to the Amboi clan which was famous for its bravery . . ." (p. 82). When he was in the Aberdare forest as a member of the Land and Freedom Army (what the Europeans called "Mau Mau"), Karari Njama reports this conversation with "Field Marshal Sir" Dedan Kimathi, the leader of all the forest fighters:

" 'And what is your clan?'
'I am *Mumbui* of the great *Wamagana,* now known as *Mbari a Kaboci,*' I replied. . . .
'Oh! you are of my clan. Have another horn [of beer]!' said Kimathi."
(*Mau Mau from Within,* p. 258).

Thus the clan of both Dedan Kimathi and Karari Njama took its name from Wamboi, "the talker," who, to judge by the dedication of *"Mau Mau" Detainee,* was the nominal source also of the clan of Kenyatta—a man in whom bravery and talking seem to be nicely balanced:

Dedicated
Kenyatta wa Muigai, our National Leader, Father
of our Nation, of the clan of Mumbui of the
Agikuyu, children of Gikuyu and Mumbi
(*"Mau Mau" Detainee,* p. v)

As will be apparent, more than one legend, past and present, informs this dedication of Josiah Mwangi Kariuki's book to Jomo Kenyatta. Of his own family, Mwangi wa Kariuki says, "We belonged to the *Mbari ya Mbogo* (Buffalo sub-clan) of the Mungari clan, who have a traditional reputation for hard work, marital fidelity and an excessive partiality for arrowroots. Mugari, founder of the clan, was the son of Wangari, who was one of Gikuyu and Mumbi's nine daughters, each of whom is the founder of a Kikuyu clan" (p. 2). This, as an introduction to a history of "Mau Mau," is rather like Sir Walter Raleigh beginning his *History of the World* (with Renaissance England and his own trials as eventual points of reference) with Adam and Eve in the Garden of Eden. The only difference is that no historian in the West any longer follows Raleigh's example, while every Gikuyu historian, even if only of the "Mau Mau," observes the same practice, at least implicitly, as Josiah Mwangi Kariuki. Waruhiu Itote ("General China" of the "Mau Mau" revolt), for example, tells us, "My mother, Wamuyu came from the Anjiru clan; her father, Matindira, had been a famous doctor. My father, Itote, was a Muicakamuyu . . ."[11]—the clan, that is, took its name from the daughter who bore the same name as Waruhiu Itote's mother: Wamuyu, "the hardworking."

"We are the clan of Achera," Charity Waciuma says of her own family, "which is also called Giceri, and we are the descendants of Njeri, the daughter of Gikuyu" (p. 13). In the Gikuyu tradition of naming, her proper girlhood name would not have been Charity Waciuma (Charity, of course, was a Christian baptismal name, like *Johnstone* Kenyatta, *Josiah* Mwangi Kariuki, *Reuel John* Mugo Gatheru, etc.) but Wanjiku wa Waciuma because her father's personal name was Waciuma and she was given the personal name of a paternal aunt, Wanjiku. "In our country names are not chosen haphazardly," the author of *Daughter of Mumbi* says. "Any name includes many people who are now dead, others who are living, and those who are still not born. It binds its owner deep into Kikuyu history, beyond the oldest man with the longest memory. All our relatives to the furthest extent of the family, their actions, their lives and their children are an intrinsic part of our being alive, of being

---

[11] Waruhiu Itote, *"Mau Mau" General* (Nairobi: East African Publishing House, 1967), p. 16.

human, of being African, of being Kikuyu" (p. 8). This Gikuyu custom of naming children for particular relatives or ancestors implies a significance that goes far beyond the mere convenience of not having constantly to look around for new and different names. Until the child is named, his being is inchoate, potential, undefined; it is as if he were still an embryo, not yet born. To name is to give specific existence; it is to shape, identify, and direct the unformed; it is to make the potential actual. Naming serves to circumscribe the general Gikuyu spirit by embodying and re-embodying that spirit in particular, familial-ancestral form. Thus, when the first male child is given the name of his paternal grandfather, it means, for the Gikuyu, that he is in essence the same as the grandfather, a reincarnation of that person, and that the spirit which both he and his grandfather embody is, through him, guaranteed a continued immortality.

The naming of Gikuyu children goes by quite clear and unvarying rules—which is to say, for the Gikuyu there are quite clear ancestral priorities in acquiring immortality. "The name given to the first male child is that of his paternal grandfather, and at the time of birth it is announced that it is 'he' who has come. Similarly the second male child will represent his maternal grandfather. In religious ceremonies the children are treated in the same manner as their grandparents. The same thing applies to a female child" (*Mt. Kenya*, p. 17). As Kenyatta implies in his reference to religious ceremonies, the spiritual affinity of the child and his ancestor goes much deeper than the fact that they are nominally identical. All the lines of relationship within the group—the family or the clan—are drawn according to the name the child bears and the being he embodies. The name he is given represents for the child not only the burden of his own being but the very considerable weight of a family responsibility as well. "If a man dies without a male child," Kenyatta says, "his family group comes to an end. This is one thing that the Gikuyu people fear dreadfully. . . . For the extinction of a kinship groups [sic] means cutting off the ancestral spirits from visiting the earth, because there is no one left to communicate with them" (*Mt. Kenya*, p. 15). Thus it is that Mugo Gatheru (who, being the first son of a first son, has the same name as his paternal grandfather: Mugo-son-of-Gatheru-son-of-Mugo) ends his autobiography, which describes his wandering far from Gikuyu land in America and England, on a note of triumph and ancestral return: "And I am happy. I am happy because I now look upon the face of my son. My first son, Gatheru, Gatheru-son-of-Mugo, for this is one tradition which I shall not be the first to change" (p. 216). Likewise, Charity Waciuma, though she has grieved for the physical death of her father, Waciuma, is content in the end for her part in perpetuating her father's real life: "To us you have never died. There are two little Waciumas now, and more to come. . . . We are increasing and growing. Our family will soon no longer be your grandfather's house, 'Nyumba ya Gacii,' but your house, 'Nyumba ya Waciuma' " (p. 153).

When she says this, Charity Waciuma, like Mugo Gatheru, has in mind, I think, something much more precise than the rather vague expression one frequently hears about parents living on in their children. This linkage of generations through names represents a real atavistic return, a lineal reincarnation and an ancestral reembodiment. "The Gikuyu tribal custom requires that a married couple should have at least four children, two male and two female. The first male is regarded as perpetuating the existence of the man's father, the second as perpetuating that of the woman's father. The first and second female children fulfill the same ritual duty to the souls of their grandmothers on both sides. The children are given names of the persons whose souls they represent" (*Mt. Kenya*, pp. 157-58). Gikuyu reincarnation is not a phenomenon that occurs here, there, or anywhere across the cultural face of the entire world; it occurs, and is more than encouraged by traditional name-giving, within the family line and between very specific family members. No Gikuyu spirit is going to turn up suddenly reborn in Peoria, Illinois, or in Accra in Ghana —not unless some Gikuyu happen to be living there for a time, and even if they were it would be dangerously far from the ancestral and ritual lands to expect the spirit to travel well without losing any of its identity. The child who is his own grandfather naturally acquires a special relationship with those people the grandfather would be particularly close to, and the Gikuyu neatly sidestep any generation gap by assuming that youth are closely bound not to their parents but, over the parents' heads, to the preceding generation.[12] "Sometimes the children spend more time with their grandparents, especially the grandmother, than with their own parents. A boy is called by his grandmother 'my husband,' and a girl is called 'my co-wife.' The grandfather calls the boy *wakine*, 'my equal,' and the girl *mohiki wakwa*, 'my bride'" (*Mt. Kenya*, p. 17). Charity Waciuma, in describing the various complex, personal, and sometimes confusing relationships indicated by different forms of address, tells how her father's father would have addressed her mother: he would have called his daughter-in-law "daughter of Wanjohi," but only until a male child was

[12] After I had written these words I came upon a very neat confirmation of their general intent in a short poem by Chinua Achebe that presents, as an Ibo sees it, the same notion of reincarnation at a remove of one generation that we find in so many Gikuyu writers:

> Generation Gap
> A son's arrival
> is the crescent moon
> too new too soon to lodge
> the man's returning. His
> feast of re-incarnation
> must await the moon's
> ripening at the naming
> ceremony of his
> grandson.

(*Beware, Soul Brother and Other Poems* [Enugu, Nigeria: Nwankwo-Ifejika & Co., 1971], p. 26.)

born. "Once she had given birth to her eldest son—in other words, to grandfather himself re-created—he would call her 'maitu' "—mother (p. 9). If a man is reborn, or "re-created," as his grandson, then his daughter-in-law would be, naturally if confusingly, his mother and would be so addressed. Similarly, Kariuki, the representative Gikuyu male in *Home Life in Kikuyu-Land*, as he lies on his death bed, calls in his son Mwangi (who, "according to Kikuyu custom, . . . had been named after his grandfather, Mwangi") and addresses him, in final words of wisdom and exhortation, not as his son but as his father: " 'Mwangi, my father,' he said to his son in the Kikuyu manner, 'come and sit by my side and listen to me' " (pp. 15 and 16).

In *Land of Sunshine* Muga Gicaru tells a rather funny but at the same time poignant story involving his grandmother and himself which came about obviously because his own generation was viewed as the reincarnation and perpetuation of his grandfather's generation:

"We spent the next night at my grandfather's house, and . . . I was greeted with great traditional solemnity and feasting. . . . I was called by the names of the people I was named after. According to custom the first son is named after the grandfather on the father's side and the second son after the grandfather on the mother's side. When all the parents on both sides have been named or 'born,' as we say, other children are named after brothers and sisters of the parents alternatively. If there are no brothers and sisters, then after the next of kin. My grandmother, in her great jubilation at seeing her first grandchild, passionately addressed me as 'dear husband,' her highest term of endearment. 'Come and sit on my lap, my love,' she cried. . . . It was, I know, a great joy for her to see her grandson for the first time; but to me, to be addressed as 'dear husband' and 'my love' was most embarrassing, to say the least."[13]

[13] *Land of Sunshine: Scenes of Life in Kenya before Mau Mau* (London: Lawrence & Wishart, 1958), pp. 66-67.

Regret comes retrospectively into this tale of generations once removed when, a year later, Muga Gicaru visits his grandfather's house again and finds there "a new grandmother" replacing the one who had loved him and who had died during the year: "Then all of a sudden I remembered the three wonderful days I spent with her and only then understood that what I had thought was fuss and foolishness was her inestimable kindness and deep love. Love and kindness that could never be repaid or reciprocated. That is what hurt" (p. 68). Unfortunately, it must frequently be the case that such a great intensity of adult emotion—the result of many years' experience of life—can be neither easily understood nor sustained by the child who, if he is conscious of his role at all, thinks of himself as a boy only beginning the story of Gikuyu rather than as a grandparent nearly finished with the tale, left now with nothing to yearn toward as an object of emotion except the child in whom the family spirit is said to be once more reincarnated and in whom the grandparents themselves are supposed to continue living. What may be incomprehensible and embarrassing to the child now, however, he will come to understand sufficiently as a parent and a grandparent: that the family and the clan, even to the whole people of Gikuyu, are bound together, link after link, in one greater family and one comprehensive unity by the atavistic return of the group spirit.

The poignancy of Muga Gicaru's story is the inevitable result of the nature of Gikuyu immortality—an immortality that, like the Gikuyu conception of existence itself, both is and is not a personal matter: it is personal in that it is familial, and the family, for the Gikuyu, is the final, the indivisible unit of personality; it is not personal in that it allows for no notion of a distinct and separated individual who will somehow continue, after death, his individuated, private-to-himself, a-familial existence. "According to Gikuyu ways of thinking," Kenyatta says pointedly in *Facing Mt. Kenya*, "nobody is an isolated individual. . . . First and foremost he is several people's relative. . . . His life is founded on this fact spiritually and economically, just as much as biologically. . . . His personal needs, physical and psychological, are satisfied incidentally while he plays his part as member of a family group, and cannot be fully satisfied in any other way. The fact that in Gikuyu language individualism is associated with black magic, and that a man or woman is honoured by being addressed as somebody's parent, or somebody's uncle or aunt, shows how indispensably kinship is at the root of Gikuyu ideas of good and evil.

"This vital reality of the family group . . . underlies the whole social and economic organisation of the Gikuyu. . . . The Gikuyu does not think of his tribe as a group of individuals organised collectively, for he does not think of himself as a social unit. It is rather the widening-out of the family by a natural process of growth and division." (pp. 297-98)

That the Gikuyu posit primary reality in the family group is, as Kenyatta says (p. 298), "an important thing for Europeans to bear in mind," since there is no doubt that for Europeans, in contrast to Africans generally, individual existence is the primary reality and individuality the highest good. The implications of the Gikuyu view of reality— implications that are religious, social, philosophical, psychological, economic, political, and literary, and that are to be found, in a variety of ways, on every page of every autobiography by every Gikuyu writer—are endless: they wind in and out of one another to form, finally, the very texture and tone of Gikuyu writing. This Gikuyu view of "the way things really are" provides the first ground from which the writer approaches and understands his own experience, and so it naturally determines the final surface of the book he writes. This Gikuyu ontology, with its ultimate communality, suggests also why Gikuyu autobiographers resemble one another so markedly and why the autobiography of *a* Gikuyu is the same as that of *the* Gikuyu.

The linked unity of Gikuyu life is not only vertical, from

generation to generation, Gikuyu and Mumbi to the most recent incarnation, but also horizontal, effected by a joining of contemporaries. The age-group brotherhood that is formed among those who are initiated together into Gikuyu adulthood relates them to one another in a different way, but almost as closely, as the vertical, generational linkage relates them to blood relatives. "The Gikuyu tribal organisation," according to Kenyatta, "is based on three most important factors": the *mbari* or *nyomba*, the family group; the *moherega*, the clan, which "joins in one group several *mbari* units who have the same clan name"; and the *riika*, the system of age-grading determined by companionship in *irua*, or circumcision rites. "As we have seen, the *mbari* and the *moherega* system help to form several groups of kinsfolk within the tribe, acting independently; but the system of the age-grading unites and solidifies the whole tribe in all its activities" (*Mt. Kenya*, p. 4). Speaking of the custom of *irua*, whereby those of an age become bound together as brothers and sisters, and referring especially to the Gikuyu practice of excising the clitoris as the essential step in female initiation, Kenyatta says, "It is important to note that the moral code of the tribe is bound up with this custom and that it symbolises the unification of the whole tribal organisation" (*Mt. Kenya*, p. 129). It may well seem strange, but is nonetheless true, that the history of modern Kenya, and especially the unfolding story of the Gikuyu people, has been to a considerable extent affected by the practice of female circumcision and by European reaction to it. Most of the schools to which Gikuyu children were admissible at the beginning of this century were C.S.M. (Church of Scotland Mission) schools, and the Church of Scotland missionaries were not slow in seeing their Christian duty: they declared that this custom, which in missionary eyes was pagan, barbaric, and savage, must be destroyed (they did not, however—presumably because of Biblical example and authority—object to the rite of male circumcision). It became one of the most important of missionary functions to rid the Gikuyu people of something that the Gikuyu had less than no desire to lose.

Charity Waciuma describes how, because she was a Church of Scotland Christian through her father, she and her sisters went uncircumcised and therefore became objects of scorn and ridicule to their contemporaries. Here again, however, there was Christian vacillation and compromise because Waciuma, the Christian father, was unable to withstand entirely the anger of his own traditionalist father and the demands of his sons: "The ban was relaxed in respect to my brothers. Being boys, they went to the hospital to be circumcised. Although this was not so significant as passing through the ceremonial operation, it was better than nothing. They were just about acceptable in proper Kikuyu society" (p. 62). That her brothers might prove acceptable provided little comfort to Charity Waciuma and her sisters and the reader of her book can often feel below the Christian surface a wish that the author might have shared in that Gikuyu custom anathematized by her church as savage. When she went away to Intermediate Boarding School, "the situation of the village was reversed," as Charity Waciuma says, but was no happier for anyone.

"One evening about a week after my arrival there was an announcement that the new girls had to go the following morning at half past nine for a medical examination at the mission hospital attached to the school. We were all surprised that there was to be this examination for we were fit and well. Along we went to find a male European doctor waiting for us. There were the usual inspections of our eyes, mouths, stomachs and so on. After that we each had to strip and lie on a wooden bench with our feet wide apart while the doctor looked to see whether anyone was circumcised. If they were, a note of it was made on their record cards. All those who were circumcised were put into one dormitory. They were segregated from the rest and we were taught to despise them. . . . They spent their three years at

101

the school in half-seclusion, where their lives were made a misery and they became very withdrawn." (pp. 82-83)

Other C.S.M. schools were less "lenient"—they simply refused to admit into school any girl who had gone through the traditional clitoridectomy to enter Gikuyu womanhood. It was in response to this inflexible missionary righteousness that the K.I.S.A. (Kikuyu Independent Schools Association) was established, largely under Kenyatta's leadership, and it was through those schools that Kenyan history very likely took a new turning. Josiah Mwangi Kariuki attended a K.I.S.A. school, Karari Njama taught in one, James Ngugi (in *The River Between*) dramatizes the operation of such a school, and Kenyatta himself was principal of the Teachers' Training College at Githunguri, which developed the teachers of K.I.S.A. schools. As one might imagine from the circumstances of their founding, and as one can see in the "Mau Mau" careers of Mwangi Kariuki and Karari Njama, K.I.S.A. schools were not likely to teach the same conduct or observe the same essentially European and Presbyterian principles as the C.S.M. schools. Implicitly at least, because they emphasized the traditional history of the Gikuyu people and their right to the land, rather than concentrating on obligations to an alien culture and a foreign government, these schools taught revolution; as we shall see later, Gikuyu education became, as it was frequently called, a "weapon" with which to defeat and expel Europeans and so regain the lost ancestral lands.

Of the Gikuyu autobiographers, only Charity Waciuma suffered the misfortune of non-initiation. (She is also, and the two facts are more than coincidental, the only woman among them.) Kenyatta devotes an entire chapter to "Initiation of Boys and Girls"; Mugo Gatheru, in a chapter on "Becoming a Kikuyu," spends seven pages describing "The Day the Knife Bit Me"; and James Ngugi describes an initiation in *The River Between* that is identical both in rationale and in ceremonial detail to the circumcision rites in *Land of*

*Sunshine* and in Karari Njama's autobiography.[14] The remarkable thing is the great similarity, amounting to essential identity, that exists among these various descriptions of *irua*. What every writer is concerned with—and this no doubt accounts for the striking similarities of phrasing and event—is life lived by rituals of immemorial age, life conducted by stages or according to a systematic pattern that has been followed by ancestors for so long that it seems, from the present view, to have been forever and to be invariable as a part of the way human life should be or must be. The child is only doing now what every Gikuyu has done before him and what, until recently, it could be expected every Gikuyu would do after him. This ritualization of life, fitting the individual within the group mold and the mythic pattern and projecting his life as an exfoliation of the legendary story, is a process of *relating*—relating the individual to the family, to the clan, to the Gikuyu people living and dead, and to the ancestral land where their spirit dwells; it makes of a Gikuyu child not merely a child of physical parents but a child of Gikuyu and Mumbi, in possession of the inheritance, in all its spiritual and material aspects, received through Gikuyu and Mumbi from Mwene-Nyaga.

Although Karari Njama, like most of the other Gikuyu autobiographers, was at least a nominal Christian, he says there came a day when "I thought it was time for me to undergo the circumcision ceremony by which members of my tribe would recognize me as a full grown man" (p. 95). Scorning the hospital operation chosen by many Christians (Charity Waciuma's brothers, for example), Karari Njama went down to the "cold, almost freezing" water of the Gura River, which would numb and anesthetize the body, and submitted to the ceremony in the traditional way, "in the

[14] *Facing Mt. Kenya*, pp. 125-48; *Child of Two Worlds*, pp. 57-63; *The River Between*, pp. 52-54; *Land of Sunshine*, pp. 114-20; *Mau Mau from Within*, p. 95. Cf. also the standard description in *Home Life in Kikuyu-Land*, pp. 10-11.

public presence." As with the others, so with Karari Njama, he showed courage, all went well, and there was rejoicing in Gikuyu land for the birth of a Gikuyu man: "With many cheers for my bravery, I returned home escorted by men and dancing women. Women danced wildly until midday." In *The River Between*, after numbing himself in the Honia River, Waiyaki sits waiting for the "surgeon" to come to him: "The knife produced a thin sharp pain as it cut through the flesh. The surgeon had done his work. Blood trickled freely on to the ground, sinking into the soil. Henceforth a religious bond linked Waiyaki to the earth, as if his blood was an offering. Around him women were shouting and praising him. . . . He was of the tribe. He had to endure its ways and be inside the secrets of the hills. . . . Women were shouting and singing their bravery. All was over. The new generation had proved itself" (pp. 52-54). Mugo Gatheru—though he hastens to let the reader know that he does not agree—says that some people explain the presence of women at the ceremony in another way: "Women stand in front of the candidates, while the men stand at the back. People joke and say that the women take an interest in watching boys' penises!" However that may be, the women in fact, when it came time, glorified Mugo Gatheru and his companions for their courage as they had Karari Njama and Waiyaki wa Chege: "I was now allowed to look down at the handiwork of the circumciser and see what had been done to me. Blood was streaming from me like water from a pipe. Thank God I did not faint for I would have been disgraced! The crowd was glad because I had shown courage. They dispersed singing and happy that another Kikuyu child had been brave and had become a man" (p. 61). Of a rebirth ceremony that precedes the actual initiation by circumcision, Mugo Gatheru earlier says, "For many years the Kikuyu tried to keep this ceremony secret and the accounts of it which they gave to European anthropologists were not always true" (p. 21). Gikuyu autobiographers, however, as will be readily apparent, have made

104

more than generous amends for this secrecy in their descriptions—frequent, detailed, and graphic—of the *irua* ceremony. Jomo Kenyatta's account both of the process and the significance of Gikuyu clitoridectomy, though it is too long for quotation, should be recommended as a classic among such descriptions of *irua*—a description of how the Gikuyu do and have always done.

Muga Gicaru's presentation of his experience of the initiation ceremony is interesting for a number of reasons, but primarily because he analyzes in some detail the psychological effect of the ceremony and also because he introduces, through the coarse humor of the older boys, a distinctly realistic touch. Forty-eight hours before the "great day" he says he gave away all his clothes and shaved his head so that during the three months of "semi-seclusion and leisure" after the ceremony (when "they are regarded as inanimate beings without sex, and are called not 'he' or 'she' but 'it' "—p. 117) he could be born again outwardly as the same new man he had become inwardly through initiation. Also before the ceremony, "The initiate receives his first lessons on the ways and behaviour of the next grade to which he is emerging, and also on his attitude and responsibilities towards the clan, the tribe, and all people at large." Though he has learned all this before from his parents and from observation of older age-groups, "Yet the psychological effect on the initiate is incredibly profound and real. One really does regard himself as a new man, or woman. . . ." Muga Gicaru's description of the edifying remarks and the antics of those who were supposed to offer encouragement to the initiates as they sat under the knife, though suggesting little of the sobriety, dignity, and even nobility of Jomo Kenyatta's account, strikes the reader as probably more realistic for that very reason:

"The Hitlers,[15] our immediate seniors, were not helpful

[15] As Kenyatta and others explain, the names given to age-grades refer to particularly noteworthy events occurring around the time of

at all. Some would come along with a 'Cheer up, old boy,
it will all be over soon.' But others would look at each other
and exclaim:

"'Oh boy, oh, boy! you remember that grass? Yes! You sit
there, and the old rogue hacks away at you, and the only
muscle you dare move is your bottom. You chew grass and
keep chewing it for eight days and eight nights, and nothing comes out through your back passage except lumps and
lumps of it. It's simply terrible! Cheer up, boys, we will see
you there.'" (p. 117)

In spite of this cheerful encouragement from the Hitlers,
"it was a simple process and was all over before I realised
that the old rogue had started. I had expected much worse
than I got." His initiation, according to Muga Gicaru, made
real to him truths about unity and solidarity and about
Gikuyu identity, especially in regard to the encounter with
Europeans, that he had been taught before as dicta but only
now felt closely and really knew because of the transforming experience he had been through. "The sharing of life
with others; the assurance that I was a member of a larger
group who were all brothers whether personally known to
each other or not; the vows never to let down my age-
group; the guarantee that wherever I went there would always be an open door for me at the house of any one of my
age-group and that I could always call on my *rika* for sup-
port when unjustly treated—all this helped me to stand on

---

initiation. "The age-grade before us, initiated in 1939, had heard so
much about the threat of Hitler and of *mbobomu*, or bombs, that they
called themselves 'Hitler'" (*Land of Sunshine*, p. 114). As for his own
age-group, Muga Gicaru says, "we could not think of a suitable name
for our age group and eventually we called ourselves 'the Forty' after
the year 1940." Mugo Gatheru was also initiated in 1940: "Those of
us everywhere in Kikuyuland who were circumcised in 1940 were
referred to as *rika ria forty*, an age-grade of 1940. I was proud to be
of the 'Forty Group'" (*Child of Two Worlds*, p. 63).

my own feet and to pass from irresponsible boyhood to the responsibilities of a man" (p. 120).

Whether they are describing *irua* as the general practice of the Gikuyu or as the specific experience they passed through, and whether or not they characterize it explicitly by the words "reborn" and "born again," all the Gikuyu writers view the ceremony as essentially a process of rebirth—rebirth as a man or woman, as a Gikuyu, as a fully privileged and fully responsible member, representative, and embodiment of the group spirit. For the Gikuyu every ritual stage or observance in life, all the *rites de passage*— and Gikuyu life is directed at every turn by such rituals: at birth, at circumcision, at marriage, at the time of warriorship and eldership, at death—represents the kind of transformation of selfhood, or the kind of change in state of being, to which one would give the name of rebirth. At each important stage of his life, the Gikuyu dies to what he has been and is reborn into a new role and into a new set of relationships with other members of the group, almost always indicated by new forms of address. Thus the effect even of the "Mau Mau" oathing ceremony, as Mwangi Kariuki, Karari Njama, and Waruhiu Itote all agree, was to establish a new alignment of responsibilities, a new state of being, a different and complexly readjusted set of relations within the community. In short, in the eyes of "Mau Mau" initiates, the oath, like any other initiating ceremony, constituted a rebirth as a new, fuller, and more intense Gikuyu. "Even my education," Mwangi Kariuki writes of his experience of the first oath, "of which I was so proud, appeared trivial beside this splendid and terrible force that had been given me. I had been born again. . . . The other three in the maize were all silent and were clearly undergoing the same spiritual rebirth as myself" (p. 27). After taking the second oath he declares, "My initiation was now complete and I had become a true Kikuyu . . ." (pp. 30-31). Whatever one may think of this identification of "Mau Mau" with Gikuyuhood

107

—many would complain, and indeed they are not synonymous—there can be no question but that for "Mau Mau"
initiates the oath was another of the ritual stages in a generally ritual life. This particular stage was instituted in response to unique historical circumstances, but in the form
observed it was anything but unique.

Members of the Land and Freedom Army, according to
Karari Njama, "all facing Mount Kenya with some soil in
our right hands" (p. 162), offered regular prayers to
Mwene-Nyaga for the success of their battle in the forest.
In one such ceremony, as all the forest fighters turned toward Mt. Kenya, Dedan Kimathi prayed: "Our forefathers'
God, we beseech you to approach us and to hear our
prayers. . . . We are the sons and daughters and heirs of Gi-
kuyu and Mumbi whom you created; your own creation
whom you gave this green fertile land, full of mountains, val-
leys and many permanent flowing streams" (*Mau Mau from
Within*, p. 323). An essential part of every important ceremony, Jomo Kenyatta says, is for the Gikuyu to face Kere-
Nyaga and to invoke the power and blessing of Mwene-
Nyaga, or Ngai, in effecting the ritual transformation of
Gikuyu spirit or energy that the ceremony itself signifies.
(This practice, of course, is the source of Kenyatta's title.)
"Then, and even now," Mugo Gatheru says, "when a most
solemn prayer is being made for help, the people turn their
faces towards the mountain. And it was to Mt. Kenya that
my father [the *mundumugo*] turned when he was healing
people. Many are the times that I have seen him do it. It
was from Mt. Kenya, too, that Ngai spoke, in the beginning
of time, and called the first man into being" (p. 3). For the
Gikuyu, Kere-Nyaga is always there looking down, the
abode and symbol of divine spirit and of Gikuyu being, the
symbolic locus of the spiritual force that founded their history and that informs every Gikuyu individual, every
Gikuyu clan, and the entire Gikuyu people. The "mountain
of brightness" is also an eternal recall and evocation of
Ngai's promise to the heirs of Gikuyu: "Before they parted,

Mogai told Gikuyu that, whenever he was in need, he should make a sacrifice and raise his hands towards Kere-Nyaga (the mountain of mystery), and the Lord of Nature will come to his assistance" (*Mt. Kenya*, p. 5).

This is not, however, to suggest that Mwene-Nyaga (under whichever of his names) is a god who occupies himself with the fall of a sparrow or the trivialities of daily existence. But though Mwene-Nyaga may be removed from the ordinary affairs of everyday life, yet his blessing is to be sought, and will surely be obtained, at each of the significant turns in the life and the unfolding destiny of his people. "At the birth, initiation, marriage, and death of every Gikuyu," Kenyatta explains, "communication is established on his behalf with Ngai" (*Mt. Kenya*, p. 225). These are the ritual stages that change the state of being of his people, and Ngai, when called, will not fail to respond, for if anything should go wrong in these critical, symbolic ceremonies, Ngai's very intention, proclaimed to Gikuyu and Mumbi and promised as heritage to their children, would be frustrated. Birth, initiation, marriage, and death are the moments of transformation not for an individual Gikuyu alone but for the Gikuyu people as a whole and as the chosen people of Ngai; nor do the Gikuyu think of these moments as involving one man only, for though the crisis is individually focussed, yet Ngai's "assistance is always obtained . . . by the family group. No individual may directly supplicate the Almighty" (*Mt. Kenya*, p. 225). The Western world may say (as C. P. Snow, in fact, has said), "Each of us dies alone"; the Gikuyu disagree. Their view is that while death, like the other major crises of life, may come individual by individual, its significance is not individual but communal: every death constitutes a realignment of the pattern, a small change in the state of being of the entire group—including the dead, who though dead still exist, and the living, who though living share their existence with the ancestors reincarnate.

"On signing the matrimonial contract," Kenyatta says, because marriage is a major "sacrament" (to adopt a Western phrase) and commits the partners to a new relationship with all other members of the Gikuyu community, "the marriage ceases to be merely a personal matter, for the contract binds not only the bride and bridegroom, but also their kinsfolk" (*Mt. Kenya*, p. 157). What the couple do now, because in marrying they assume the obligation and the "sacred duty" of extending ancestral lines through procreation, is done for all the family and not for themselves alone. "A childless marriage in a Gikuyu community is practically a failure, for children bring joy not only to their parents, but to the *mbari* (clan) as a whole" (*Mt. Kenya*, p. 158). Likewise, though "Mau Mau" and marriage may be alike in no other way, the psychological effect of the oath administered by the "Mau Mau," who were astute enough to give their ceremony the traditional form of an appeal back through family and clan, through Gikuyu and Mumbi, to Ngai, was, according to Mugo Gatheru (p. 171), "literally terrifying to the Gikuyu. If a man lied, he lied not only to society but also to the ancestors' spirits, whom [sic] we have seen could cause great suffering if displeased, and still more he lied to the Creator, Ngai himself." In the oathing ceremony, as in the marriage contract, though to a different end, the initiate bound himself and at the same time his "family and even his entire clan . . . to the success of the rebellion by the traditional, most solemn method of the Kikuyu oath—for that is all the Mau Mau oath was essentially, the Kikuyu oath adapted for war, a religious expression or [of?] moral intent" (pp. 171 and 172). The marriage contract, the "Mau Mau" oath, the ceremony of *irua*, the rites associated with birth and with death—these are all affairs of family and of clan, unified in supplication to Ngai. Traditional Gikuyu philosophy, in its analysis of social structure, does not descend beyond the family as a unit; in particular, it provides no place for individual psychology and individual will as distinct from, or as acting in contrast to, family psychology and family will.

110

The history of the Gikuyu—indeed the very essence of the Gikuyu as a people—has always been intimately bound to the land they occupy, the heritage of Gikuyu and Mumbi kept in trust by all the generations that succeeded them. No African people (and no non-African people for that matter) identifies itself more closely with its ancestral land than the Gikuyu. "Although some of the clans are despised," Charity Waciuma says of the various clans and their differing personalities, "each man is extremely proud of his own and its rights. So conscious is he of its importance, that he spends his life within the boundaries of his clan land. Although my parents were Christians, they could not risk moving out of our clan land because they thought they would be persecuted by the spirits of their own place or of their ancestors" (pp. 19-20). It is in Gikuyu land that the ancestors are located, both literally and symbolically; hence it is through the earth that the present generation contacts past generations, communicates with them, and so continues their existence in present time. In *The River Between*, it will be recalled, Waiyaki establishes "a religious bond" with the earth as the blood of his intiation ceremony sinks into the earth[16] and satisfies the ancestors that he is living the traditional Gikuyu pattern, for the land, as Kenyatta says, "not only unites the living members of the tribe but also the dead ancestors and the unborn posterity" (*Mt. Kenya*, p. 205). And Mugo Gatheru, describing his wanderings far from Gikuyu land, tells of his ambiguous attachment to West Hampstead where he lived for two years—ambiguous because it was in West Hampstead that his daughter was born, but the birth was unattended by the ritual that would link the child with the ancestors and the land. "I felt sad,"

[16] Cf. John S. Mbiti's description of initiation by circumcision: "The shedding of his blood into the ground binds him mystically to the living-dead who are symbolically living in the ground, or are reached at least through the pouring of libation on to the ground" (*African Religions and Philosophy* [Garden City, N.Y.: Doubleday & Co., 1970], p. 161).

he says of the move from West Hampstead to Hammer-smith, "to leave the birthplace of my daughter. In fact, I still feel sentimental about it because it was there that the placenta of my daughter was disposed of as soon as she was born; if she had been born in Kikuyu Country, the placenta would have been buried near our gate by the old woman who acted as midwife. At the hospital I was told that it had been burned. I wished it had been buried instead of being burned" (p. 215). It may seem insignificant, to the "unsenti-mental" Westerner, whether placenta is burned or buried and whether the operation in either case is carried out in London or in "Kikuyu Country," and it may seem unlikely, to a man born in a hospital and circumcised there, that blood dripping on the ground will satisfy ancestral spirits and provide them a continued existence, but this only means that Western man in general does not live a life of traditional ritual and that Western man, again in general, does not bear anything like the relationship to ancestral lands that the Gikuyu bears, both as a heritage and as an obligation.

Burying placenta, like dripping blood into the ground, unites the individual with the ancestors and both with the will of Ngai, for "it is in the ancestral lands that the ances-tors lie buried," and it is through communion with ancestral spirits and through "incarnation [that] the future generation is linked up with the past, thus bringing spiritually the three groups, i.e. dead, living and unborn, into one organic whole" (*Mt. Kenya*, p. 205). Though Gikuyu ownership of land is, as Charity Waciuma's phrasing ("clan land") would suggest, a family and clan affair, yet as a whole, "The Gikuyu consider the earth as the 'mother' of the tribe. . . . [T]he earth is the most sacred thing above all that dwell in or on it."[17] The buying and selling of Gikuyu land, as Ken-

[17] *Facing Mt. Kenya*, p. 22. Cf. this similar passage in *My People of Kikuyu* (p. 22): "The Kikuyu have a saying which means: 'There can be no ground for friendship with one who seeks to deprive you of

yatta outlines that complicated ritual (*Mt. Kenya*, pp. 38-39), is all done symbolically in the form of a wedding cere-mony, since, as is natural, the Gikuyu do not think that it shows proper respect or reverence to sell "the mother of the people," or any part of her, in a straight cash transaction. An earth nexus, not Carlyle's cash nexus, binds the children of Gikuyu and Mumbi. This mystical union through the earth of child and grandparent, of the living and the dead, and of present age-grades with similar groups in the an-cestral past all depends, however, on tenure of the land. The man who is deprived of his piece of earth, his *shamba*, suffers "a spiritual loss," as Ngotho thinks in *Weep Not, Child*. "When a man was severed from the land of his ances-tors where would he sacrifice to the Creator? How could he come into contact with the founders of the tribe, Gikuyu and Mumbi?" (p. 110). In this same novel, which adopts the universalizing form of fiction only to present once again the autobiography of the Gikuyu, James Ngugi draws a sig-nificant contrast between the feelings for the earth of Ngotho and of Mr. Howlands, the British settler now occu-pying the land formerly claimed by Ngotho's clan. "Both men admired the *shamba*. For Ngotho felt responsible for whatever happened to this land. He owed it to the dead, the living and the unborn of his line, to keep guard over this

---

your land, your women, and your cattle.' For they hold that without these three a nation is dead. The earth is the mother whose breast gives suck to the children of the nation. She supplies both men and women with the material comforts of life, and thus enables them to bear many children, and during their infancy they receive the nourish-ment of Mother Earth through the breast of a woman; and when this natural food fails in the woman, there is the cow to fill the need." Kenyatta's conclusion, coming down from Mother Earth and the maternal breast to the cow's udder, may strike the reader as some-what bathetic, but it points up one fact of the Gikuyu economy: the Gikuyu are both herdsmen and farmers, and as such they are attached to their domesticated animals—cattle constitute the chief symbol of wealth for the Gikuyu—as well as to their women and their land.

**113**

*shamba.* Mr. Howlands always felt a certain amount of victory whenever he walked through it all. He alone was responsible for taming this unoccupied wildness" (p. 55). In Howlands' view, the land is his because he, acting alone and individually, has subdued it; Ngotho, on the other hand, finds in the same piece of land his own ancestry, his inalienable share in the being of "the mother of the people," his piece of life coming down to him from Murungu. From these thoroughly opposed attitudes toward land and people and human existence "Mau Mau" eventually arises in Ngugi's fiction as it arose in historical fact. Through violence—because it appeared the ancient prophecy would be fulfilled in no other way—the Gikuyu reclaimed from the Europeans their heritage and their destiny.

It was Mugo wa Kibiro who, years before any white man had been seen in Gikuyu land, foretold from dreams and visions the arrival of a people who would be dressed in "clothes like butterflies" and carrying sticks that produced killing fire; these mysterious people, he said, would later bring a huge iron snake (the Uganda Railway) that would move from the ocean westward across the country; but, most important of all, these people would want the ancestral lands of the Gikuyu for themselves—"Land which could not be given away. Land which meant everything to the tribe. Land which belonged to the Kikuyu. Land, land, the precious land. The land of our forefathers. They coveted our land" (*Daughter of Mumbi,* p. 91). Mugo wa Kibiro advised his people, however, that they must not try to oppose the butterfly people with force, for their fire-making sticks would be too powerful; instead they were to be hospitable but suspicious, learn the magic of these foreigners, and then drive them out by turning their own magic against the intruders. If the Gikuyu began by fighting the white man openly, Mugo wa Kibiro warned them, they would all be destroyed; if, on the other hand, they used the white man's power and knowledge to strengthen themselves, they would one day produce a "Black Messiah," a latter-day Gikuyu savior, to free them from foreign bondage.[18] There is certainly, according to Mugo wa Kibiro, a medicine more powerful than the white man's, but to possess and control that superior power requires first a knowledge of what the white man's magic is. "Mugo often said you could not cut the butterflies with a panga [a sort of machete]," Chege tells his son Waiyaki in *The River Between.* "You could not spear them until you learnt and knew their ways and movement. Then you could trap, you could fight back" (p. 24). Chege goes on to reveal to his son that he may be the promised savior, and tells him how to realize his greatness. The strategy he urges is that same one suggested by Mugo wa Kibiro and is essentially the strategy followed by several generations of Gikuyu of this century: "Arise. Heed the prophecy. Go to the Mission place. Learn all the wisdom and all the secrets of the white man. But do not follow his vices. Be true to your people and the ancient rites."

One of the sources of "Mau Mau" strength was that they claimed to know the white man's secrets, or at least the important ones, and they claimed to carry the power of Ngai's salvation, thus to represent the fulfilment of Mugo's prophecy. Without questioning whether a panga would have much success against a tank or an airplane, Karari Njama describes how, "Moved by emotion and will, I quickly believed that the time had come for all prophecies to be fulfilled—for such had turned out to be common gossip. The prophecy of the Kikuyu's honored witchdoctor, Chege Kibiro, who foretold the coming of the whitemen, the building of the railways and the going of the whitemen out of this country. I remembered the star that brilliantly shown [sic] in 1946 and moved from southwest to northeast which was claimed by witchdoctors that it indicated their departure

---

[18] The Mugo wa Kibiro story is told by Charity Waciuma (*Daughter of Mumbi*, pp. 15-16), Karari Njama (*Mau Mau from Within*, pp. 175-76), James Ngugi (*Weep Not, Child*, pp. 48-50, *The River Between*, pp. 2, 8, and 22-24, and *A Grain of Wheat*, pp. 13, 15, and 83), and Jomo Kenyatta (*Facing Mt. Kenya*, pp. 41-47).

115

and showed the whitemen the way out" (*Mau Mau from Within*, pp. 175-76). Even the "Mau Mau," however, saw that in this contest of opposed cultures—although Ngai might be supporting their cause by Mugo's prophecy and by signs in the stars—the essential thing was to know the enemy's special magic and to turn it into a weapon to destroy him. So Karari Njama says, of his schoolteaching days, "We preached to them [pupils and parents] that ignorance was our chief enemy, and that education was our best weapon" (*ibid.*, p. 101). One can be sure that this "best weapon" is not just the cliché of year-end commencement addresses directed against who knows what, but a device to be directed very specifically against usurping Europeans and against "colonial policy." Waruhiu Itote describes "how essential a weapon it [education] was in our fight for freedom" (*"Mau Mau" General*, p. 19) and refers to one particularly valuable aspect of his own Western education: "While we were at Gatundu, I blessed the circumstances which had made me join the army. Although at times I regretted having fought for our Colonial masters, on that day I was glad, for I was now going to use the knowledge they had given me, against them" (p. 46). Likewise, Charity Waciuma, who, though not precisely "Mau Mau," was a determined daughter of Mumbi, says of her educational intentions, "I was filled with a desire to study and become educated in the White Man's ways and in his knowledge so that I could help in turning him out of my country" (p. 59). Muga Gicaru quotes approvingly the remark of a shepherd who expressed Muga Gicaru's own sentiments: "Education is our only major weapon left . . ." (*Land of Sunshine*, p. 65).

It is a remarkable fact that in none of the Gikuyu writers does education, even though it be primarily Western and Christian, divide the literate and the illiterate—quite the contrary. Each of the writers sees his education as something not drawing him away from his people but binding him yet closer to them in their fight for land. Education commits the Gikuyu individual to special service of his community, and he becomes, in the process of educating himself, not less of a Gikuyu but more of one. "Somehow the Gikuyu people always saw their deliverance as embodied in education. When the time for Njoroge to leave came near, many people contributed money, so that he could go. He was no longer the son of Ngotho but the son of the land" (*Weep Not, Child*, p. 148). Education has the same effect as the Unity Oath, the same effect as the placenta burial in the birth ritual, the same effect as initiation. Of the Gikuyu who journeyed far to acquire education with the single intention of bringing it back as a weapon in the fight to reclaim the land, Mzee Jomo Kenyatta was, of course, the chief. Even those who thought him the very incarnation of evil and a threat to the whole British empire—the magistrate at his trial in Kapenguria, for example, or such writers as Ione Leigh and C. T. Stoneham, or the whole body of settlers who would have preferred a summary execution to a lengthy trial—even these bitterly opposed critics of Kenyatta never denied that he was an educated man.[19] Indeed

[19] See Montagu Slater's excellent book, *The Trial of Jomo Kenyatta* (London: Mercury Books, 1965) for the magistrate's views; also the account of the trial given by the chief defense counsel, D. N. Pritt, in the third volume of his *Autobiography: The Defence Accuses* (London: Lawrence & Wishart, 1966), pp. 71-136. Ione Leigh (*In the Shadow of Mau Mau* [London: W. H. Allen, 1954]) and C. T. Stoneham (*Mau Mau* [London: Museum Press, 1953]) may fairly be taken to represent those who, like the magistrate, apparently felt themselves threatened by unspeakable evil when in the proximity of Kenyatta. Ione Leigh, though she is rather confused as to which way she wants it about Kenyatta—once he is a "suave and ingratiating . . . diplomat of the first order" who, with his "guile" (p. 32) and "shrewd cunning" (p. 43), has subverted the government and perverted the simple, uneducated Gikuyu; another time, "In spite of the education he has received abroad, Kenyatta is extremely primitive" (p. 41)—is nevertheless quite confident in pronouncing on African character in general: "The uneducated African is a child in many respects. He is forgetful and irresponsible, careless and idle, ungrateful and often quite stupid, but if he is not practised upon he is amiable and trusting" (p. 16). Again, with the same mixture of bland certainty, colonial superiority, and meanness of spirit she says: "The fact that they are

117

it seems fairly obvious that the reason for the especially violent rancor in regard to Kenyatta was precisely his education, his worldliness and sophistication. He was not at all,
to the Kenya government and to the settlers, the fondly
imagined "simple native," cheerful, childish, happy-go-
lucky, and subservient, of smug colonial tradition. Kenyatta was far too "cheeky" for the settlers' taste—not to say
often disdainfully superior to their parochial, small-minded,
and nasty politics. But what hurt was that he had been to
England for too many years and he knew the white man's
magic and his secrets—all of them. He knew his people also,
better perhaps than any other man of his time. In their eyes
and in his own, and often in the eyes of the Kenya government as well, Kenyatta *was* his people. While he was in
England and after his return, Kenyatta was the subject of
stories and legends and songs, many of them based on fact
and all of them bearing religious overtones. "All of us
knew," Mugo Gatheru says, "that Jomo had gone to Britain
in 1929 to protest about the taking of the land and that he
had started to study there at the London School of Economics with the great anthropologist, Malinowski, and that
he had written a book about the Kikuyu people called *Facing Mount Kenya*" (*Child of Two Worlds*, p. 105). There
were other rumors, too, told most often in the accents of
legend and myth: "that he had journeyed into the land of
the Russians and stayed there for some time; that he had
married an English woman and had had a child by her; that
he was known to all the powerful politicians in Britain . . ."
(*ibid.*, pp. 105-06). As Mugo Gatheru goes on to say, "Although to the older people Kenyatta was the man who
would restore the land, to the young people of Kenya in

---

committing the most savage and brutal murders is simply because
brutality is a part of the native character. It is prevalent in all Africans" (p. 205). In her conclusion, Ione Leigh advances what is perhaps the most arresting, novel, and astonishing solution ever offered
for "Mau Mau": "the only hope for Kenya is a widespread European
immigration" (p. 216).

1946 [the year of his return] he was an African Messiah . . ." (p. 106). Few Gikuyu of the time doubted that Kenyatta represented the fulfillment of Mugo wa Kibiro's prophecy. What James Ngugi says of Ngotho in *Weep Not, Child* was equally true for a great many other Gikuyu—true for Charity Waciuma and Mugo Gatheru and Muga Gicaru, for Karari Njama and Waruhiu Itote and Dedan Kimathi, for Josiah Mwangi Kariuki and Joseph Kariuki (the author of a resounding and slightly fulsome "Ode to Mzee")[20]—and perhaps true for Jomo Kenyatta as well: "To him, too, Jomo had been his hope. Ngotho had come to think that it was Jomo who would drive away the white men. To him Jomo stood for custom and tradition purified by the grace of learning and much travel" (*Weep Not, Child*, p. 110).

There can be no doubt that in the course of the thirty-five years that transpired between Kenyatta's departure for England and his election as the first (and to this date, only) president of the Republic of Kenya, he gradually assumed the dimensions of a mythic figure to the Gikuyu. Tragically but compulsively the Kenya government acted their part in the mythic drama to perfection: they persecuted the political-spiritual leader, they tried him as if he were any Messiah, they banished him to the wilderness, and they only

[20] "Ode to Mzee" (Nairobi: Chemchemi Cultural Center, 1964). These are some representative lines (in which one sees reference also to the particular myth that Kenyatta lived between 1946 and 1963):

"Many years of subjection had subdued the people,
Many years of little hope, for Pharaoh was strong,
Well-grounded, and armed with confidence.

. . . . . . . . . . . . . . . .

So when the hero came
The ground was prepared.
'This is our country,' his voice pierced incredulous ears,
'Ngai gave it to us, and to our children for ever.'
The story will be told to generations hence
How the bowed stood upright, and the cowered became bold
With a new heart and courage rose to defy foreign rule."

(pp. 4-5)

119

barely failed to crucify him.²¹ This merely made the Gikuyu more certain that Kenyatta was indeed the promised savior and that through him their providential destiny would be realized. "There was a man sent from God whose name was Jomo. He was the Black Moses empowered by God to tell the white Pharaoh 'Let my people go!' "²² The parallel between the Gikuyu story and the Biblical tale of deliverance was one drawn by many people. In it Kenyatta was invariably cast as the African Messiah, the Black Moses, even the Gikuyu Christ who would take on himself the suffering of his people and who would eventually make the foreigners

²¹ Cf. *Suffering Without Bitterness* (Nairobi: East African Publishing House, 1968), a curious book that claims to be written by Kenyatta—he is simply listed as author—and that certainly is about him, yet is in the third-person throughout. Some details, and very likely the spirit of the book, could have come only from Kenyatta, but actual descriptions appear frequently to have been written by another hand. I assume that the two members of Kenyatta's staff whom he thanks in his first-person "Foreword"—Duncan Nderitu Ndegwa and Anthony Cullen—were given access to his papers and requested to write an apologia for "Mzee." Whatever the case of the authorship, the book describes a good deal of "suffering," but it is not quite accurate to say that the description is "without bitterness." No doubt the bitterness is justified; in spite of the title it is certainly there and obvious. Besides being an apologia, the book is a denunciation of fools, charlatans, criminals, and traitors and—in addition—an exercise in hagiography (which is perhaps a good reason for its being in third-person). Though the title may not be altogether accurate as a description of its contents, its sentiment is, of course, one befitting a saint.

²² *Weep Not, Child*, p. 88. *A Grain of Wheat* is studded throughout with Biblical quotations and allusions (e.g., pp. 1, 37, 147, 229, 247) nearly always of an apocalyptic flavor pointing to the messianic destiny of Jomo Kenyatta and his independent Kenya.

Though he firmly and somewhat ostentatiously disavows Christianity in his most recent book (*Homecoming*), Ngugi continues to avail himself of Christian rhetoric and to draw a parallel between Biblical events and twentieth-century African experience. For example: "One could say that if Christ had lived in Kenya in 1952, or in South Africa or Rhodesia today, he would have been crucified as a Mau Mau terrorist, or a Communist" (*Homecoming* [London: Heinemann, 1972], p. 34).

120

"let my people go." Dedan Kimathi, who at times saw himself in some rather grand roles, nevertheless knew who the ultimate Gikuyu leader was; as he told Karari Njama, "Kenyatta is a very wise man, in fact he had predicted many of the emergency events. He is a prophet chosen by God just like Moses, who [sic] God chose to deliver the Israelite nation out of the Egyptian slavery; so is Kenyatta chosen to deliver the Kenya people out of the colonial slavery" (*Mau Mau from Within*, p. 440). But Dedan Kimathi need not have pointed out the parallel to Karari Njama, for that Christian-educated forest fighter had long since realized that "the Holy Bible is mostly Israelite or Jewish religion which in *all* respects agrees with the Kikuyu religion before the arrival of the Europeans. This only makes a Kikuyu believe that our religion was the right one. I had a strong thought that the Kikuyu were one of the twelve Israel tribes" (*ibid.*, p. 101).

Very much like Karari Njama's "strong thought," the education of Njoroge in *Weep Not, Child* mixes elements of traditional religion and Christianity until he comes to believe "in a God of love and mercy, who long ago walked on this earth with Gikuyu and Mumbi, or Adam and Eve. It did not make much difference that he had come to identify Gikuyu with Adam and Mumbi with Eve. To this God, all men and women were united by one strong bond of brotherhood" (p. 78). In spite of this brotherhood, however, only one people is chosen at a time—there is only one people descended from Gikuyu and Mumbi—and the consequence of Njoroge's education, as with so many Gikuyu, is that "there was growing up in his heart a feeling that the Gikuyu people, whose land had been taken by white men, were no other tribe than the children of Israel about whom he read in the Bible. So although all men were brothers, the black people had a special mission to the world because they were the chosen people of God. This explained his brother's remark that Jomo was the Black Moses" (*ibid.*). Carrying the parallel to the events of the New Testament, "in

121

Mathenge's song book," Karari Njama says, "Jesus Christ's name has been substituted for by Jomo Kenyatta's" (p. 121). This, which was a stage in Kenyatta's messianic progress, was also one of the points of bitter contention in his trial, evoking expressions of deep horror and breathless shock from the prosecutor and the magistrate. But to the Gikuyu it was no more than their Leader's due. By joining legend and autobiography—Kenyatta's autobiography, any individual autobiography, the autobiography of the Gikuyu nation—the Gikuyu transform their life into myth. This way of seeing life in mythic terms, whereby every man—or at least every Gikuyu—is living out his proper role in an unfolding universal drama whose ultimate author is Yahweh or Ngai, gives a weight and meaning to individual life by placing it within the patterns of ritual history and invests that individual life with a much greater than individual responsibility and significance.

Finally, there is the apotheosis of Kenyatta in the marvellous description by Josiah Mwangi Kariuki of his pilgrimage to visit the Leader, still detained at Maralal, shortly after Mwangi Kariuki had himself been released from detention: "There, framed in the doorway, waiting for us, was *Mzee*. He greeted us in a wonderful manner and as he embraced me to him I felt like a tiny chicken being folded under its mother's wings; all my worries and troubles now belonged to him. This would be a small burden indeed for a man who had already taken the suffering of all our people on himself" (*"Mau Mau" Detainee*, p. 178). Mwangi Kariuki, grateful to the Gikuyu Messiah, does not stand off as did those people who once might have been chosen—"O Jerusalem, Jerusalem. . . , how often would I have gathered thy children together, even as a hen gathereth her chickens under her wings, and ye would not!" Mwangi Kariuki, secure under his "mother's wing," held warmly in the embrace of the man-god who had suffered for all his people, goes on: "Kenyatta is greater than any Kikuyu, he is greater than any Luo or Nandi or Masai or Giriama, he is greater than any Kenyan, he is the greatest African of them all. He knows no tribe, no race, he bears no hatred or malice for the past; he is human and yet wiser than any other human being I have ever known. They are all his people, his responsibility and his children . . . " (p. 179). Greater than any Gikuyu or Luo or Masai he may be, yet Kenyatta does not for a moment forget the Gikuyu or neglect them, "his people" and his Jerusalem, and in their mythic character as well as in his, they are all his children even as they are the children of Gikuyu and Mumbi: "I am the leader of Mumbi . . ."—no doubt that same leader promised by Mwene-Nyaga from the heights of Kere-Nyaga, foretold by Mugo wa Kibiro, and, finally, so long awaited by the children of Gikuyu and Mumbi.

# CHAPTER III

# "Ces pays lointains"

THE WORD "nostalgia," according to the dictionary, is derived from two words, both of them Greek in origin: *nostos* ("a return") and *algos* ("pain"). *Algos* is the symptom of a sickness or a disease, the sign of some disorder, some disharmony, some illness in the organism; *nostos* provides evidence of the nature of the illness and a clue to its diagnosis, if not always to its cure, by specifying the kind of pain and its provenance. The pain, which is presumably to be cured by a return of some sort or in some form, is psychological and apparently is caused by separation from that to which the sufferer would return. That a man can feel a painful yearning to return suggests an incompleteness, a disjunction in his present condition, and, as a corollary, it implies either that he had previously known a state of unified being and of non-separation or that his imagination, with or without the aid of memory, has contrived to create such an ideal state for him to yearn toward. The first is the case of the man who was happy in his childhood and who, in the more complicated and troubled days of his maturity, wishes to have again the simplicity of his earlier years. (This is the motive, pure and simple, for a good many autobiographies; the product is usually rather bland and almost always ephemeral. *Kossoh Town Boy* is a good example from African literature.) The second is the case of the artist who creates the ideal object of his heart's desire and so possesses in imagination what he may never have known in fact. (Yeats, for example, created many such unified worlds for his emotional satisfaction—one he called *The Land of Heart's Desire*—but in those creations he was looking to his own vi-

124

sionary construction and not back to his childhood, for he tells us in *Reveries* that "I remember little of childhood but its pain. I have grown happier with every year of life. . . .")

Camara Laye's *Dark Child* (*L'enfant noir*)[1] is a classic expression of nostalgia of both kinds, an autobiography with the double motivation of the man remembering his happy childhood and the artist creating his ideal world. Recalling the marvels of his childhood, which are also the elements of the artist's vision, Camara Laye exclaims in *L'enfant noir,* "Ces prodiges—en vérité, c'étaient des prodiges!—j'y songe aujourd'hui comme aux événements fabuleux d'un lointain passé" (p. 91). *Dark Child* is a book in which the pain to return impels the writer to re-evoke a lost world of grace and union, to recapture "les événements fabuleux d'un lointain passé," and in so doing to cure, by the artist's powers, the illness and the disharmony of which the pain is only symptomatic. The merger of the man who was the boy and the artist who creates his own imaginative world is complete as Camara Laye continues (in the English of the Kirkup-Jones translation) in his recall of that "far-off past": "That past is, however, still quite near: it was only yesterday. But the world rolls on, the world changes, my own world perhaps more rapidly than anyone else's; so that it appears as if we are ceasing to be what we were, and that truly we are no longer what we were, and that we were not exactly ourselves even at the time when these miracles took place before our eyes" (p. 75). The man's memory and the artist's imagination—where does one leave off and the other begin? The sense of a unified world recalled from childhood is too real and the feeling of disunion in adulthood too immediate to say which is a more powerful emotion or which the dominant motive in Camara Laye's auto-

---

[1] *L'enfant noir* (Paris: Presses de la cité, n.d.); *Dark Child,* trans. James Kirkup and Ernest Jones (New York: Noonday Press, 1954). Page references in the text when in French are to the Presses de la cité edition, when in English to the Noonday edition.

biographic act. *Dark Child* is consequently both an autobiography and a work of art, and it is a supremely fine book.

In everything he has written—a more or less pure autobiography (*Dark Child*), a more or less pure novel (*Le regard du roi*, translated as *The Radiance of the King*), and a book that is half-and-half (*Dramouss*, translated as *A Dream of Africa*)—different as the books may be formally, Camara Laye develops a single theme that he works out in two opposed, complementary, and joined movements, movements that are the mirror opposites and the reversed images of one another. Separation and return, disunion and reunion—they are like the two sides of a single coin, or like an event and an image of that event reflected in the artist's eye. When Camara Laye's father, in *L'enfant noir*, murmurs distractedly of "ces pays lointains" (p. 247), he is thinking of the imminent separation that will take his son away to France, to Europe, to the non-African world; spiritually as well as physically the boy is about to depart, as his father recognizes, for a country that is distant in all ways from the country of his own being. But when the young man sits down (as Camara Laye has described himself doing) in a cold and cheerless hotel room in Paris to try to recapture his past experiences, a complete transformation has been effected: it is now Kouroussa, the African world of his father and mother and the town of his own childhood, that is "un pays lointain." Through ambition he was separated, in nostalgia he returns. In *Dark Child* the two-fold theme revolves about the unified community on the one hand and the separated individual on the other; paradoxically it is the separated individual who recreates, in an act of memory and artistry, that world that in fact no longer exists—if it ever did exist in fact. In *Dark Child*, Camara Laye has said, "je traçais de ma Guinée natale un portrait qui certainement n'était pas celui de la Guinée d'aujourd'-hui."[2] Out of his disunion Camara Laye makes a reunion;

[2] "Entretien avec Camara Laye," *Afrique*, No. 26 (juillet 1963), p. 55.

in describing his separation he achieves a symbolic return. By the very act of writing *Enfant noir,* according to Camara Laye, "je regagnais par la pensée mes amis, mes parents, le grand fleuve Niger—et j'étais heureux, inexprimablement heureux: je ne me sentais plus seul ni abandonné" ("Entretien," p. 55). This disunion and reunion, this separation and return, and the mystery wherein they are made one and the same, has been the theme of all of Camara Laye's writing. In *Dark Child* the return is achieved through the artist's imagination; in *A Dream of Africa* the return is literal (and disappointing); and in *The Radiance of the King* the return is symbolic and vicarious, the white man Clarence discovering in Africa the world of simplicity that Camara Laye had lost through experience and had refound through art.[3]

At much the same time that Muga Gicaru was being addressed as "husband" by his grandmother and Mugo Gatheru was being bitten by the knife in Gikuyu land, Camara Laye, some four thousand miles away across the hump of Africa, was being called "little husband" by his grandmother in Tindican and was being initiated into Malinké manhood by circumcision ceremonies remarkably similar to those described by both Mugo Gatheru and Muga Gicaru. One of the movements of *Dark Child* rediscovers that same world of atavistic reincarnation and of social and psychological synecdoche that all the Gikuyu autobiographers detail. In Camara Laye's childhood too, as his autobiography remembers it, there was a belief that ancestors returned in the newborn child and that every individual, especially after his ceremonial rebirth, was really something other and more than an individual: he was the embodiment of a communal soul, the personfication of a

---

[3] According to an interview in *Africa Report,* 27, No. 5 (May 1972), Camara Laye has almost completed a new book, to be called *L'Exil,* which will apparently continue his autobiography from *A Dream of Africa* on. Dissatisfaction with the government of Sekou Touré in Guinée has caused Camara Laye to live in exile in Sénégal since 1965.

group spirit, the representative of Malinké manhood. To the ceremonial dance that preceded circumcision, "The whole town came," Camara Laye says, "because the test, so very important to us, was equally important to all. No one could be indifferent to the fact that this second birth, our real birth, would increase the population of the town by a new group of citizens" (p. 114). The shots that signalled the successful conclusion of the circumcision ritual "would announce to all that one more man, one more Malinké, had been born" (p. 123). The ceremony, in addition to binding the initiate to the land and reviving the ancestors through him ("Life itself would spring from the shedding of our blood" [p. 113]), made the individual entirely at one with, indistinguishable and inseparable from, the group. Thus it is that the black snake which the young boy is cautioned not to harm is described both as "your father's guiding spirit" (p. 22) and as "the guiding spirit of our race" (pp. 24, 25, 26). Socially and psychologically Camara Laye's father and the "race" are essentially and indistinguishably one in the extent of their being and embodiment of the spirit. Likewise, the workers, as they harvested the rice at Tindican, seemed to the boy to be participating in a single existence, a communal soul: "They sang and they reaped. Singing in chorus, they reaped, voices and gestures in harmony. They were together!—united by the same task, the same song. It was as if the same soul bound them" (p. 61). Though at the time Camara Laye already sensed that he would break free from this communal existence, yet he recalls the joy of oneness that work in the fields inspired. "Above us the swallows were already flying lower, and, although the air was as clear as ever, the end of the day was near. We were happy as we entered the village, weary and happy. . . . The scent of flowers, awakened by the approach of evening, seemed to clothe us in fresh garlands. If our song had been less noisy we would have heard the familiar sounds of the day's end: cries and laughter mingled with the lowing of cattle returning to the corral. But we were singing. We were singing. Ah! how happy we were in those days" (p. 64). A large part of *Dark Child* is an exaltation of what Camara Laye calls "farm ceremonies and manners" (p. 62), or the ways of country people, as against the artificiality of city life, where men are removed from natural rhythms, natural relations, natural observances. "Farm ceremonies and manners," in the view of the man looking back from Paris to his childhood in Guinée, are the outward forms of grace, the ritual gestures of a ritual life, the traditional observances of an organic community.

The primal world that Camara Laye recalls in *Dark Child* is much the same as that described by another writer, also born in Guinée but long separated from it, in his autobiography: Prince Modupe's *I Was a Savage* (more recently and less foolishly called *A Royal African*).[4] What Prince Modupe, like Camara Laye, remembers in his book is a community (Soussou in his case rather than Malinké) closely unified by recurrent and virtually ageless rituals marking every stage in the life of the individual and celebrating in his triumph the increase of being in all Soussou manhood; and celebrating too, as they do in Gikuyu land, the slight change in the character of the whole group which this new individual achievement represents. Initiation into Malinké or Soussou manhood meant surrender of any individual claims in favor of group responsibility: the part had to stand for the whole as the whole was concentrated in the part. "It was a sense of brotherhood which although it did not extend beyond the tribe, was vitally alive within it. Mutual help was the rule, even the condition, for life. Common concern for the common good was uppermost in all tribal training of youth. . . . Also present in tribal life was a deeply

---

[4] *I Was a Savage* (London: Museum Press, 1958); *A Royal African* (New York: Praeger, 1969). There are a number of minor differences in phrasing between the two books. References in the text are to the Museum Press version called *I Was a Savage*.

felt sense of symbolism, the communion of friendship in eating together for instance" (Modupe, pp. 123-24). In *Dark Child* Camara Laye describes a similar "communion of friendship" in the lavish banquets prepared for the initiates and for all the family and clan to celebrate the successful circumcision ceremonies; they all celebrate together because they have all been changed, they have all, in the experience of one and one on behalf of all, come through a ritual ordeal into a new state of being. Kouroussa and Dubreka alike, according to the biographers of those villages, were communities in which group well-being circumscribed, fortified, and defined individual existence—and also, therefore, limited that existence. "Any destiny apart from the tribe was, of course," Prince Modupe declares, "beyond the limits of either imagination or intuition. It was as unthinkable as that one of the bright orange legs of a millipede should detach itself from the long (eight inches or so) black body of the creature and go walking off by itself" (p. 47).

For such an eventuality, such a breach in nature, such an adventure in individual assertion, nothing in their village training had ever prepared Prince Modupe or Camara Laye. Both men did, of course, separate themselves from the communal body—both went first to Conakry and then out to the Western world, Prince Modupe to the United States, Camara Laye to France—but the experience, as they describe it, was more akin to the tearing of a closely woven fabric or the violent rending of an organism than to a normal and natural, expected and necessary event in the life of the maturing individual. It was expected of the individual that he would mature into an epitome of the group, not tear himself from it to end up isolated in Paris or Los Angeles, rootless in a distant country, alien to his people and thus, in the eyes of that group that defined him in their own image, alien to himself. "No, I do not like to remember that parting," Camara Laye says of his separation from his

130

family and from the ancestral lands. "It was as if I were being torn apart" (p. 187). Prince Modupe's departure, which
was like the rupture of a vital organ, was naturally intolera-
ble to all other members of the interdependent group: to
leave he had to break free of traditional restrictions, escape
from the community, and flee from his own father, who
pursued him as a representative of his people to insist on
Prince Modupe's responsibilities to the group and to try to
enforce a return to a communal, non-individualized existence.

The dedication of Prince Modupe's book reads "For my
mother, whose first words after she had paid the pain price
of my birth were of gratitude for my being." There is no
doubt that he means to give homage to his physical mother;
but when he describes the traditional ceremonies observed
after his birth it becomes abundantly clear that the mother,
like every Soussou individual, lives a symbolic role and
bears much more than merely individual significance. "The
placenta must be buried with ceremony in the compound
with the witch-doctor present. As the navel cord ties an unborn child to the womb, so does the buried cord tie the
child to the land, to the sacred earth of the tribe, to the
Great Mother Earth. If the child ever leaves the place, he
will come home again because the tug of this cord will always pull him toward his own" (p. 7). As Matara was
mother to the infant Modupe, so the Soussou group is
mother to every Soussou individual and the land of Africa
is the Great Mother to all her children. In the dedication of
Camara Laye's book—also to his mother—the significance
of the individual woman is infinitely expanded beyond the
personal to include the communal, the continental (Mother
Africa), and the universal; memories of her, as in the case
of Prince Modupe and his mother, are memories of the land
of Guinée and of the mysterious state of childhood union.[5]

[5] For some reason the first part of Camara Laye's dedication (the
part quoted above) is not included in *Dark Child*. It seems to me,

131

> Femme noire, femme africaine,
> ô toi, ma mère, je pense à toi . . .
>
> O Dâman, ô ma mère, toi qui
> me portas sur le dos, toi qui
> m'allaitas, toi qui gouvernas mes
> premiers pas, toi qui la première
> m'ouvris les yeux aux prodiges de
> la terre, je pense à toi . . .

Except for "Femme noire, femme africaine," which might suggest a representative and archetypal significance, Camara Laye's words up to this point would seem to refer only to his own mother; but the dedication continues in such a way as to identify her with nothing less than the whole natural landscape and, in his memory, with that psychological condition which we call childhood.

> Femme des champs, femme des
> rivières, femme du grand fleuve, ô
> toi, ma mère, je pense à toi . . .
>
> O toi Dâman, ô ma mère, toi
> qui essuyais mes larmes, toi qui
> me réjouissais le cœur, toi qui,
> patiemment, supportais mes ca-
> prices, comme j'aimerais encore
> être près de toi, être enfant près
> de toi!

This is the mother both historical and mythic, both personal and symbolic, in yearning for whom *Dark Child* was written. As, in the memoried re-creation, she is both herself and all mothers to all children, so the child is simultaneously both himself and all *enfants noirs*. This is partly because of Camara Laye's artistry, which enables the reader to identify

---

however, rather more interesting than the last part, which is printed as the entire dedication in the English translation. The ellipsis marks are in the original.

132

himself with the child and his experiences, but it is also partly because life itself, in the traditional African community, is conceived as having a symbolic element: as Prince Modupe and Camara Laye were both taught at the time of initiation, the individual lives the life of the people and the people live in the individual.

"The way up," as Heraclitus pointed out, "and the way down are one and the same." Even as Camara Laye re-creates the unified community in *Dark Child*, he is simultaneously narrating the events by which he, now sitting in Paris, became separated from that organism. The way into the forest and the way out are identical (indeed in *The Radiance of the King* Clarence thinks the path through the forest is circular and endless); a movement toward union, one discovers in the description of initiation ceremonies in *Dark Child*, is also paradoxically a movement toward separation. This is the double movement—or the pair of simultaneous mirror-image movements—informing Camara Laye's vision everywhere. The boy, upon being circumcised, becomes a man, an adult, a full Malinké, and so finds himself united indistinguishably with the group. As this union of the individual with the group occurs and as the boy becomes a man, the relationship of the African mother, the "femme africaine," and her dark child, the "enfant noir," necessarily alters: no longer a boy, he is thus far separated from her and in becoming the child "of the whole tribe," as Jomo Kenyatta puts it, he ceases to that extent to be simply the child of his mother. When the mother comes to see her son after the initiation ceremony in *Dark Child*, something new, something psychological, keeps them from communing in the old way. "When I had left her I was still a child. Now . . . But was I really a man now? Was I already a grown man? . . . I *was* a man! Yes, I was a grown man. And now this manhood had already begun to stand between my mother and myself. It kept us infinitely further apart than the few yards that separated us" (p. 131). Though Camara Laye's mother opposed it in all ways possible because of her

133

conservative maternal instinct to preserve the emotional status quo, she was to find that her son would be separated ever further from her with every stage in his growing up. Camara Laye's own comment on the separation caused by initiation has behind it essentially the same feeling as the nostalgia that impelled him to recall his childhood when he was in a far distant country:

" 'Mother!' I said again.

"But this time I spoke very low, as if lamenting sadly, as if it were a lament for myself."

Indeed it is a lament for himself—for his vanishing childhood and for the loss of the internal psychological unity and the external family unity signified by the relationship with his mother. This movement, viewed in one way, is toward union; but viewed in another way it is toward disunion. For, as Birago Diop points out, in becoming a man the individual falls into incompleteness, he loses touch with that mystic oneness in which he participated as a child. In the apologia that introduces the first of his *Contes d'Amadou Koumba*, Birago Diop says, "Si je n'ai pu mettre dans ce que je rapporte l'ambiance où baignaient l'auditeur que je fus et ceux que je vis, attentifs, frémissants ou recueillis, c'est que je suis devenu homme, *donc un enfant incomplet*, et partant, incapable de recréer du merveilleux."[6] Camara Laye, I suspect, would be willing to affirm every word of this explanation, his intention in *Dark Child* being the same as Birago Diop's ("recréer du merveilleux") and his vision of childhood and manhood and of the relationship between the two being identical with Birago Diop's.

For a reason that is not immediately apparent—but that one can, I think, figure out by considering the intention and the achievement of Camara Laye's autobiography—many commentators have regarded *Dark Child* as fictional narrative or as an "autobiographical novel" or even as a novel

[6] *Les contes d'Amadou Koumba*, 3d ed. (Paris: Présence Africaine, 1969), pp. 11-12; italics are mine.

pure and simple.[7] Camara Laye himself has never claimed that the book is anything but "memories" or autobiography, a record of his childhood viewed from the detachment of maturity. No doubt this record is arranged to an artistic end, but every book, autobiography or not, is arranged, more or less effectively, to a particular end more or less clearly conceived, an end that might be described as "artistic." The mistaken assumption that *Dark Child* is fictional is a result of the intention from which Camara Laye began to write and—a corollary of his intention—the understanding or the vision he held of his own experience, that subject about which he was writing. Because it is one and the same person in an autobiography who experiences and who later narrates that experience, we cannot legitimately expect to separate the attitudes of the writer from the events described; we cannot deny the autobiographer his understanding or his vision of his life any more than we can deny him the events of his life—they are both, and equally, his material. In *Dark Child*, in addition to describing details of his childhood, Camara Laye presents his own vision and his

[7] A. C. Brench, for example, claims that *Dark Child* "is not meant to be a political manifesto, an indictment of colonialism but a novel and, as in all good novels . . ." (*The Novelist's Inheritance in French Africa* [London: Oxford Univ. Press, 1967], p. 37); Janheinz Jahn (*Muntu* [New York: Grove Press, 1961], p. 213) refers to *Radiance of the King* as Camara Laye's "second novel," which it would be only if *Dark Child* is his first; Oladele Taiwo groups him together with Prince Modupe, Robert Wellesley Cole, and William Conton as one of "those writers who use the medium of the novel to record their childhood memories" (*An Introduction to West African Literature* [London: Nelson, 1967], p. 54); Robert Pageard (*Littérature négro-africaine* [Paris: Le livre africain, 1966]) calls *L'enfant noir* "un des romans africains les plus lus" (p. 24) and refers to *L'enfant noir* and *Le regard du roi* as "deux romans édités par Plon" (p. 122); Jahn and Dressler classify the book bibliographically as ARo (i.e., "autobiographischer Roman"); and Jeannette Macauley (*Protest and Conflict in African Literature*, ed. Cosmo Pieterse and Donald Munro [London: Heinemann, 1969], p. 82) declares that "His novel *L'Enfant Noir* . . . [is] a very self-centred novel."

135

achieved understanding of those details. "Quand j'ai commencé à écrire," Camara Laye told an interviewer in 1963, "il m'a semblé que ce qui distinguait le plus l'ancienne Afrique de l'Europe, c'était l'omniprésence du mystère. Mon ambition était de révéler tout ce qui, dans mes souvenirs, relevait du mystère."[8] The essential spirit of African life, especially for the youth growing up, Camara Laye says, was determined by a sense of mystery infusing the quotidian, a sense of the ineffable pervading the most ordinary events, a sense of love human and divine binding families and clans into unified groups and joining them all mystically together in a vast organism with the surrounding natural world. Recounting the events of an African childhood, the acts and situations in which he was involved as "l'enfant noir," Camara Laye is looking to convey a depth of meaning, a universal rhythm, that far transcends the individual but that finds its realization only in his experience. In thus communicating a feeling of the supernatural operating in his own experience, Camara Laye ascribes to his life —specifically to his life as an African—a profound and important meaning which those who do not believe in the daily supernatural could only suppose to be "imaginary" or "fictional" or, in literary terms, "thematic." Camara Laye, in the view of such shortsighted critics, must have fictionalized his memories, must have imposed themes and meanings where there was really only experience, only acts and events without any significance beyond themselves. Life, they would say, has nothing of the mythic about it; hence autobiography must be meaningless and only fiction capable of embodying meaning. An artist and autobiographer (and occasional mystic) like Yeats would have disagreed, and so does Camara Laye: "Et pourquoi n'y aurait'il pas eu ces choses mystérieuses? La réalité du monde n'est-elle pas précisément autre chose que ce qu'un regard distrait aperçoit? Le mystère est inhérent à notre condition hu-

[8] "Entretien avec Camara Laye," p. 55.

136

maine, à cette union qui se fait en nous entre le ceil et la terre et que nous partageons avec toutes les civilisations" ("Entretien," p. 55). For Camara Laye, both art and life are symbolic and both have meaning, so that life, viewed in perspective, becomes, like fiction, "thematic." This does not make of *Dark Child* a novel; it is, rather, the autobiography of a man possessed of a comprehensive, and specially African, vision.

Every reviewer of *Radiance of the King* and every commentator on that novel has remarked that it is a symbolic work or, in Janheinz Jahn's rather vulgar phrasing, which suggests that the book is formally like an overstuffed and lumpy bag, "The whole book is full of symbolism."[9] What has not been so often noticed—indeed, has not been noticed at all—is that *Dark Child*, in discovering and adumbrating a meaning for past experience, renders the events of childhood in the symbolic mode while never departing from historical narrative. The earlier book does not have in it the accumulation of symbolic details, amounting almost to an overload, that characterizes *Radiance of the King*; instead, *Dark Child* suggests that life itself is symbolic and that every individual, ignorant though he may be of the fact, is living out the mysterious patterns of humanity. There is a tale of a student in a creative writing class who declared that his story was all finished except that he had to go back and put in the symbols. Camara Laye's artistry in *Dark Child* is never so painful as that: all he had to do was describe his life and the "symbols" were there. A symbol, according to Coleridge—and his words might stand equally well as a description of the African concept, or at least Camara Laye's concept, of the most ordinary human existence—"is characterized by a translucence of the special in the individual, or of the general in the special, or of the uni-

---

[9] "Camara Laye's Symbolism: Another Interpretation," in *Introduction to African Literature; An Anthology of Critical Writings from "Black Orpheus,"* ed. Ulli Beier (London: Longmans, 1967), p. 201.

versal in the general. Above all by the translucence of the eternal through and in the temporal."[10] If, as Camara Laye suggests, every individual life exhibits the typical curve of the species, if the boy, through initiation, becomes not only a man but in himself embodies Malinké manhood generally, and if the eternal mystery is thus translucent "through and in" the years of childhood and youth, then the life of the individual is rich in natural symbolism. The pattern of the boy's life in *Dark Child* is precisely a symbolic pattern, virtually an Aristotelian action with beginning, middle, and end; it portrays the eternal human dilemma of growing up and separating, of gaining knowledge and losing innocence, of falling from union and seeking reunion. Though eternal and universal, however, the pattern is neither abstract nor theoretical but embodied and real, the record of a life lived: fixed temporally in the specific years of Camara Laye's youth, located geographically in Kouroussa, Tindican, and Conakry.

This is not to suggest that Camara Laye had no choices to make in realizing the pattern of his life. There were, as he tells the story of his childhood, multiple possibilities before him: he might have been a craftsman in metal and in wood like his father; he might have developed in himself the talent for traditional artistry of his father or the supernatural powers of both his father and his mother; he might have been, or have remained, at one with his uncles and the other farm workers at Tindican; he might have attended an academic rather than a technical school in Conakry; he might have gone to Dakar rather than to Paris. Given the number of paths available to him (in the original French "les chemins" and "les voies" form a recurrent motif—le chemin de l'école, le chemin de la vie, le chemin de Dieu, le chemin de notre exil, etc.), it is significant that even before he could imagine that one day the railroad ("Nous

[10] *The Statesman's Manual*, in *The Complete Works of Samuel Taylor Coleridge*, ed. W.G.T. Shedd, 1 (New York: Harper & Bros., 1884), p. 437.

habitons en bordure du chemin de fer," p. 14) would take him far away from Kouroussa, far away from his father's "case" and his father's traditional life, and far away from the various "chemins" that, if chosen, would have brought him back home again for life, Camara Laye should have spent "much of my time . . . watching the iron rails" (p. 21) leading out from Kouroussa to Conakry, to another world and another life. This "chemin de fer," whose rails "glistened cruelly in a light which nothing in that place could relieve" (p. 21), is the first of those "chemins" that the child has to contemplate, the beginning of his puzzlement about which should be his proper path, his own way. "And I was no longer sure whether I ought to continue to attend school or whether I ought to remain in the workshop: I felt unutterably confused. . . . Ah! what was the right path for me? Did I know yet where that path lay? My perplexity was boundless as the sky . . ." (p. 27). When the boy sets foot on "le chemin de l'école," though he could hardly have known it at the time, he seals his destiny, for, as his father realizes from the beginning, after this first school there will be another and yet another after that until his path finally leads the boy all the way from Africa to Paris and then back to an alien land.[11]

[11] In *The African* William Conton repeats Camara Laye's picture of the African child drawn away from the known and the traditional by a Western education and in so doing he echoes the phrasing of *Dark Child*: "My parents started me off that day on the long, endless road of schooling; a road on which, for me, every milestone was to be a signpost pointing ahead, and every step of the way a sharpener of the intellectual appetite" (*The African* [London: Heinemann, 1964], p. 4). In *Kotia-Nima* (Paris: Présence Africaine, 1968-1969), Boubou Hama, like Camara Laye, sees Western education as a tearing apart of a unified organism—"Quatre-vingt-dix enfants furent arachés [sic] à leurs parents" (i, 119)—and when he goes to school for the first time (in Téra) the way there is "le chemin de l'exil" (i, 33); when he goes yet farther away to Dori it is "la route sans retour de l'exil" (i, 81). Western education, especially as it affects the African individual and the traditional community, is a very common theme in autobiography and fiction from Africa. Some very interesting contrasts might be made

Coupled with this motif of the many paths possible is another that refers to the "warmth" of the family home, "la chaleur de la case natale," from which the boy is progressively led away by the path he chooses to take. His father's embrace when he goes to meet Kondén Diara (the test of courage preparatory to initiation) warms the child—"He drew me to him, and I could feel his warmth; it warmed me, too, and I began to feel less frightened (p. 95)—with something of that same blessed "chaleur" that Camara Laye associates with his mother and with the state of childhood in his dedication: "ô Daman, ma mère, comme j'aimerais encore être dans ta chaleur, être enfant près de toi." When the "lions" of Kondén Diara start roaring, however, the memory of his father's warm embrace is hardly enough to sustain the boy's spirits: "Ah! how I wished this roaring would stop! How I wished I was far away from this clearing, back in the concession, in the warm security of the hut!" (p. 102). But more than the roaring of Kondén Diara, "le chemin de l'école" threatens and finally obliterates "la chaude sécurité de la case" (p. 130). As the boy starts out for the railroad station, leaving his mother and father behind in the compound, to take the train to Conakry, and as all the other children gradually join him on the road to say a last farewell on the platform, he comforts himself with the thought that what he is doing is after all no different from what he has done every day when he left home to go to school in Kouroussa. But the comfort is short-lived because this road, "le chemin de fer," though the logical extension of the other, "le chemin de l'école," goes much further and carries him far beyond the reach of the warmth of his mother and father and the warmth of his home. This is the road of growth and maturity, of separation and disunion; it is the road which makes him, in the Western sense, an individual and alone, no longer a Malinké among

---

between the treatment of the theme in works in French and works in English.

Malinkés but a disjunct fragment torn from the living body, an isolated individual unnourished by the organic community. "A mesure que nous avancions, des amis se joignaient à nous; Fanta aussi rejoignit notre groupe. Et c'était un peu comme si de nouveau j'avais été sur le chemin de l'école. . . . Et, de fait, n'étais-je pas sur le chemin de l'école?" To solace them both, he remarks to Fanta (his childhood girl-friend) that "nous sommes sur le chemin de l'école," but neither of them is much comforted, for the path and the school alike signify separation and loss of an intimate warmth. "J'étais en vérité sur le chemin de l'école, mais j'étais seul; déjà j'étais seul! Nous n'avions jamais été plus nombreux, et jamais je n'avais été si seul. Bien que ma part fut sans doute la plus lourde, nous portions tous le poids de la séparation . . ." (p. 188). As he waits on the platform for the train to come and listens to the *griots* singing his praises, the boy's mental anguish comes back more poignantly than ever when he thinks of leaving his brothers, those last two contacts with the warmth of his home. "Mes jeunes frères avaient glissé leurs petites mains dans les miennes, et je pensais à la tendre chaleur de leurs mains; je pensais aussi que le train n'allait plus tarder, et qu'il me faudrait lâcher leurs mains et me séparer de cette chaleur, me séparer de cette douceur. . . ."[12] The train

---

[12] P. 190. Because the translation gives little of the effect of Camara Laye's use of the recurrent motifs of "le chemin" and "la chaleur," I have found it necessary to quote from the original here. The final clause in this quotation for example—"il me faudrait lâcher leurs mains et me séparer de cette chaleur, me séparer de cette douceur" —in the translation becomes simply "I should have to release those small hands" (p. 144). Thus one loses not only the "chaleur" but the emphasis on separation from family unity. The "chaleur" of the dedication—"Dâman, ma mère, comme j'aimerais encore être dans ta chaleur, être enfant près de toi"—is translated as "How I should love to embrace you again, once again to be your child." And "le chemin de l'école" is regularly translated as "my way to school"; but when Camara Laye extends the motif (see below) to include reference to "le chemin de la vie" and "le chemin de notre exil" (translation: "the highway of life" and "the highways of our exile," p. 178) all verbal con-

comes, as he wishes it would not, on those same tracks he had stared at as a small child, to carry the boy to Conakry, to a Western school, finally to "un pays lointain," where, in a cold hotel room, he would remember this last warmth of his boyhood. "Était-ce leur chaleur qui imprégnait encore mes mains et me rappelait que mon père, tout à l'heure, m'avait pris la main? Oui, peut-être; peut-être cette dernière chaleur qui était celle de la case natale" (p. 191). Even the first night away from his family, which he passes at Mamou in the house of a former apprentice of his father's, Camara Laye describes as chilly and uncomfortable for him; the overwhelming impression one gets of his years in Paris (described in *A Dream of Africa*) is of his being always cold and always alone.

A third motif, again verbal and recurrent, accompanies these two of "chaleur" and "chemin" to describe the effect on the whole organism of separating off an individual part: "déchirer" (to lacerate, to mangle; to tear, to rend, to rip). For the individual perfectly at one with his community, separation is an internal as well as an external process, a rending that is psychological as well as familial and social, agonizingly painful from either perspective. Thus Camara Laye describes himself as being torn apart within at the same time as and because he is torn away from the integral family and the organic community. Though he spends his first night in Conakry in the family of his uncle, his state of mind is painfully split: "Ma pensée demeurait toute tournée vers Kouroussa: je revoyais ma mère, mon père, je revoyais mes frères et mes sœurs, je revoyais mes amis. J'étais à Conakry et je n'étais pas tout à fait à Conakry: j'étais toujours à Kouroussa; et je n'étais plus à Kouroussa! J'étais ici et j'étais là; j'étais déchiré. Et je me sentais très seul, en

---

nection is lost between the two "chemins," though Camara Laye surely intends the reader to make the connection and to understand the two as essentially one. This is not offered as a censure of the translation by James Kirkup and Ernest Jones—it is generally a fine translation—but only as an explanation for reverting so often to the original French.

dépit de l'acceuil affectueux que j'avais reçu."[13] This internal "déchirement," which is the consequence of an external
one, is as nothing compared to the psychological-social
"déchirement" that tears him from his family at the end of
the book and takes him to a far distant and totally foreign
country. "Oh! ce fut un affreux déchirement!" Camara Laye
says of this last and most symbolic separation. "Je n'aime
pas m'en souvenir. J'entends encore ma mère se lamenter,
je vois mon père qui ne peut retenir ses larmes, je vois mes
sœurs, mes frères. . . . Non, je n'aime pas me rappeler ce
que fut ce départ: je me trouvai comme arraché à moi-
même!"[14]

For Camara Laye it would not be at all hyperbolical to
say that the individual dies a little with each separation
from those he loves; indeed, death, as he came later to
think, is less fearsome than separation, for death, being a
great reuniter, reverses the movement of life, which is a
progression from one separation to another, or a regression
from original union to eventual disunion. Life, then, is exile:
growing up and apart, leaving childhood and innocence
and happiness, being separated inevitably from the Edenic
union within the family and the community (returning
home from school in Conakry, Camara Laye says, "I set off
for Kouroussa as if for the promised land," p. 155); death

[13] Pp. 196-97. The central phrase—"j'étais déchiré"—becomes in
translation, "I was ambivalent" (p. 148).
[14] Pp. 253-54. "It was as if I were being torn apart" is the way
Kirkup and Jones translate the last sentence quoted. Cf. the similar
phrasing in Camara Laye's account of his writing *Dark Child*—an
account delivered to the Dakar Conference in 1963 and translated
into English as "The Soul of Africa in Guinea" in *African Literature
and the Universities*, ed. Gerald Moore (Ibadan: Ibadan Univ. Press,
1965), p. 65: "Memories jostled each other; they came so fast that
my pen sometimes stopped abruptly because I did not know which
recollection to take first. I wanted to take them all at once. And sometimes it stopped because my father or my mother were actually there
in front of me and I saw them again as on the day I said goodbye
to them, *when I literally tore myself away from them* to take the plane
for Paris, and because I could see the tears in their eyes." My italics.

143

repairs the "déchirements" that, added together, constitute a life, and it restores the mystic oneness lost in innumerable separations. "Je songe à ces jours," the mature Camara Laye says of the death of his boyhood friend Check, "et très simplement je pense que Check nous a précédés sur le chemin de Dieu, et que nous prenons tous un jour ce chemin qui n'est pas plus effrayant que l'autre, qui certainement est moins effrayant que l'autre . . . L'autre? . . . L'autre, oui: le chemin de la vie, celui que nous abordons en naissant, et qui n'est jamais que le chemin momentané de notre exil . . ." (p. 242). Life, as Camara Laye envisions it, is made up of those countless roads of exile—to school, to France, to adulthood—that lead away from the warmth of one's brothers' hands, the security of a father's embrace, the "chaleur" of a mother's presence, "cette dernière chaleur qui était celle de la case natale."

Thomas Melone in his book on *Négritude* comments on the two worlds of Kouroussa and Conakry in *Dark Child*—the one characterized, he says, by happiness and familiar faces, by freedom and intensity of living, the other by sadness and indifference, by individualism and the severity of a student's life—and concludes with this remark: "Camara a vécu ces deux vies et, il sait apprécier la distance qui les sépare; il sait aussi apprécier leur rapport en valeur absolue. On comprend son déchirement au moment de son départ vers cette France étrangère et inconnue. L'espoir du retour vers les siens, cri de la Négritude!"[15] Whether this is especially or uniquely a "cri de la Négritude," there can be no question about the "déchirement," nor can there be any doubt but that "l'espoir du retour vers les siens" provides the major motive for the writing of *Dark Child*. In Paris, where he found himself "cold, terribly cold,"[16] in the

---

[15] *De la Négritude dans la littérature négro-africaine* (Paris: Présence Africaine, 1962), pp. 89-90.

[16] *A Dream of Africa*, trans. James Kirkup (New York: Collier-Macmillan, 1971), p. 77.

evenings of "longues journées d'hiver froides,"[17] Camara Laye, through his memory and his art, made the symbolic return to his parents, to his childhood, and to the warmth of his "case natale" that soothed the pain of nostalgia and partly cured it. When he had restored himself to a state of paradisal union, he says, "I felt inexpressibly happy and I no longer felt alone. I felt as though I was with my father and mother, as though we were talking to each other. I felt their warmth all round me once more" (*African Literature and the Universities*, p. 65). The return is only in imagination, yet the warmth is as comforting psychologically as if the return were physical and literal.

Or one should say rather that the warmth is more comforting and more real than if the return were physical, for this is the warmth, whether imagined or remembered, of pre-separation days, and it is not to be rediscovered in any literal return. Once the organism has been rent, once the internal and external union has been destroyed, there is no restoring it, except in an imaginative vision, to its pristine state. This is what Camara Laye, under the name of Fatoman, discovers in *A Dream of Africa*, his third book in order of publication but in chronology of events the immediate successor to *Dark Child*. "C'est une suite de *L'enfant noir*," he told an interviewer, in which "je raconte . . . ma vie de vingt à trente ans" ("Entretien," p. 57). Unfortunately, *A Dream of Africa* is not an exception to the rule that sequels are seldom as good as the successful books they follow. The reasons for the failure of *A Dream of Africa* are interesting and they reveal, by way of contrast, a good deal about what it is that makes both *Dark Child* and *Radiance of the King* such fine achievements. The pattern of *A Dream of Africa* exactly reverses the pattern of *Dark Child*: the earlier book concludes with the boy (Laye Camara as he is called; this is the proper order for his name) leaving Guinée to fly to Paris ("The earth, the land of Guinea began

[17] "Entretien avec Camara Laye," p. 55.

145

to drop rapidly away," p. 187); the later book begins with his return to Guinée after six years in Paris ("the land gradually rose. . . . And then there took shape the island of green. . . . Conakry! Conakry!" p. 20), and then proceeds to reverse the events, but not the spiritual condition, of separation as narrated in *Dark Child*. After Conakry and the reunion there with the uncle and aunts with whom he lived in *Dark Child* and with the girl-friend (Marie) of the earlier book, Fatoman continues his journey of return to Upper Guinea and Kouroussa, to his "case natale," to the scenes of his childhood and to his parents. But of course he does not find there what, when in Paris, he had remembered leaving behind. After experience—Paris gives Fatoman plenty of experience: from the homosexual caresses that revolt him in La Pergola to a game of hide-and-seek as he evades the hotel manager and his demand for money—he can never recover his innocence. Moreover, it is not only that Laye Camara-Fatoman has changed; so have his parents, so has Kouroussa, so especially has Guinée herself changed. "Heraclitus somewhere says," according to Plato, "that all things are in process and nothing stays still, and likening existing things to the stream of a river he says that you would not step twice into the same river."[18] It is a mistake for Fatoman to suppose, or for the author of *A Dream of Africa* to suppose, that he can step back into the river that is Guinée and find it or himself unchanged. If *Dark Child* describes the separation of the individual from the body and from the life of the community, *A Dream of Africa* presents the alienation, accomplished during Fatoman's absence, of an entire people from their own traditions and from their corporate self.

As fiction or as autobiography—the recall and renewal of experience—*A Dream of Africa* is a dead thing: a view from outside on a totally alien and unsympathetic scene quite unlike the evocation in memory of a past experience,

---

[18] G. S. Kirk and J. E. Raven, *The Presocratic Philosophers* (Cambridge: Cambridge Univ. Press, 1966), p. 197.

146

once lived and now again made to live, that we get in *Dark Child*. In Kouroussa Fatoman finds that the unified and interdependent world of *Dark Child* is entirely gone and that the life of ritual and of traditional community has been replaced by a westernized life of material possession and individual acquisition.[19] This new attitude, which values the shoddy and the showy rather than the solid and the well-made, is symbolized in the person of a boyhood friend (Bilali), who, instead of building a real concession in the old style (cf. "the nobility" of Fatoman's mother's hut, p. 129), lives in a hovel while driving an American-made limousine originally turned out for the president of Liberia (pp. 94-98). Or it is symbolized in the fact that Fatoman cannot find any of the old leather goods because they have been driven out of the market by cheap Lebanese trash (pp. 125-28); thus the craftsman, the artist representative of the old community, is gone, replaced by the foreign huckster: a money economy and a spirit of money has replaced the barter economy and the spirit of craftsmanship. Camara Laye's attempt to make this spiritually dead world come to life in autobiographic re-creation is a failure virtually from the start. Were the book a satire throughout,

---

[19] Cf. the very similar experience in Bernard Dadié's heavily autobiographical novel *Climbié* when the hero (Climbié) returns to the Côte d'Ivoire after a number of years away to find himself "plus qu'un étranger" in the country of his birth (*Climbié*, in *Légendes et poèmes* [Paris: Seghers, 1966], p. 211). What Climbié, like Fatoman, discovers is that the old unified community has fallen apart under the pressure of the Western world and no possible replacement has been provided by that foreign, colonial world.

In an essay that he calls "Et demain?" (*Présence Africaine*, Nos. 14-15 [juin-septembre 1957], pp. 290-95) Camara Laye begins with the autobiographical experience that links *L'enfant noir* and *Dramouss*: "L'étudiant africain qui regagne son pays natal, après avoir passé cinq ou six ans en Europe—le temps d'achever ses études—a d'abord quelque peine à se figurer que ce pays natal est bien le sien. Il y a plus peine encore si ce pays est la brousse ou une petite ville de la brousse, et si l'Europe où il a vécu durant ces cinq ou six années, est une grande ville, une ville comme Paris . . ." (p. 290).

and not, for the most part, an autobiography, it might have succeeded in that totally different genre; but *A Dream of Africa* does not come off, except very intermittently, as satire precisely because Camara Laye is trying, from unsympathetic materials, to re-create a world in his later book ("une suite de *L'enfant noir*") that will be something like the world of the child in his first book, and satire had nothing whatever to do with that earlier world. In Camara Laye's case, successful autobiography could be written only in Paris and satire successfully only in Guinée. There are few books, whether fictional or autobiographical, with conversation as stiff and as wooden, as unlikely and as unreal as the conversations of *A Dream of Africa*. The effort to create something positive—for example, by having Fatoman's father talk about his art—to set against the lifeless world of the new generation in Guinée is simply still-born. The discourse on the nature of art and the African artist put into the mouth of Fatoman's father, and claimed as recollection of his conversation (pp. 129-33), is obviously Camara Laye's own best thought on the subject: the speculations of an intellectual with six years of France behind him, now returned to Guinée and looking for something that is no longer there. The conversations of father and son read more like "philosophic dialogues" than they do like anything anyone ever said in conversation or ever could say; rather than dialogue in fiction or conversation in autobiography, they might stand as a neat and solid, half-dramatized essay for an exhibition—in Europe obviously—of African art. It comes as no surprise to the reader of *A Dream of Africa* to learn that this same discourse on the arts of traditional Africa was presented to the Dakar Conference in 1963 by Camara Laye as being his personal experience (observations of his father's craft and thoughts about it) and his own aesthetic theory (*African Literature and the Universities*, pp. 70-73). A month later Camara Laye did much the same thing when he narrated to the conference at Fourah Bay College in Sierra Leone a long dream that is virtually the

148

same one as the dream at the center of *A Dream of Africa*[20] —a dream that in both cases, like the discourse on art, strikes the reader as being about as heavy in significance as it is light in verisimilitude. *A Dream of Africa* proves that no amount of talk about how things are different can replace the creative effort of reenacting the way they were in the past or the way they are in memory.

The world of *Dark Child* is a world of childhood that may or may not have existed as Camara Laye describes it— may or may not because it is altogether a subjective world anyway and hence immeasurable, inexperienceable by anyone but the author, who is no longer the child—but in any case certainly does not exist in the present time of the book except in the creative imagination of Camara Laye. To this world there are, one would have supposed, two kinds of return: the re-creative, evocative return of art as in *Dark Child*; or the unsuccessful, frustrated, actual return as narrated in *A Dream of Africa*.

With remarkable genius Camara Laye discovers a third mode of return in *Radiance of the King*. When Socrates remarked to Meno that "seeking and learning are in fact nothing but recollection," he was referring to the knowledge that the individual carries over from one incarnation to another; he was not speaking of rediscovery or recollection, nor of literal return, within the span of a single life. In *A Dream of Africa* Fatoman comes to realize that he cannot go home again, and he is right: neither he nor the Heraclitean stream allows a return to the childhood he once knew. In *Radiance of the King* the European Clarence, discovering a world of mystic union that he has never known before, almost feels that he is recollecting something from a previous existence, or realizing a Socratic, potential awareness, a possibility of perfect and primal union, hitherto present but unrecognized within himself. That is to say, Clarence can become like an African child in a way that

[20] See *African Literature and the Universities*, pp. 124-28 and *A Dream of Africa*, pp. 155-79.

149

Fatoman paradoxically cannot—precisely because Fatoman has already in this life *been* an African child. Clarence matures in *Radiance of the King* by growing up enough to be as a child, and not as a child once more but as a child for the first time. For in Africa, but also potentially within himself, he discovers that unified existence where body and soul are not separated and at odds with one another but perfectly joined and indistinguishable as expression and essence the one of the other. He discovers, that is, the mysterious world of childhood of *L'enfant noir* that he had never previously known because he had been born into the analytical, individualistic, materialistic, physically energetic but spiritually dead Western world of separation. What for Fatoman is regression and hence a failure is for Clarence progression and a wonderful triumph. By the end of *Radiance of the King* Clarence is no longer, in Birago Diop's phrase, incomplete, no longer incapable of sensing and participating in the "merveilleux."

*Radiance of the King* represents, much more successfully than the abortive *A Dream of Africa*, for Clarence an initiation into and for Camara Laye a return to that organic state of being from which the individual was seduced by a foreign education in *Dark Child*. Clarence's journey to the South in search of the king, from Adramé through the dense and overwhelming forest to Aziana—a journey to the heart of Africa not as a place but as an experience—constitutes his "dematerialization." In the symbolic progress of Clarence's quest, Africa does to the white man what in reverse Europe does to the African: it provides an education in the spiritual-sensory versus an education in the material-mental. The South into which Clarence penetrates, and where he finally receives the glance of the King, is a place of heightened sensuality and organic unity, an existence untouched by Cartesian dualism: there spirit is dissolved to become the surface receptors of open senses, and there body is the perfect expression, the very being, of spirit. Of the pervasive impression of the jungle entrance to the South

—the initiatory gate through which Clarence passes to reach a non-Europeanized Africa—Camara Laye says: "It was an odour in which the body and the spirit, but above all the spirit, were gradually and imperceptibly dissolved. One might have to call it, to be precise, an emollient."[21] It is an exact and felicitous stroke to characterize "the South" as a place, or a state of being, where both body and spirit are nourished by the senses, a place where both are bathed in a constant sensory flow, for it is the fantastic, overwhelming richness of sensory experiences that first strikes the visitor to Africa, especially West Africa (for example, Clarence) and comes to stand in his mind for the experience of Africa herself: the calls of strange birds, the chattering of monkeys, the unidentifiable cries of unidentifiable animals in the night, and the sounds of drums and men's voices when the moon is full, carrying so far and seeming to mean something so mysterious; the smell of dried fish and palm oil, the smell of coffee-blossoms and orange-blossoms, so sweet, so pervasive, so insidious it finally, as if from within, drowns the sense of smell; the taste of cayenne pepper and the taste of palm oil and palm wine and palm butter and of the marvellously named butter pear; the taste of pineapples, oranges, limes, bananas; the red-brown earth and the intensely green forest; the sharp, almost painful yellow-white of the moon in dry season, the apocalyptic colors of sunset; the purple-black skins of the people and the brilliant indigoes, whites, greens, reds of women's garments in Dakar; the moisture of the atmosphere that surrounds and embraces one like a damp cloth, a flannel that touches the skin at every point and gives a sense of pressure, of resistance to movement in the circumambient air. Immersed in this amniotic, total experience of the senses, Clarence is reborn at the end of the novel into a new and integral existence. It is relevant to remark that the symbol for this new state of being—perhaps one should say for this immensely

[21] *Radiance of the King*, trans. James Kirkup (New York: Collier-Macmillan, 1971), p. 94.

old state of being: a pre-lapsarian, organic unity—is precisely an *enfant noir*: the ages-old child King in whose antiquity and youth, in whose frailty and strength, and especially in whose Africanness and blackness ("the midnight of this slender body," p. 252), Clarence finds his apparent salvation.

In an ingenious variation on the theme of nostalgia, Camara Laye shows us in *Radiance of the King* not the *enfant noir* returning (he has never been away, has never lusted after foreign gods or known anything but his own self and his own being) but a representative of the other, the foreign, world discovering and participating in that internal-external union from which the hero fell away in *Dark Child* and from which he is effectively excluded in *A Dream of Africa*. "Puis c'est le voyage sans fin dans la forêt mystérieuse," as Claude Wauthier puts it, "où Clarence perd toute notion du temps à la recherche d'un lieu qu'il ignore: paraphrase sans doute du rhythme et de la géographie d'une Afrique sans montres ni cartes."[22] It is also a metaphor for the rhythm and the geography of a psychological, a philosophical Africa existing in the spirits and bodies, in the minds and souls, of men. What Clarence finds without knowing he was looking for it is that unity of being that Léopold Senghor claims is peculiarly African, or that oneness of being that Senghor associates with "*négritude*": "On l'a dit souvent, le Nègre est l'homme de la nature. Il vit traditionnellement de la terre et avec la terre, dans et par le *cosmos*. C'est un sensuel, un être aux sens ouverts, sans intermédiaires entre le sujet et l'objet, sujet et objet à la fois."[23] Whether or not one should take this psychological oneness described by Senghor as a corollary of *négritude* is less important than the fact that Camara Laye sees this

[22] *L'Afrique des Africains; Inventaire de la négritude* (Paris: Éditions du Seuil, 1964), p. 74.

[23] "L'esprit de la civilisation ou les lois de la culture négro-africaine," *Présence Africaine*, Nos. 8-10 (juin-novembre 1956), p. 52; reprinted, under the title "L'esthétique négro-africaine," in *Liberté I: Négritude et Humanisme* (Paris: Éditions du Seuil, 1964), p. 202.

mystic unity as the presiding and sustaining spirit of the South, of the King, and of Africa, and especially as the spirit of "the forest, where everything attracts and is attracted, where everything is split open like a ripe fruit bursting with warm and heavy juices, where everything opens itself to every other thing, where everything is penetrated by everything else."[24] This is none other than Marvell's "Garden" where

> Stumbling on Melons, as I pass,
> Insnar'd with Flow'rs I fall on Grass,

but for most of the novel Clarence resists the appeal of the "Garden" and the forest, being too filled with the white man's pride and with Western individualism to accept what is lying all about him and to be dissolved in that mystery which is an expression of essential love.

In the course of the novel, however, Clarence gradually discards his pride, his individualism, his materialism as he symbolically divests himself of his clothes—the white hotel-keeper has taken his trunks of belongings; Clarence gives his coat to the black inn-keeper and then to the boys Noaga and Nagoa; in Aziana he assumes a *boubou*; and finally he is entirely naked when he comes before the King—until his humility is total and he is purged entirely of the philosophic and material trappings of his Western civilization. Eventually, when Clarence succeeds in

> Annihilating all that's made
> To a green Thought in a green Shade,

[24] *Radiance of the King*, p. 98. Cf. the similar expression in Cheikh Hamidou Kane's *Ambiguous Adventure* (New York: Collier-Macmillan, 1962), when Samba Diallo describes what he has lost in going from Africa to Paris: "It still seems to me that in coming here I have lost a privileged mode of acquaintance. In former times the world was like my father's dwelling: everything took me into the very essence of itself, as if nothing could exist except through me. The world was not silent and neuter. It was alive. It was aggressive. It spread out. No scholar ever had such knowledge of anything as I had, then, of being" (p. 139).

and when he resolves the Marvellian "Dialogue of Body and Soul" by surrendering both in an act of humility to the simplified and unified vision—then he is capable of the paradisal rebirth (which for Camara Laye himself is not a rebirth but a symbolic return); he exists not in part but in full, he knows even as also he is known, and he sees, at the end of the novel, not as through a glass darkly but face to face with the *enfant noir* "qui, dans mon livre," Camara Laye has said, "symbolise Dieu" ("Entretien," p. 56). In the artistry of these two books, Camara Laye claims thus much for his own childhood, since what Clarence finds in the King is that sense of the "ineffable," that pervasive "mystery" and "love" that he says he was trying to realize as the essence of African existence in *Dark Child*. When Clarence kisses the faintly beating, calling heart of the King at the end of the novel, he is, among other things, putting away his highly prized individualism to come to a state of innocence and of African childhood, "a condition of complete simplicity," in Eliot's phrase, "costing not less than everything."

No longer talking about "luck" as if this were a universe of chance and accident, and no longer insisting on his "rights" or his "merit" as a white man, Clarence comes to understand that the dark child's glance, his embrace, and his love are a matter of "favor," as the beggar says, or of "pity," as Diallo, the blacksmith, calls it (pp. 247-48). It is this spiritual world of grace and this supernatural love displayed in the being of the child that Camara Laye takes as the deepest reality of human existence and that he tries to present as such in *Dark Child* and in *Radiance of the King*. Camara Laye himself grew up, according to his own account in a short piece entitled "Kafka et moi," into such a world of the spirit until that world became his world, the necessary condition and accompaniment of his existence. "Si . . . je crois 'qu'il n'y a rien d'autre qu'un monde spirituel,' c'est que ce monde-là est le mien depuis mon enfance, c'est que je n'ai jamais séparé le monde Visible de l'Invisible.

154

J'étais, en Afrique, naturellement plongé dans ce monde spirituel; j'y suis resté en Europe, comme en Afrique. Je ne puis entrevoir d'en sortir jamais. La mort même ne devra que m'y intégrer plus intimement."[25] Though Clarence does not die at the end of *Radiance of the King* he does for the moment—and in that moment forever—participate in that spiritual condition symbolized by the child; he is united with that same spiritual world into which, as Camara Laye says, he himself expects to be yet more intimately integrated at death.

"When he had come before the king, when he stood in the great radiance of the king, still ravaged by the tongue of fire, but alive still, and living only through the touch of that fire, Clarence fell upon his knees, for it seemed to him that he was finally at the end of his seeking, and at the end of all seekings.

"But presumably he had still not come quite near enough; probably he was still too timid, for the king opened his arms to him. And as he opened his arms his mantle fell away from him, and revealed his slender adolescent torso. On this torso, in the midnight of this slender body there appeared —at the centre, but not quite at the centre . . . a little to the right—there appeared a faint beating that was making the flesh tremble. It was this beating, this faintly-beating pulse which was calling! It was this fire that sent its tongue of flame into his limbs, and this radiance that blazed upon him. It was this love that enveloped him.

"'Did you not know that I was waiting for you?' asked the king.

"And Clarence placed his lips upon the faint and yet tremendous beating of that heart. Then the king slowly closed his arms around him, and his great mantle swept about him, and enveloped him for ever."

[25] From "Kafka et moi," *Dimanche-Matin, Nouvelles des Lettres* (2 janvier 1955); reprinted in *Camara Laye: écrivain guinéen* (Paris: Fernand Nathan, 1964), p. 37.

The achievement of Camara Laye's writing—as in this passage which concludes *Radiance of the King* (pp. 252-53)—is a double but unified thing: a portrait of the organic community and an autobiography of the individual separated from it; an autobiographical recall of a meaningful existence and a fictional representation of the same meaningful pattern; a merger and reversal of the symbolic places and conditions of Guinée and France, of childhood and maturity, as "ces pays lointains"; an imitation of a movement away from union and a simultaneous return to union; a rendering of human experience in which, by fidelity to the memory of that experience, the author, and with him his reader, discovers nothing less than the divine mystery infusing life. Camara Laye has twice given us, in two of the finest books in contemporary African literature—two books that are the equal, I should say, of the finest autobiographies and the finest novels of contemporary Western literature— a vision of the dark and divine child powerful enough and persuasive enough, if we live into it, to sustain us, African or not, as it sustained him, on all our roads of wandering, in all our years of exile.

# CHAPTER IV

# Love, Sex, and Procreation

THE LIFE of the Ibo of Eastern Nigeria—a very highly
unified and closely integrated community life, as one can
gather from all the various accounts of it—has been described from within, preserved for later generations, and
transmitted to the Western world in a number of autobiographies and quasi-autobiographies, including among them
one of the first from an African born south of the Sahara:
Olaudah Equiano's *The Interesting Narrative of the Life of
Olaudah Equiano, or Gustavus Vassa, the African* (published in 1789). Like the A-Gikuyu autobiography, the Ibo
portrait of experience seems to be fashioned after a proto-
typical pattern: Ibo autobiographers, that is, like their
Gikuyu counterparts, all seem to be writing their versions
of one and the same essential story. Victor Uchendu, who
presents a Kenyatta-esque mixture of anthropology and autobiography in his *Igbo of Southeast Nigeria*, indicates, both
in his practice (basing an anthropological monograph on
autobiographical authority) and in his observations, the
dual nature, simultaneously personal and communal, of Ibo
experience and Ibo writing about that experience. Discussing the geographical division of the Eastern and Western
Ibo, he says that in spite of separation they have nevertheless "retained their cultural as well as their psychic unity."[1]
For Victor Uchendu as for other Ibo portraitists, culture,
though a community matter, is manifest in the individual,
his beliefs and his actions; and, turning the personal-com-
munal coin over, psyche, though the Western world may
consider it an individual affair, is also in this case the spirit,

[1] Victor C. Uchendu, *The Igbo of Southeast Nigeria* (New York:
Holt, Rinehart & Winston, 1966), p. 1.

157

the personality, the soul and the self of a people. Psyche contains and reflects the total culture in the same way that any Ibo individual, at least until recently, could be taken to embody and represent the group soul. The fullest and most exact picture of Ibo personality and of Ibo life is to be found, however, not in anthropology nor in autobiography in the strict sense but in the novels of Chinua Achebe, which present the student of African literature with an interesting, and I should say paradigmatic, case. If we take his novels as a single, coherent body (and Achebe encourages this in certain remarks on his art as well as in his reuse of settings and characters), then those novels can be seen to constitute an "autobiographical" dramatization of three-plus generations of Ibo experience. So typical is that experience and so faithful is Achebe's representation that the significance of the drama is vastly increased to encompass the experience of modern Nigeria and of West Africa; it expands finally into a vision and representation of the archetypal experience of Anglophone Africa from the end of the nineteenth century to the present.

There can naturally be no question of maintaining that this archetypal narrative is Achebe's own private story or his personal autobiography; but neither can there be any doubt about its being the Ibo story and the Ibo autobiography, a story or an autobiography that Achebe discovers in a reading of his own generational experience. Asked by an interviewer from the periodical *Afrique* whether *No Longer at Ease* could be considered a sequel to *Things Fall Apart*, Achebe (in 1963) responded, "Oui et non, puisque dans 'No Longer at Ease' il s'agit du petit-fils du héro du premier livre. Il s'agit en fait de l'histoire de mon pays natal Oguidi, dans l'Est nigérien. Dans le premier livre, je raconte les traditions du village au moment où les premiers contacts ont lieu avec les Européens, avec les espoirs et les peurs de tous les habitants. Dans le second, qui est en fait le troisième de la trilogie, il s'agit de ma génération. Dans le livre qui manque ce sera celle de mon père, la génération

158

de ceux qui ont été christianisés."[2] Earlier in the same interview, Achebe described his novelistic intentions thus: "Je
voulais en fait écrire un long roman, dont l'action devait se
dérouler sur une centaine d'années. J'ai partagé en trois
parties." Beginning with the traditions of the village—those
ceremonial traces which are both the residue and the evidence of cultural and psychic unity—Achebe winds his narrative down through "l'histoire de mon pays natal," down
through a story that is Achebe's story, his family's story, and
the Ibo story, to a resolution—if it can be called a resolution
—in the author's own generation and in the present where
community traditions are little more than a fine memory
and where the "pays natal" has been transformed so thoroughly that its original character seems only a dream of
glory from earlier days. In drawing such a picture, Achebe
is telling what he has seen in his own life and in the life of
his ancestors; what he has seen in that life, in his own field
of action, becomes nothing less than the seventy-five-year
drama of nearly half a continent. Achebe's fiction grows out
of Ibo life and is an accurate reflection of that life, but it
also imitates a corporate experience that has been known
not in Iboland alone, nor only in Nigeria, but in all the nations that have recently become independent of the British
colonial empire. Thus Achebe is not only the best of the Ibo
self-portraitists but also the quintessential and most completely representative of African novelists writing in English. If we consider Achebe's fiction and the curve described
by the body of his work—that is, the development of his
themes, the evolution of his vision, and the progress of his
technical concerns—first in relation to other portraits of Ibo

---

[2] "Entretien avec Chinua Achebe," *Afrique*, No. 27 (octobre 1963),
pp. 41-42. This was before the publication of *Arrow of God* (1964)
and *A Man of the People* (1966). *Arrow of God* is presumably "le
livre qui manque," an omission that Achebe repaired in the year following the *Afrique* interview. In *Arrow of God*, however, Achebe does
not center his story on the Okonkwo family; this is one reason for not
giving an extensive consideration to that novel in a discussion of his
generational "autobiography" of the Ibo people (see note 5 below).

life and second in relation to the development of the African-English novel generally we shall, I think, discover some very interesting and relevant things about Achebe's writing, about Ibo life, about the African novel, about African history, and about the African conception of existence.

What one finds in reading Achebe's fiction against the autobiographical descriptions of Ibo life presented by such writers as Olaudah Equiano, Victor Uchendu, Mbonu Ojike, Dilim Okafor-Omali, Onyenaekeya Udeagu, Rems Nna Umeasiegbu, Nnamdi Azikiwe, and Onuora Nzekwu[3] is that the Ibo personality has changed hardly at all in the course of two hundred years, but the Ibo community, under the pressure of an outside world and of passing time, has changed very markedly and so has the relation of the individual to the community. What has occurred might best be described as a group dissociation of personality. This psychological disintegration, which takes place in the whole community and which we can follow most comprehensively in Achebe's novels, also informs the writing of other Ibos and provides the cultural background to the African-English novel in general.

In the introduction to *Africa in Prose*,[4] O. R. Dathorne speaks of two stages of development in African fiction, but he outlines, in fact, and conveniently for our purposes, three: the earliest fiction, given over for the most part to

---

[3] Olaudah Equiano, *The Interesting Narrative of the Life of Olaudah Equiano, or Gustavus Vassa, the African. Written by Himself*, 2 vols. (London: Printed for and sold by the author, 1789); Victor Uchendu, *The Igbo of Southeast Nigeria*; Mbonu Ojike, *My Africa* (New York: John Day Co., 1946); Dilim Okafor-Omali, *A Nigerian Villager in Two Worlds* (London: Faber & Faber, 1965); Onyenaekeya Udeagu, "Ibos as They Are," in *An African Treasury*, ed. Langston Hughes (New York: Crown Publishers, 1960), pp. 16-19; Rems Nna Umeasiegbu, *The Way We Lived: Ibo Customs and Stories* (London: Heinemann, 1969); Nnamdi Azikiwe, *My Odyssey: An Autobiography* (London: C. Hurst & Co., 1970); Onuora Nzekwu, *Wand of Noble Wood* (New York: New American Library, 1963).

[4] *Africa in Prose*, ed. O. R. Dathorne and Willfried Feuser (Harmondsworth, Middlesex: Penguin Books, 1969), pp. 13-14.

preserving traditional customs and dramatizing cultural conflicts with the European invaders; an intermediate fiction that shows the individual separating from the group; and contemporary fiction that concerns itself with personal fulfillment in a world divided and confused by the European/African encounter. Almost exactly this same progress is to be discovered in the fiction of Achebe, with a novel devoted to each stage of thematic development:[5] "At the start," as Dathorne puts it, "there was the anthropological concern with tribe, and later with the coming of the white man" (thus, *Things Fall Apart*); more recently, "there emerges the theme of the individual struggling against the pressures of the tribe and breaking out of the enclave in which custom would seek to restrict him" (thus, *No Longer at Ease*); "latterly there has been a concern in depth with the person, his private predicament in a world he seeks to salvage from the chaos of a divided inheritance" (thus, *A*

---

[5] To date, Achebe has published four novels: *Things Fall Apart* (1958); *No Longer at Ease* (1960); *Arrow of God* (1964); and *A Man of the People* (1966). *Arrow of God* treats the generation between *Things Fall Apart* and *No Longer at Ease* but does not focus on the Okonkwo-family representative of that generation. I have excluded *Arrow of God* from the remarks that follow because, though it deals with the intermediate generation, the world of *Arrow of God* is very similar to the world of *Things Fall Apart*, and the curve I am concerned with can be more precisely traced by considering *Things Fall Apart*. On the other hand, I have included *A Man of the People*— which, like *Arrow of God*, has nothing to do with the Okonkwo line— because it seems to me that that novel advances the dual theme of cultural disintegration and personal reintegration in a way that Achebe's other novels do not. Though *A Man of the People* has to do with much the same generation as *No Longer at Ease*—only some seven or eight years later—yet the worlds of these two novels are quite different. From Achebe's picture it would appear that cultural processes in African society have accelerated drastically in recent times, so that a few years now accomplish more in the way of change than did two generations fifty years ago. References are to the following editions: *Things Fall Apart* (New York: Astor-Honor, n.d.); *No Longer at Ease* (London: Heinemann, 1963); *A Man of the People* (Garden City, N.Y.: Doubleday & Co., 1967).

161

*Man of the People*). In Ogbuefi Okonkwo, Obi Okonkwo, and Odili Samalu, the figures in and around whom the various conflicts focus in these three novels, Achebe embodies and dramatizes, in a sort of summary form, Ibo and African experience of the past century as seen by the Ibo and African novelist. That experience, as Achebe imagines and represents it, is one of progressive cultural disintegration and moral confusion; at the same time, however, Achebe's drama hints at new, if difficult, possibilities, and seems to suggest almost a new morality growing out of a personal reintegration. The movement, in largest outline, is from cultural tragedy to personal tragedy to personal comedy.

Another way of describing the curve of Achebe's fiction would be to say that it begins as a kind of cultural autobiography with the beliefs, the customs, and the personality of the group summarized and symbolized in their fullest embodiment, Okonkwo (much as the Gikuyu realize their homogeneous society in the fully representative figure of Kenyatta); it progresses to the autobiography, if one may so put it, of a society with a split personality—but still viewed objectively from without as if it were possible yet to find a sufficiently representative figure (Obi) to stand for his whole generation; and it concludes with the individual and isolated figure who must make his own way with neither guidance nor restraint from a unified culture—without the positive direction that his society afforded Okonkwo or the taboos and restrictions that bound Obi. For Odili there is no community voice at all and he represents no group: there are no ties that bind nor roots that nourish and so, though *A Man of the People* is fiction, it is also an "autobiographic" portrait of the modern Nigerian, who is hardly even seen as Ibo, déraciné, socially functionless because the old social roles, indeed the old society, are gone. In Odili we have a portrait of the modern Nigerian—not of course Achebe, but rather like something one could call a spiritual autobiography of the individualized man of post-independence Nigeria. Mbonu Ojike, in an odd and unexplained re-

mark that nevertheless throws some light on Achebe's role
as Ibo, Nigerian, and African novelist, says that the artist
"is the only individualistic personality in Africa. We the un-
artistic live communally, think nothing, and act like a
crowd" (*My Africa*, p. 202). The novelist's art, if one may
thus interpret Ojike's comment and apply it to Achebe's fiction, provides individualistic and conscious expression for
an experience that is in itself communal, unconscious, and
dumb. To a degree, the African artist embodies the Western
ideal of individualism—on behalf of the "crowd," however,
not for himself alone. This, at any rate, is what Achebe does
in his novels, which are an individualized expression of a
group experience.

Achebe writes from within; we read, in hopes of understanding, from without. Obvious dangers attend such a situation. It is a principle of cultural anthropology, and undoubtedly a valid principle, that one should not try to judge
the works of one civilization by the standards of another or
try to understand the culture of one people in the philosophical terms of another. Thus, to view the traditional
dance of Africa through the assumptions of European ball-
room dancing is, at best, misguided and, at worst, vicious.
So also with other art forms or cultural manifestations that
have shaped themselves out of the African experience over
those centuries when Africa had no essential contact with
other, and especially European, civilizations. But is not the
case somewhat different with the novel? The novel is primarily and in origin a Western, as distinguished from African, art form; this is not true, for example, of the dance, of
poetry, of song in general, of sculpture. The comments that
one makes about novels are, I am certain, fortunately or
unfortunately, colored by this fact. We often judge the African novel by standards and ideals that are non-African.
The African writer who chooses the novel form thereby
commits himself to a mode of expression developed by the
Western world and hence, probably, to some of the ideas
and ideals of that Western world—ideas and ideals, after

163

all, that have shaped the novel form and to which it gives expression. At least this is importantly true with Achebe, and in his novels, as I have suggested, we can see a paradigm of the African novel.

The ideal that we find embodied countless times in the characters and the actions of Western fiction is what we call "love." Love may or may not make the world go round, but it undoubtedly keeps the novelist in business. The question, then, is whether, in drawing his characters, in setting his men and women in relation to one another, the African novelist will incline to do the same sort of thing as a Western writer, or something quite different. To see how Achebe handles his characters, both in themselves and in interrelation, it will be well to place the question in context by reminding ourselves of what love is, of where sex figures, of what place procreation occupies in the Western world. Thus we shall be in a position to see where Achebe resembles and where he differs from the Western novelist in this matter of love.

The fable that Aristophanes relates in *The Symposium*, to explain the origin of sexual desire and the nature of love, gives a clear and finely ironic picture of the idea of love (leaving practice out of consideration) in the Western world. From an original state of circular wholeness and perfection, according to Aristophanes, man has fallen into his present condition of incompleteness and fragmentation. Zeus, so that man would learn better than to overreach himself, cut the members of the human race, as originally constituted (four arms, four legs, two faces on a circular neck, a double component of generative organs), in half. "Man's original body having thus been cut in two, each half yearned for the half from which it had been severed. When they met they threw their arms around one another and embraced, in their longing to grow together again." This is the love, romantic and sentimental (though anything but sentimental in Aristophanes' fable)—or, again, the *idea* of love—that has obtained in the Western world for twenty-five hundred years. Man, before he was split in two, was entire in himself, the Greek equivalent of pre-Eve androgynous Adam. The instinct that remembers wholeness and yearns to have it again is the motive force that we call love and that draws the lines for the relations of the sexes.[6] Thus love, according to this Western fable, is suprarational or irrational, going beyond or against reason and logic; it is an entirely individual matter, but leaves its victim without choice as to whom he shall love. Furthermore, there is no

[6] One might note in passing that this theory of love serenely recognizes homosexual and heterosexual love as essentially the same in motive and validity (for there were originally three sexes: pure male, pure female, and hermaphrodite, only the third of which would lead to heterosexual love). I mention this sidelight on love in the Western world to point up the fact that the same is distinctly not true in African sexual theory and that, because of this, homosexuality was virtually unknown, according to many writers, in traditional African communities, such as the one Achebe describes in *Things Fall Apart*, before the arrival of Western man with his "new" ideas of love and sex. To the traditional African it would seem obvious, from implicit assumptions about the nature of human existence and from the very physical make-up of man and woman, that their *raison d'être* is to reproduce.

In his introduction to the Penguin translation of *The Symposium* Walter Hamilton says, "The love with which the dialogue is concerned, and which is accepted as a matter of course by all the speakers, including Socrates, is homosexual love; it is assumed without argument that this alone is capable of satisfying a man's highest and noblest aspirations, and the love of man and woman, when it is mentioned at all, is spoken of as altogether inferior, a purely physical impulse whose sole object is the procreation of children." I imagine that this view would seem so perverse to an African of traditional attitudes that he would scarcely know where to begin to demonstrate its madness; but if he began, in the Socratic manner, by seeking a definition of "a man's highest and noblest aspirations," there can be little doubt that this would, in the end as in the beginning, turn out to be "the procreation of children." That is to say, in the traditional African community these are not opposed but identical. Though the African characters in Wole Soyinka's *The Interpreters* can hardly be said to be deeply imbued with village tradition, notice their attitude toward the homosexual Joe Golder, who is, significantly, an American (one-fourth Negro): revulsion, disgust, horror, disbelief.

165

necessary connection between love (an individual necessity) and marriage (a social arrangement); children are
altogether incidental and secondary to love. Finally, Aristophanes' tale suggests that love is not a means to an end
(pleasing society, producing children, acquiring money or
a name) but the end itself (being made whole, complete,
perfect again).

*Things Fall Apart*, the first of Achebe's novels, both in the
chronology of its events and in the chronology of its author's career, begins a story that is continued in *No Longer
at Ease* and establishes the theme of African/European conflict that we find at the center of all of Achebe's works. The
story told in this first novel, if we neglect the anthropolog-
ically interesting but fictionally irrelevant descriptions of
traditional ceremonies spotted throughout the book, is a
vastly simple tale of cultural conflict resolved in tragedy.
Ogbuefi Okonkwo, a Herculean strong man and representative of the old, coherent community, is so frustrated and
discouraged with the arrival of the white man and with
subsequent defections among his own people (including his
son Nwoye, rechristened Isaac in the new faith) that he
commits suicide. Achebe complicates the action with a good
many details of what happens in Iboland from day to day
and year to year, but essentially this is the whole story of
*Things Fall Apart*. If one examines the characters involved
in Okonkwo's tragedy, one finds that they have the same
exaggerated simplicity, the same representative significance
as this outline of action, which might serve equally as a
sketch of Achebe's plot and his theme. Internal division, the
theme says, results in self-destruction, and the plot "proves"
this theme dramatically. Characterization in *Things Fall
Apart*, like plot and theme, is simple, rigid, and abstract:
there is, indeed, really only one character in the novel—
Okonkwo. Okonkwo, it is true, has three wives and a number of children; friends and townspeople move in and out
of the action involving him; elders meet to judge disputes
and to pronounce traditional wisdom—but there is not an-

other distinct and distinguishable figure in the novel. His wives, his children, his friends and enemies exist only as shadow figures that help to define the character and the significance of Okonkwo. The most obvious instance would be the wives who claim none of the novelist's attention as people interesting in themselves; in fact, they are not people at all but devices used (by Achebe *and* Okonkwo) to define the central male. None of the women is particularized beyond being numerically 1, 2, and 3. We never learn the name of Wife No. 1; we only hear of her as "Nwoye's mother," a designation of considerable significance when one considers the role of women in this book and in the society it describes. There is nothing in *Things Fall Apart* resembling a physical or mental description of these adjuncts to Okonkwo's masculinity: they seem simply to represent "woman," that useful creature who fetches water, bears children, plants female crops (coco-yam and cassava), cooks, and keeps her personality (if, indeed, she has one) very much to herself. These three women are in no sense and never individuals but rather generic representatives of Ibo wives and abstractions from Ibo womanhood.

What shall we say of the character of Okonkwo himself? Achebe is at considerable pains to let us see, know, and understand his hero; yet, in spite of the fact that he sacrifices all other characters to the definition of Okonkwo, Achebe draws in him no more than the generalized portrait of a man whose character is deliberately and significantly without individualizing traits. We learn of Okonkwo, and this is really about all, that he is physically powerful, ambitious, generous and honest, proud, quick to anger, hard-working, a great wrestler. To the reader who is at all familiar with the peoples of West Africa, this picture begins to suggest something. Any observer naming the African cultures that have unique and distinct characters unto themselves will invariably place the Ibos near the top of the list. An Ibo will not easily lose himself in a confusion of peoples. Historically, he has resisted any blurring of the group character,

167

any melting down of the Ibo personality that would render it indistinct within the larger agglomeration. He has refused to be Nigerian because that might prejudice his remaining distinctly Ibo; he retains his Ibo personality and will not surrender it for the less distinct "African Personality" of Kwame Nkrumah. On the other hand, he will not go the step in particularity that lies beyond Ibo character: with the assurance of group definition behind him, the Ibo does not insist on his own and individual, perhaps eccentric, personality. For the Ibo who considers himself an embodiment of a group spirit evolved over generations and centuries, a communal identity is a much more real, powerful, and secure thing than any identity he could hope to work out for himself individually and alone in the few years available to him.

What is this tenaciously maintained group identity? Descriptions of the Ibo personality, whether by insiders or outsiders, whether done two hundred years ago or today, are remarkably consistent. All of them agree in virtually every detail with the characterization that Achebe presents in the representative personage of Okonkwo. Nearly two hundred years ago Olaudah Equiano gave a brief character to his people as he remembered them from the time before he was kidnapped at the age of ten and sold into slavery; his account differs hardly at all, as a general character, from what we are told by Achebe and Onuora Nzekwu and Rems Nna Umeasiegbu, by Victor Uchendu and Mbonu Ojike and Dilim Okafor-Omali, by M. M. Green and C. D. Forde and G. I. Jones. According to Equiano specifically and according to all observers generally, the Ibo "are habituated to labour from our earliest years . . . and as we are unacquainted with idleness we have no beggars."[7] Equiano goes on to speak of the "hardiness, intelligence, integrity, and

[7] Reprint, with a new introduction by Paul Edwards (London: Dawsons of Pall Mall, 1969), of the first edition of *The Interesting Narrative*, I, 20-21.

168

zeal" of the Ibos, of "the general healthiness of the people, and . . . their vigour and activity"; he concludes with the Ibo women (may God bless them for propagating, on behalf of Ibo men, a pure line): "nor do I remember to have ever heard of an instance of incontinence amongst them before marriage" (*ibid.*, p. 22). Again, here is the description by a contemporary Ibo (not, as it happens, Achebe but Onyenaekeya Udeagu) of "Ibos as They Are": The Ibo is physically powerful ("He is," as Udeagu puts it, "strong and able to work or fight"); ambitious ("He likes to advance and he is quick to learn"); generous and honest ("They are very generous and approachable. . . . He likes to give rather than take"); quick to anger ("Ibos are an argumentative set of people. . . . Their expressive mentality . . . does not always allow them to gulp in false charges without defense"); proud ("This pride enhances the prestige of an Ibo wherever he goes"); hard-working ("They possess high aptitude for hard work and learning. . . . An Ibo prefers to die than to be idle"); a great wrestler ("Wrestling forms the best and most remarkable Ibo game").[8]

Now what is it one has to do with here? Is it the traditional Ibo character or the character of Ogbuefi Okonkwo? The two, it becomes apparent, are coterminous, and we soon come to the conclusion that Achebe has not been concerned to create Okonkwo, any more than his wives, as a unique, living and changing human being. Okonkwo's inability to change, for one thing—seen otherwise as an uncompromising devotion to the ancestral past—leads him to self-destruction. The inflexibility of his character ("inflexible" both in a moral sense and in a technical, novelistic sense) leads inevitably to Okonkwo's tragedy, since the world, with the arrival of the white man, insists on change and has the power to enforce its will. This is not the tragedy of a mere individual. Like his women, Okonkwo is an "ideal" standing for the characteristics of a whole people. He too is a sort of

[8] Onyenaekeya Udeagu, "Ibos as They Are," pp. 16-19.

abstraction: Ibo-man incarnate, Ibo manhood to the tenth power, specifically as it was before the arrival of the European.

Wole Soyinka, the Nigerian poet and dramatist, once asked Achebe a pertinent question about the character of Okonkwo during a filmed interview and Achebe returned an equally pertinent answer. "I'd like to take as my point of reference," Soyinka said, "the last carving you showed me here in the museum—the carving of Ikenga. This represents, as you said, the spirit of manhood, of strength, of real masculine energy in Ibo society. In *Things Fall Apart*, the character of Okonkwo seems to me to represent a kind of figure in society who's acted upon . . . by this kind of strong spiritual quality. Was there a conscious derivative in the creation of this character?" Achebe's response, pointing up the ideality of Okonkwo's character, went thus: "Not conscious, but I wanted a character who could be called representative of this particular group of people." A little later in the conversation, Achebe commented on the group character represented in Okonkwo: "The weakness of this particular society is a lack of adaptation, not being able to bend. . . . I think in [Okonkwo's] time, the strong men were those who did not bend and I think this was a fault of the culture itself."[9] There is a virtual one-to-one relationship between Okonkwo as an individual and the Ibo as a people,

[9] Lewis Nkosi, "Conversation with Chinua Achebe," *Africa Report*, 9, No. 7 (July 1964), p. 19. Lewis Nkosi conducted this and other interviews in the series, but Wole Soyinka and others participated in the "Conversation" with Achebe.

William Fagg, in exhibition notes for the display of African sculpture at the National Gallery of Art in Washington, D.C. in 1970, says of "Ikenga": "It is specifically an embodiment of male power and there are no female *ikenga*. In principle, it is a means of externalizing powers which are by their nature internal to one's self, of 'feeling' one's self-confidence without limit until one is ready to take on the world." As one can see from the remarks of Soyinka and Achebe, however, "Ikenga" is as much an embodiment of a communal personality as of an individual one.

170

in just the same way as the Ibo spirit is entirely present in and identified with the effective power of "Ikenga" in the carving. Thus one must read Okonkwo's fate, he being representative and typical, as nothing less than the symbolic fate of the traditional Ibo society with the advent of the white man.

With this picture of ideal Ibo-man and Ibo-woman, we are ready to question the motive and basis for sexual relations in the world of Achebe's novel. Why *do* man and woman come together in this society? Is it because "love" draws them together, even, at times, against their conscious will? Hardly. Is it, as in Aristophanes' fable, because they have an ineffable yearning to be made whole again by union with the separated half (or, in Okonkwo's case, the separated fourths)? Obviously not. Is it because the man requires a woman to do his cooking, water-fetching, cassava and coco-yam planting? Perhaps, in part. But the primary reason and the essential motive is to produce children and so to continue the line.[10] Why should he want to continue the line? In a profoundly circular response that allows no further questioning, the answer is that this is why man was created. Christianity says, in a typical formulation, "Man was created to praise, reverence and serve God Our Lord, and by so doing to save his soul." This emphasis on individual salvation would constitute virtual heresy for the Ibo of Okonkwo's character. For the pre-colonial Ibo, the truth would be: "Man was created to procreate, and by so doing to continue the ancestral line." It is the will of the ancestors or of the spirit of the clan to continue living, and that can be only if the present embodiment of the ancestral past produces a future embodiment, an ancestral reincarnation, in

---

[10] Cf. the remark of a villager in *Arrow of God* during a marriage dispute: "Different people have different reasons for marrying. *Apart from children which we all want*, some men want a woman to cook their meals, some want a woman to help on the farm, others want someone they can beat" (*Arrow of God* [London: Heinemann, 1964], pp. 76-77). Italics are mine.

171

the form of children. Wives are naturally a valuable commodity—almost, if not exactly, a necessary evil—from the
Ibo husband's point of view, for how shall he have children
without a wife or wives? On the other hand, any woman's
value is entirely contingent on her fulfilling that child-bearing role assigned to her by tradition. What is a woman good
for, according to the understanding of this male-dominated
society, if she fails to reincarnate, by propagation, her husband's ancestors and so to give at least provisional immortality to the husband himself? Mbonu Ojike explains that
in Iboland women are held in high esteem and for a very
good, very specific reason: "women must be kept sacred
and undisturbed so that they may bear children safely"
(*My Africa*, p. 172). The same Ibo autobiographer, though
he maintains that women should be considered the equals
of men, reveals the typical bias of Ibo assumptions about
the relations between men and women, when he refers to
the latter, in a somewhat less than exalted phrase, as "the
future breeders of posterity" (p. 159) and again when he
declares that "When they [women] desire to pray to village
ancestors"—than which no desire is more human or more
sacred for the Ibo—they must "do so through men"
(p. 173). Men must procreate through women, so it seems
only fair, Mbonu Ojike implies, that women should be able
to contact past segments of the line only through men.

Until very recent times, as Victor Uchendu points out, the
options of the marriageable Ibo girl were few in number;
hers, in fact, was no more than a Hobson's choice: "She remembers the advice her mother and other relatives gave
her. She knows that her great objective in life is marriage;
that a woman's glory is her children, and that to have children she must have a husband. This is a chance she cannot
afford to miss" (*My Africa*, p. 53). The premises of Ibo belief bind the girl, one, two, three, willy-nilly and very
tightly to the conclusion: gather ye husbands while ye may
—"a chance she cannot afford to miss." This is not to suggest that men in traditional Ibo communities had so much

more choice than women; the men could, and still can, take several wives, but the aim of Ibo life is invariable, the same for men as for women: to produce as many legitimate children as possible. The first sentences of the first "custom" related by Rems Nna Umeasiegbu say very simply that "A married couple is looked upon with contempt if the marriage is not solidified with a child. The first prayer on the lips of all couples, therefore, is that God will give them children."[11] This reads like the first principle of the relationship of men and women in Iboland, which is why an Ibo mother, as Victor Uchendu says, precisely because she "has increased [her husband's] lineage membership" (p. 57), is infinitely more worthy and more honored than the childless wife. In a similar vein, after his father and mother had "lived together for a few years without a child," Mbonu Ojike tells us, "My father was . . . seriously worried about the situation. The death of his father accentuated the tension. He must have a son or be written off the dynasty."[12]

In all these observations by Ibo writers, there is little

[11] Rems Nna Umeasiegbu, *The Way We Lived: Ibo Customs and Stories*, p. 1.

[12] *My Africa*, p. 6. Cf. the comment of Akiga (who was not an Ibo but a Tiv; the Tiv are, however, next-door neighbors to the Ibos): "However successful in life a man may be, if he has no heir to his house, to the Tiv he is a useless person and a standing butt for their scorn. 'What sort of a man is So-and-so without children?' they sneer. 'Who is there to carry on his line when he dies?' So also a woman, if she does not bear children, falls in Tiv esteem, however excellent she may be in other ways. And she herself is never happy, though she may be very well treated by her husband, because when she dies there will be no one to mourn for her. It is for this cause above all others that women desire a child. They are not so concerned as men about the founding of a family.

"If it were not for the family, many men would not marry at all; their relationships with women would be entirely promiscuous. But because of it, every Tiv when he reaches manhood sets his heart on taking a wife and producing a son to carry on his line, that his heritage may not pass to another" (*Akiga's Story: The Tiv Tribe as Seen by One of Its Members*, trans. and annotated by Rupert East, 2d ed. [London: Oxford Univ. Press, 1965], p. 312).

173

mystery and less variety in the motives for the coming together of men and women. It is this consistency of belief
and attitude that accounts for the tone of deep shock and
horror, for the note of moral repulsion and stern reproba-
tion, in Mbonu Ojike's comment on sexual mores in modern
Africa: "The most lamentable degradation that Western science has introduced into Africa," he says, obviously measuring his words very carefully, "is not machine guns or
bombs; it is contraceptives. This most ignoble commodity
could by itself lead African womanhood into social deca-
dence and moral degeneracy." When this happens, he continues, then "caring for children and families no longer remains the progressive motive that unites man and woman"
(p. 160). The new motive, regressive it would seem, that
unites man and woman is not named by Mbonu Ojike, but
it is clearly that thing that is forever rearing its ugly head
in the Western world: sex, it is sometimes disparagingly
called; true love, it is termed by sentimentalists; Aristophanic love, we have named it. Whatever it is called, it is
destroying the old ways and relations in Iboland. The sad
fact that an Ibo has to contemplate is that things were once
so different. "Before the European era," Onyenaekeya
Udeagu claims, and he echoes in his remark the statement
of the pre-European Olaudah Equiano, "there was no har-
lot in Iboland. Every man and woman married and perpetuated that end which nature ordains for reproduction.
There is no excuse for not marrying except extreme poverty
and deformity."[13] Not so, according to the Western notion.
"It is better to marry than to burn," St. Paul says; that very
cautious, grudging, backhanded approval of marriage expresses well the Christian and generally Western attitude
toward the non-primacy of the procreative motive in matters of the spirit. In the Western world, every man is responsible for his own soul and his own emotional needs, but
only for his own; he must take on himself one burden only
—getting himself together according to his individual ne-

[13] "Ibos as They Are," p. 19.

cessities and individual conscience. This is as true of Christian doctrine as of Aristophanes' love ethic.

The picture that Achebe gives us in Part I of *Things Fall Apart* is of an "Ibo community in the past" (as he says in a note appended to the American edition), an Ibo community not atomized by the agonies, the attitudes, and the appetites of individual members, an Ibo community with one soul rather than a multitude of souls, held together by the will of the ancestors, who speak group wisdom and timeless desires through the mouths of the present ruling elders. It is only when foreign ideas and beliefs are imposed that this community begins to disintegrate. One of these foreign ideas is that sex and love, rather than sex and marriage, should go together, and that love is a personal matter, an individual pleasure and necessity, a private question; that love is the end and not the means; that man seeks love because he wants love and not because he wants children in order to continue the ancestral line, or to appease and to express it. Another foreign and dangerous idea is that you can love only one person. This strange Western notion says that, of course, it is possible to produce children by several women, but love is given only to that one, unique, separated half. Love, according to the West, is the big thing—not procreation, not the ancestral voice. When these two different views of sexual relationships come into conflict, and when some members of the Ibo community start to follow one belief and, for example, employ contraceptives, while others follow another, then things start to fall apart in the world of Achebe's novel. "We must all hang together, or assuredly we shall all hang separately." In becoming an individual personality or soul, or by adopting the Western ideal of individualism, the single figure separates himself from the homogeneous and coherent group character. In becoming uniquely himself, he ceases to be specifically Ibo. Okonkwo's son, Nwoye/Isaac (who, we later learn, takes only one wife), goes over to the other side, which means symbolically that the center, both of the family and of the

175

people, "cannot hold," and from here on, the old community all hangs separately—as, in fact, Okonkwo does hang himself.

When we say that Okonkwo is not individualized or that he is a representative character, we are saying something not only about the techniques of Achebe's fiction but also, perhaps more importantly, about the society, the culture, the world, that informs that fiction. Implicit in the characterization of *Things Fall Apart* is the cultural belief of the Ibos of the old order that individualism, if it is conceived of at all, is a positive evil. W. E. Abraham, in *The Mind of Africa*, makes the case for the existence of a group character that transcends the personal when he says that "A lineage . . . has a personality which may in fact be called its group personality. . . . The inter-relation of the several lineages in the community in a definite way bestows a certain formality on the larger society too, and creates the foundation of the community personality."[14] The Ibo, on the other hand, are often said to be highly "individualistic," and while this may be true in comparison to other African peoples, their individualism must be sharply qualified when taken in a Western context.[15] Victor Uchendu, for example, though he argues that the Ibo "lay a great emphasis on individual achievement and initiative," is quick to acknowledge that this individuality, when considered in a Western perspective, is a partial and non-extreme thing: it is *Ibo* individual-

[14] *The Mind of Africa* (Chicago: Univ. of Chicago Press, 1962), p. 64.

[15] Cf. Dilim Okafor-Omali, *A Nigerian Villager in Two Worlds*, p. 75: "Every family, every extended family or group of relatives, every village and village-group, managed its own affairs and tolerated no unnecessary outside interference. Though there were occasions when activities were communal, there was a strong individualistic tendency in all institutions." One may if one wishes call this tendency strongly individualistic, but it is to be remarked that the tendency manifests itself at the level of "institutions" or at the level of family, extended family, village and village-group rather than at the level of the Western individual.

176

ity, not personal, private individuality. "Igbo individualism is not 'rugged' individualism; it is individualism rooted in group solidarity. . . . There is a great emphasis on communal cooperation and achievement. The 'communal' character of the Igbo must be traced to the formative influence of their traditional social patterns, the influence of their nucleated residence pattern, and the ideological urge 'to get up' " (*The Igbo of Southeast Nigeria*, p. 103). This communal character, to describe it somewhat more simply, is rooted in the family extended so far as to include the clan and the whole Ibo people; in other words, it is the reverse of what a Westerner would mean by individualism. Peter Abrahams, the South African novelist, looking at the matter from within as an African but also from without as one in exile, put it all much more directly, more abruptly, and more succinctly: "Tribal man," he declared, "is not an individual in the western sense. Psychologically and emotionally he is the present living personification of a number of forces, among the most important of which are the ancestral dead."[16]

Mankind, according to African thought, includes more than the sum of those now living, for the dead, though no longer alive, continue to exist and to exert a tremendous force on and through their living descendants. Hence, in a tradition-oriented novel like Achebe's, "man" must be understood in the sense of man in the living present and man in

[16] "The Blacks," *Holiday*, 25 (April 1959), p. 120. On the relation between living and dead and on Ibo ideas of reincarnation, cf. Victor Uchendu: "In the Igbo conception, the world of the 'dead' is a world full of activities; its inhabitants manifest in their behavior and thought processes that they are 'living.'. . . An Igbo without . . . a patrilineage . . . is an Igbo without citizenship both in the world of man and in the world of the ancestors. In the Igbo view, there is a constant interaction between the dead and the living: the dead are reincarnated, death making the transition from the corporeal to the incorporeal life of the ancestors possible. . . . For the Igbo, death is a necessary precondition for joining the ancestors, just as reincarnation is necessary for the peopling of the temporal segment of the lineage" (*The Igbo of Southeast Nigeria*, p. 12).

177

the ancestral ages. Achebe, who after all chose a quotation from Yeats as the title of his first novel and a quotation from Eliot as the title of his second, may seem a rather unlikely candidate to be the subject of these remarks about the ancestral dead, about a peculiarly African way of conceiving of human character and personality, and about a specifically non-Western vision and sensibility. Yet Achebe himself gives us the clue to reading his fiction—reading any individual book or the progress and the curve of his career —when he says, "I regard myself as very much an African writer. I think I'm basically an ancestor worshipper, if you like. Not in the same sense as my grandfather would probably do it, you know, pouring palm wine on the floor for the ancestors. . . . With me, it takes the form of celebration and I feel a certain compulsion to do this."[17] The ancestors are there, very much there, dead perhaps but awful in their power, in the being and in the experience of Ogbuefi Okonkwo and Obi Okonkwo; they are there paradoxically even in the experience of Odili Samalu—they are there, that is, by their felt absence. In each of these figures, and especially in Okonkwo, we have much more than an individual character living his moment in time, for the character is both in and out of time, is himself and is also the focus of the ancestral will stretching as far back as the line goes. Like ritual masks that are not ordinarily drawn directly from life or intended to represent particular individuals, but rather to symbolize the being or the existence of ancestral force in composite, character in the traditional African novel is not likely to be drawn from an individual; for it is not, any more than a carving of "Ikenga" or any more than a Dan mask or a Benin bronze, a living likeness, but rather a sum of existing, informing forces. Fictional character in *Things Fall Apart*, like ritual sculpture, is more a significant and affective or symbolic figuration than a mimetic one.

The techniques and intentions of a novel like *Things Fall Apart* have much in common with the techniques and inten-

[17] "Conversation with Chinua Achebe," p. 20.

tions, with the manifest attitudes and the unspoken assumptions, of African art more generally. Léopold Senghor, writing of "L'esthétique négro-africaine"—which he maintains is quite different from the aesthetic that has prevailed in the Western world since the Renaissance—makes some suggestive comments about sculpture and poetry that apply *mutatis mutandis* to a Western-influenced yet still tradition-directed novel like *Things Fall Apart*. African art and literature, he says, "engagent la *personne*—et non seulement l'individu—par et dans la communauté, en ce sens qu'ils sont des techniques d'*essentialisation*."[18] In drawing a character whose outlines coincide with the personality of the community, Achebe presents us, in the figure of Okonkwo, with essences rather than accidents, with the typical and eternal rather than the individual and temporal. His fictional technique is to "essentialize," as Senghor puts it, and to "idealize" rather than, as the Western novel most often does, to individualize and to particularize. "Le récit négro-africain," according to Senghor, whether it be myth, legend, fable, or story, "prend, naturellement, les formes de la parabole, de l'image en mouvement dans le temps et l'espace. . . . C'est parce que l'ontologie négro-africaine est existentielle, que le conte et la fable sont tissés de faits quotidiens. Il ne s'agit pas d'anecdotes ni de 'tranche de vie.' Les faits sont images, ont valeur exemplaire" (*ibid.*, p. 211). Elsewhere (in a preface to the *Nouveaux contes d'Amadou Koumba*), but developing a similar idea about African narrative techniques, Senghor says of the traditional story teller, "Le Négro-africain répugne à la 'tranche de vie,' qui n'est qu'anecdote. Même lorsque le conteur nous promène à travers le monde factuel des besoins animaux, les héros du récit se haussent aux archétypes, les faits les plus singuliers s'élargissent à la dimension du général: ils sont images, partant symboles. . . ."[19] And so also Achebe's characters

18 "L'esthétique négro-africaine," *Liberté I: Négritude et Humanisme* (Paris: Éditions du Seuil, 1964), p. 207.

19 From Senghor's preface to Birago Diop's *Les nouveaux contes d'Amadou Koumba* (Paris: Présence Africaine, 1958), p. 10.

"sont images, ont valeur exemplaire. . . . sont images, partant symboles"; they are like masks being danced from whom all traces of mere individuality and of time fall away and in whom is contained the essence, the spirit, the personality of a people, some dead but now back in time, some living but now out of time, great archetypes distilled from the experience not of one man alone but of generations of men bound together by the one soul of which the living individual or the fictional character is but an embodiment, or of which he is an image, therefore a symbol. African art and literature, if one may introduce Western terms, is more Platonic than Aristotelian, more "idealistic" than "realistic," positing its ultimate reality in pre-existent and transcendent Ideas rather than in the appearances and the categories of the created world.[20] The whole difference, for the work of art as for the society that it reflects, turns on the question of the unique individual and the representative type; the one is a Western ideal, literary and social, the other an African. This is why, to the non-African reader, *Things Fall Apart* seems, in a sense, both more and less than a novel— as an African mask seems both more and less than a portrait.

One could say, if one chose, that African literature, like African art, is representational but then only in a very special sense. It is not representational of the particular, the unique, the individual, the external, nor of appearance at

---

[20] Cf. Jean Laude, *Les arts de l'Afrique noire* (Paris: Librairie Générale Française, 1966), p. 293: "Tout ce qu'il y a de diffus, de transitoire, de périssable, d'irremplaçable dans la création, '*la minute du monde qui passe*,' comme disait Cézanne, tout cela ne peut concerner l'Africain qui, à la lettre, vit dans l'éternité, ignore l'individu et ne se conçoit que dans son rapport avec l'archétype, l'ancêtre dont c'est même trop dire qu'il est issu, puisqu'il en est l'émanation dans un présent sans histoire. . . . Dans un monde qui ignore l'individu, le temps, le spectacle, il n'y a pas de place pour la peinture, pour la représentation du monde. Le cheval, le crocodile, l'antilope, le lièvre, l'Africain ne les voit pas comme des animaux, mais comme des espèces, au sens presque platonicien du terme."

180

all; it is representational of the general, the communal, the essential, the spiritual, of the typical and the archetypical. So if, in *Things Fall Apart*, Achebe is going to present his reader with an imitation of African reality (African ontology being, as Senghor implies, different from Western ontology), it will be a reality transcending the particular individual and the single moment of the present. If Peter Abrahams and Léopold Senghor are right about "tribal man" or the "Négro-africain," then the novelistic result will be precisely as we have discovered it in our analysis: individual characterization will give way before non-specific ancestral embodiment or group representation, and character development will yield to the one great monolithic fact of cultural conflict. Until it begins to disintegrate under the impact of a foreign civilization, the old Ibo community, manifest in the person of Okonkwo, is untroubled by internal dissension or individual conscience, by moral hesitation or disunity of purpose. Conflict in such fiction as this will always be large and simple, external rather than internal, intertribal or intercultural or even international rather than interpersonal or intrapersonal. Okonkwo, though he destroys himself, does so not from individual motives, but as a representative of Iboland beaten down by something too foreign, too external to himself, even to understand.

"I am also interested," Achebe continues in the note already quoted from the American edition of *Things Fall Apart*, "in the problems of present day Nigeria and intend in my next novel to bring the story of Okonkwo's family up to date." The time of the events in *Things Fall Apart* is never specified, but would appear to be the end of the nineteenth century. *No Longer at Ease*, the lineal sequel to *Things Fall Apart*, skips over one generation of the family to pick up its hero in 1957, the generation it skips over being Nwoye/Isaac, the son of Ogbuefi Okonkwo, who accepts all the religious belief and the colonial system of the European white man. Whatever Christian belief and practice may do to an Ibo, and how it may change his personality,

181

is assumed, rather than dramatically represented, in the character of Isaac. Isaac's son Obi Okonkwo is of the third-generation Nigerians after the white man. He is one of those who have necessarily accommodated themselves, at least to a certain degree, to the white man's world while living in the village of their ancestors. Education for a Nigerian of this generation and condition is like a confusion of tongues: the personality of the group, with all its affective power, undoubtedly remains in him as an educative and moral force, but his conscious, formal education is according to the white man's ways and values. The Western world may be able to remove the Ibo from his ancestors, but removing the ancestors from the Ibo is another matter. In passing over Isaac to concentrate on Obi, Achebe chooses a hero who is in reaction against the Christian father, a pagan of the old community. However, anti-antipaganism in the third generation does not necessarily produce a pagan, and Obi Okonkwo is too many removes in experience from his grandfather, and too advanced in moral confusion, ever to inhabit a world at all like Ogbuefi Okonkwo's in *Things Fall Apart*.

How the world of *No Longer at Ease* came about, how it could be the grandchild of the world of *Things Fall Apart*, and how the personal and group unity of the earlier novel could give way to the cultural schizophrenia of the later fiction can be traced most conveniently in a little book by Dilim Okafor-Omali in which the author intends to render homage to his personal, his familial, and his cultural past: *A Nigerian Villager in Two Worlds*. Ostensibly the book is a biography of Okafor-Omali's father, Nweke, but as happens so frequently in African biography and autobiography, the life of the biographical subject takes on a representative and typical figuration, and it expands outward to a significance far beyond the personal. Nweke, who was of precisely the same generation as the fictional Nwoye/Isaac and of the same generation as Chinua Achebe's father, realized in the contours of his own life, as that

182

life is described by his son, the course of cultural and political history in modern Nigeria and twentieth-century Africa. Though his declared subject is the life of his father, what Okafor-Omali begins with and what he really succeeds in evoking for the reader is the corporate life and the inclusive spirit of all his Ibo ancestors rather than the single existence of the one man, Christopher Nweke Okafor. In his moment, of course, Nweke did represent and embody the existence of the family and the clan; which is to say that in writing the biography of his father, Okafor-Omali is in effect also writing the autobiography of his people even down and into his own present life. The story he tells is the story of the clan and of the Ibo people realized and re-realized in all its successive embodiments. "Thus, my father's genealogy," Okafor-Omali says, "was as follows: Nweke, son of Ókafó Omali (founder of the extended family of that name), son of Ómali Ukam, son of Cheche (founder of the quarter of that name), son of Ezeunó, son of Ike, son of Ezunebete (founder of the village of Enuagu), son of Ókpalakanu (founder of the village group of Enugwu-Ukwu)."[21] On the next page, Okafor-Omali makes it clear that this line could and should be extended one more place at either end to include himself as the son of Nweke and to include Nri, founder of Nri clan and father of Ókpalakanu, from whom it is only a step backward (though that step is lost to our sight in the depths of time) to the first Ibo, the founder of all Ibo lines.

Because the "life" he writes is one generation removed from his own, Okafor-Omali can perceive the entire pattern in which that life is a detail; he can, like the novelist who looks to the past as necessary prologue to writing about the present, view the experience at arm's length and see more than the isolated, engulfing consciousness of the present moment. This detached view—the view of ancestral recall —is most clearly seen in the fact that Okafor-Omali is able to give us what no autobiographer in a strict sense can de-

[21] *A Nigerian Villager in Two Worlds*, p. 40.

183

liver: a description of the end of his subject, the death of his father. On the other hand, however, while this conclusion represents the death of a generation, it does not signify the extinction of the father's being, for his existence continues in the family line. As Okafor-Omali says near the end of his book (giving a precise statement of his particular motive in writing biography/autobiography): "It is, of course, very necessary for us to know what other people do; but how can we make the best use of the experience of others if we do not sufficiently understand ourselves? Self-knowledge is the beginning of wisdom. And since our grandsires live in us, to know ourselves we must know them!" (p. 158). There can be little doubt that this "self," of which we may hope to gain knowledge, is a corporate self, the family and clan self; and that one way we may gain such knowledge, whether we are insiders or outsiders, is through the kind of biography and autobiography that Okafor-Omali writes—or the kind of fiction that Achebe writes. After his comment about being "an ancestor worshipper" who feels a compulsion to celebrate those who have gone before, Achebe goes on to give a reason very like Okafor-Omali's reason for re-creating the past: "It's not because I think this will appeal to my readers, but because I feel that this is something that has to be done before I move on to the contemporary scene" ("Conversation," p. 20). The present, for both Achebe and Okafor-Omali, has too much of the past in it to be understood without taking bearings by referring backward over several generations.

Because the two writers are dealing with the same material, even though they have chosen different forms in which to present that material, it is not surprising that Okafor-Omali's account of Ibo experience should, both in narrative details and in the overall pattern of his story, resemble and parallel the picture of Chinua Achebe's novels. There is, in the biography and in the fiction, the same traditional, old culture, the same conflict with a new culture, the same individual alienation, and the same eventual attempt

184

to reconcile—necessarily on an individual basis—the demands and the best features of the old and the new. There exists, likewise, a striking similarity in specifics within this pattern: the ritual practices, beliefs, observances of the old culture; the arrival of the white man; the burning of guns; the defections to Christianity; the move to the city; the formation of unions in the city (village-group unions); the occasional alien returns to the village (Okafor-Omali's return, for example, and Obi Okonkwo's). It is a single pattern of cultural history, too, that is realized in the work of the two writers: the generation before Nweke's generation (i.e., Okafo Omali) was the same as Ogbuefi Okonkwo's generation; Nweke himself (a Christian convert) stood in the same historic position as Nwoye/Isaac;[22] Okafor-Omali, though he was educated in Africa rather than Europe, suffered the same split heritage as Obi Okonkwo; and, with his last words, Okafor-Omali seems to look hesitantly forward to the sort of private, individualistic solution that Odili Samalu painfully advances toward in *A Man of the People*. As to his father and the disintegration of heritage that occurred in his time, with some hint also of an attempt at reintegration, Okafor-Omali says: "He was intimately connected with social changes in his village-group from the 'Old World' of indigenous culture to the 'New World' of Western or European culture. In this process, four distinct stages appear: the first when the way of conducting village affairs was entirely indigenous; the next, when the white man came and a conflict broke out between the Indigenous

---

[22] See Okafor-Omali, pp. 129 and 153-54, on traditional African naming and Christian baptismal naming. Nweke's baptismal name was Christopher, Okafor-Omali's was Sigismund. With the birth of his daughter Nweke attempted to reconcile the old and the new: he had her baptized in the Christian faith but with an African name chosen in the African tradition of "significant" naming; she was baptized "Chukwuebonamilo which means 'let God not mark me out' " (p. 153). According to Okafor-Omali, this minor device of his father's for reconciling the two worlds was at first scorned, but later other Ibos "understood his idea and followed suit."

185

Culture and Western Culture; the next again when Indigenous Culture gave way and the aping of Western Culture followed. The villagers at first accepted this third stage, but later the tragic implications of it dawned upon them. Then came the fourth and last stage, when individuals and later the whole people made strenuous efforts to revive and conserve the best of the indigenous customs and behaviour" (p. 19). At the second stage of this cultural process Ogbuefi Okonkwo, the representative of the "indigenous culture," was destroyed in the conflict with "Western culture." At the third stage (Nweke and Nwoye/Isaac, who drew away a part of the community to the white man's ways) the division was not between the community and something outside but within the community itself; still, however, it was a social rather than an individual matter. Toward the end of the third stage, however, the "tragic implications" became apparent in the fate of such young men as Obi Okonkwo who tried, and found it impossible, to exist in two irreconcilable worlds. For them—the "tragic generation"—the split was no longer external or social but internal, personal, and psychic.

The conflict between African and Western values that determines the action of all of Achebe's fiction becomes progressively more internalized and individualized, which is true both in terms of theme and in terms of technique. *No Longer at Ease* is the crucial novel in this process of internalizing and individualizing. It is also—and the coincidence is more than fortuitous—the crucial novel in the depiction of changing sexual mores. This is Obi's story as that novel tells it, a story considerably more complicated than his grandfather's, just as Obi's character is the more complex of the two. Returning to Nigeria after four years' schooling in England, financed on a loan from his Ibo compatriots, Obi Okonkwo goes to Lagos, takes a job in the civil service (on a scholarship-granting committee), and resolutely opposes the corruption and bribe-taking evident all around him. In England he had met Clara Okeke, another Ibo, had met her again on the return boat, had fallen in love, and back in Lagos becomes "loving to" her, i.e., takes her as his mistress. Though they become engaged, Clara, who has always acted rather peculiarly when the question of marriage has come up, now says that they can never marry because she is "an *osu*"—that is, a person dedicated to serve a god, "thereby setting himself apart and turning his descendants into a forbidden caste to the end of Time" (p. 72); one who is *osu* cannot marry outside the caste.[23] Obi romantically intends to marry anyway, goes back to his home village to persuade his parents, and there meets flat refusal because, though his parents are Christians, marriage to an *osu* would mean family destruction and ancestral annihilation, since any children of the marriage would automatically become *osu* to all Ibos and could never marry within the culture. Obi's mother dramatizes the refusal by telling her son that she is dying, but, if he marries before her death, her blood will be on his head for she will in that case commit suicide. Obi, stunned by this pronouncement, returns to Lagos and tries to reason with Clara and to postpone marriage; Clara, however, is both indignant and pregnant, and Obi, caught between his ancestors and his fiancée, between the African ideal of procreation and the Western ideal of love, can find no solution but to finance an illegal abortion. The abortion puts him seriously in debt, and when he learns that his mother is dead and that Clara has disappeared, Obi breaks down, takes bribes, both of love and money, is caught and convicted. So the story ends in unqualified personal tragedy.

Obi's tragedy, though in a sense equally great with his

[23] To be *osu* is, in effect, to be of a slave caste; as Achebe puts it in "Chike's School Days," a short story of earlier date than *No Longer at Ease*: "Strangely enough, a slave to a god was worse than a slave to man. A slave to man could buy his freedom. But an *osu* was condemned forever, and his generation after him" (*The Sacrificial Egg and Other Stories* [Onitsha: Etudo Ltd., 1962], p. 16). "Chike's School Days" has now been reprinted in *Girls at War* but without the foregoing quotation.

187

grandfather's, is personal rather than communal or cultural. Again, unlike his grandfather's, Obi's tragedy is a result not of powerful external forces but of inner confusion, and consequently the technique of Achebe's presentation is quite different in *No Longer at Ease* from what it was in *Things Fall Apart*. The two central figures of *No Longer at Ease* are more individual and distinct, more separate in themselves and more clearly characterized than the figures of *Things Fall Apart*. They stand for nothing and represent no group, but simply are, more or less successfully, themselves; they are, as it were, characters in a novel rather than symbols of a force. Clara, a modern woman at loose ends in the world and thrown back on herself, has no traditional, clearly defined role in a society that knows what it is, who its women are, and how they relate to their men. Having lost her innocence to a Western education, she cannot be Ibo Woman; she has no choice but to try to be herself. Obi likewise, with his English education, is an individual, one divided and troubled by the voice of his personal conscience—that being a peculiarly modern difficulty entirely unknown to the massively simple Grandfather Okonkwo. For Obi, who is torn in two different directions—toward his Western love for Clara and toward his African loyalty to the family—the conflict that resolves itself in tragedy is an internal affair. Instead of a conflict that exists out there between representatives of two cultures, Achebe shows us a conflict that is really a projection of Obi's character. Yet the conflict is not merely personal, not simply psychological, but involves loyalty to two different and irreconcilable ways of life.

With the conflict thus internalized and his characters individualized, Achebe draws a relationship between Obi and Clara that accords with all the notions of romantic, sentimental, Western love: Clara, as Obi thinks in the best manner of any popular song of the West, is the only one for him. She is not, as Wife No. 1 was to Grandfather Okonkwo, one of several adjuncts to Obi's manhood, a sort of possession

188

by which he is known; instead, she embodies for Obi, and she alone, the power of love—a power entirely different in effect and significance from the power of either the dead ancestors or the living family. Clara is, as it were, that separated half which can complete Obi's being. In *Wand of Noble Wood*, a novel of Ibo life that is strikingly similar to *No Longer at Ease* in its action and its themes, though nothing like as good a novel as Achebe's, the narrator, Peter Obiesie, says of his great romance, "We kissed, and it was heavenly."[24] The reader need not be an addict of popular

[24] Cf. the remark of a nameless "African Sociologist" in an odd little essay-cum-questionnaire-cum-symposium in *Présence Africaine* titled "Love in Africa" (NS No. 68 [4th Quarter 1968]), p. 52: "Much of our mating is controlled by social elements. . . . The individual bond is completely established by the society. . . ."

These traditional attitudes are no doubt changing, and changing rapidly, as Achebe's novels themselves demonstrate, especially among villagers who find themselves transplanted in urban surroundings. The chapbooks that are generally referred to as "Onitsha Market Literature" give perhaps the best picture of the new, and distinctly Western, ideas of love and the individual now prevalent in West African cities. In his introduction to a selection from this literature, Emmanuel Obiechina says, "Love is often associated with marriage in the pamphlets though sometimes marriage does not result. It is worthwhile to note however that the impulse which drives the pamphlet authors into championing Western marriage practices in preference to traditionally-based marriage customs also propels them towards an undisguised acceptance and promotion of notions of romantic love. To them, romantic love and marriage are the channels through which their characters express their individuality, their liberation from the rigours of traditional constraint and the authoritarain imposition of the older generation" (*Onitsha Market Literature* [London: Heinemann, 1972], pp. 17-18).

*The Game of Love*, a short play included in Obiechina's selection, displays the typical progress of love in an urban African situation under Western cinematic influence. The love of Edwin and Agnes in this drama culminates in "a kiss which lasted for over five minutes" (p. 61). The Nigerian who will kiss in public view at a taxi rank is far removed from Mbonu Ojike's *Africa*, and the Nigerian who can sustain the single kiss for five minutes must certainly have put himself to school to Western romantic love as it might be found in popular

189

culture to hear in Peter's phrase, as in Obi's expression of undying devotion, echoes not of the music of the heavenly spheres but of all the songs of sentimental love of the 1950's —songs originating, of course, in the West. Six pages earlier, in fact, the girl-friend (Nneka)—who, like Peter, found their kiss "heavenly"—has herself supplied the essential reference in her counselling of her beloved on what "true love" is: " 'A man says to a girl, "I love you." It is because she is as beautiful as our proverbial Angelina, because of her face, her well-formed breasts, her shape, her gait, her understanding, her dowry, or her family. He does not understand that these things are not enough. They change with the passing years. By all means let him love her for these things, but let him, as the song goes, love her most because she's herself. That is the love that lasts,' she concluded." "But most of all I love you 'cause you're you," is how "the song goes," and it is what Nneka would like to hear from Peter or Clara from Obi. It is all very pretty, this sentimental, individualistic, Western love; but when "you" happens, as in the case of Clara, to be an *osu*, and when "I" is an Ibo who only imagines himself free of the ancestors, then it is very hard going. "Obi knew better than anyone else that his family would violently oppose the idea of marrying an *osu*. Who wouldn't? But for him it was either Clara or nobody. Family ties were all very well as long as they did not inter-

---

songs and in "cinema show." Agnes' mother, too, demonstrates her expertise in the language of love when she says, in a fine and mysterious phrase that transcends all mere meaning, "Love is the kingdom of marriage" (p. 62). Even Agnes' father, who is unread in Western ways, uninterested in songs, cinemas, and kisses, and untutored in book generally, finally comes around but not before he asks, in response to Agnes' announcement that she is "in love with one young man by name Edwin," an acute and relevant question: "Wethin you de say my pickin? Who been that man? Wethin be love? You no go marriam" (p. 62). What indeed is love to Chief Bombey, and what has it to do with marriage? The chief may in the end agree to their marriage, but it is only because he understands a dowry, not because he comprehends the fine emotion of love.

190

fere with Clara" (p. 75). Family ties, however, prove to be not only "all very well" but, in fact, very powerful too— more powerful, indeed, than a mere momentary, Western-inspired passion for a woman. Love, as Obi experiences it in *No Longer at Ease*, is a distinctly equivocal thing: the most powerful emotion in the Western lexicon, yet, as Obi discovers, impotent in the face of opposition from the African ancestors.

Victor Uchendu's comments on the *osu*—specifically on the legal and the actual status of the *osu* in 1965—demonstrate to what a great degree Achebe is simply doing the portrait from within of a schizophrenic society in *No Longer at Ease*. "Although legally abolished, the *osu* system is not dead," according to Uchendu. "The *osu* lineages are still a living social reality; their residential segregation has not been abolished by law. . . . There is no generally acknowledged intermarriage or willingness to intermarry between *diala* [free-born] and *osu*, even among the most acculturated Igbo. However, sexual relations which were tabooed between the two groups do occur, especially in cities" (*op.cit.*, p. 90). The pictures Uchendu and Achebe give us—one in the dress of anthropology, the other in the language of fiction—could hardly be more identical. It is one thing, as both Uchendu and Achebe suggest, for an Ibo to romance a girl who is *osu* while in London or aboard ship back to Nigeria; it may even be feasible to sleep with her in a city like Lagos: westernized young men have these fancies nowadays about *osu* being the same as anyone else, and they may as well be allowed such notions so long as they are living in the West or in a westernized city. But it is something else again, a matter of family disaster and outrage, to talk of marrying an *osu* (no matter how "acculturated" the man may have become and no matter how much he may "love" the girl), or to think of taking her back to Iboland as the girl of his dreams and as a suitable candidate to become a "future breeder of posterity." Oh no: the parents won't have it, the ancestors won't have it, Iboland

191

won't have it, Africa herself is outraged—all this nonsense of public spooning and private affairs, this foolishness of "being in love" and mooning around about dying if deprived of the beloved. Take it right back to Lagos and to the West where it came from is the answer Obi gets from his parents, from his ancestors, from all of Iboland when he declares to them his irresistible and consuming passion for Clara.

Mbonu Ojike pleads an odd argument in *My Africa* when he declares the reason Africans give no public show of affection is that they consider love a private matter. On the subject of kisses, heavenly or otherwise, he tells how he and his schoolmates once saw a popular European teacher kiss his fiancée and then goes on to describe their dismay and revulsion. "Some Africans," he says, "protested against the demonstration. It was corrupting the youth. The protest was eased off by the principal and staff, who explained that the couple were engaged, and that it was their European love custom to hug, kiss, and hold hands in public. We tolerated it, but wished it had not happened in the face of the Africans" (p. 69). To public signs of affection—the observances and rituals of romantic love—the Ibo of traditional attitudes and mores responds with unbelief and incomprehension; he is disgusted, embarrassed, or scandalized, or perhaps all three. Kissing, like more complete expressions of love, is a halfway house to, or a symbolic gesture toward, full reunion in the Aristophanic sense, which has no place in African sexual tradition. No ancestral line has ever been perpetuated merely by kissing, which will moreover very likely go on from nonsense to real trouble since once the kissing starts any inquiry as to family origins (is she an *osu*?) and maternal suitability (will she breed pure?) will probably stop. But "love," Mbonu Ojike says, taking over a Western word and misapplying it to an African relationship, "love is so sacred an affair between two persons that no third party has the privilege of seeing them in action" (p. 158). It is difficult to imagine that there are so many

192

voyeuristic anthropologists around "curious," as Ojike claims, "to probe into the sanctum sanctorum of African love life" and desirous of "seeing them in action"; but in any case all the evidence, even from Ojike himself, indicates that the interpretation he offers here to account for the apparent absence of romantic love in African life is a mistaken one. Ojike may say that sex is a personal matter and that this is why there is no public display of feeling between boy and girl, husband and wife, or lovers of any age, station, and sex. But all other writers agree, either in direct statement or in the assumptions of their fictionalized presentations, that sex is precisely *not* "an affair between two persons" and *not* a personal matter; that it is *not* something in which the individual engages for his own pleasure, his personal satisfaction, or his private enjoyment. When a couple embrace they do so in the name of the ancestors, in their spiritual presence and under their aegis, and for the perpetuation of those powerful beings. There may be a little pleasurable excitement there for the couple, but no writer whose concern is with the traditional African community has ever suggested that such excitement is the motive for sex and marriage. Not at all: sex in marriage satisfies the ancestors' desires and therefore the couple's—not vice versa and not otherwise. If love and sex could really be only "an affair between two persons," Obi Okonkwo would have no problem in *No Longer at Ease*, but in Iboland they cannot be only that, and consequently his problem is inevitable and insoluble.

What can Obi do, hung up as he is between two worlds? In the course of the novel and at the end, he is "loving to" other women; this is not at all, however, the same as "being in love"; it is not, as the movies and songs say, "the real thing." That his love for Clara is the genuine article, tinselly though that may be, is made eminently clear by Achebe:

"Until Obi met Clara on board the cargo boat *Sasa* he had thought of love as another grossly over-rated European

193

invention. It was not that he was indifferent to women. On the contrary, he had been quite intimate with a few in England—a Nigerian, a West Indian, English girls, and so on. But these intimacies which Obi regarded as love were neither deep nor sincere. There was always a part of him, the thinking part, which seemed to stand outside it all watching the passionate embrace with cynical disdain. The result was that one half of Obi might kiss a girl and murmur: 'I love you,' but the other half would say: 'Don't be silly.' And it was always this second half that triumphed in the end when the glamour had evaporated with the heat, leaving a ridiculous anti-climax.

"With Clara it was different. It had been from the very first. There was never a superior half at Obi's elbow wearing a patronising smile." (p. 70)

When Obi kissed Clara, it was undoubtedly, as Peter Obiesie would say, "heavenly." This deep and sincere uncynical emotion felt by Obi for Clara and by Peter for Nneka has a powerful champion in the person of Nora in Onuora Nzekwu's *Wand of Noble Wood*. When she discusses Ibo ideas about marriage with Peter and a friend in Lagos, Nora, a West Indian, speaks up consistently for Western individualism, for women's rights, and—incessantly—for love, love, love. Nora finds that because she has been severed from her African roots for four hundred years, the mere fact of her being black does not help her; consequently she cannot understand the Ibos nor can she ever hope to persuade them that the fancy Western views she prizes so highly are anything but destructive modern nonsense. "Fortunately," she says at one point (and says it "hopefully"), "this traditional social setup is breaking down and will soon be completely gone. Africans are becoming more individualistic nowadays" (p. 27). The marital result of their becoming more "individualistic," as she recognizes, would be for Africans to adopt that attitude that she herself espouses: "Love should be your first consideration in mar-

194

riage" (p. 34). Nora is only a West Indian after all, so she cannot be expected to understand, and therefore she can be allowed to pronounce this sort of heresy and folly, at least in Lagos; but neither Peter nor Obi is well advised to proclaim it as truth to the parents and the ancestors, and both discover the disaster of trying to live it.

In *No Longer at Ease* Achebe presents a sexual relationship that is motivated not by an urge to procreation and ancestral appeasement—which makes it quite different from anything in *Things Fall Apart*—but by, quite simply, an Aristophanic yearning for reunion. Indeed, the illegal abortion that Obi provides for Clara is a powerful symbol suggesting how drastically different is the motivation for sexual relations here from what it was in pre-European Ibo society. The voice of the ancestral past can only be very confused, in itself and to Obi's ears, when he, the ancestral present, decides to marry an *osu* anyway, in spite of fathers and forefathers, and then agrees to abort the child which would, paradoxically, both continue the ancestral line and simultaneously corrupt and destroy it. Nearly all the difficulties that Peter Obiesie encounters from his family in *Wand of Noble Wood* when he goes down the list of prospective brides have to do with whether or not the women in question could perpetuate the line undefiled, for no one in his family, as also in Obi's family, needs bad blood introduced. For Obi or for Peter to fail to consider whether their girl-friends are suitable as "future breeders of posterity" would be to offer the ultimate insult to the ancestors; even worse, it would be to deny those ancestors the unbroken and uncorrupted immortality—an immortality very much of this world—so bravely and so tenuously maintained from generation to generation. Corrupt the line by marrying an *osu*, or fail to produce children—the worst fate imaginable to an African of traditional beliefs[25]—and you have once and

---

[25] "You must remember," Peter Obiesie's sister writes to him, apropos of the necessity of his marrying soon and getting at the business

for all destroyed the ancestors and their spiritual power, which is effective only in and through their living heirs: the ancestors have no life in time—that is, they have no life at all—unless through lineal reincarnation and descendant procreation. Once that thread is broken, those great spirits are deprived of being forevermore. By a terrible irony, and in total moral confusion, it is Obi himself who pronounces the curse of childlessness not only for his own self but for the ancestors who are, by that act, not simply dead but finally, irremediably, eternally powerless and non-existent. Obi, as he finds when he returns to the ancestral village, is "no longer at ease here, in the old dispensation,/ With an alien people clutching their gods." But neither is he at ease in the new dispensation, and therein lies his personal tragedy: for the Western gods withhold from him that same personal fulfillment through love with which they tempted him away from the traditional gods of the Ibos. Fittingly, it is the Western world, i.e., the British administration, that prosecutes Obi and clucks its tongue at this most recent "na-

---

of propagating, "that, among us, celibacy is an impossible prospect, and that to be childless is the greatest calamity that can befall any woman who becomes your wife" (*Wand of Noble Wood*, p. 57).

Speaking to an audience in Texas on the subject of Greek influence on his *Song of a Goat*, John Pepper Clark, the Nigerian playwright and poet, drew a contrast between African ideas about procreation and Western ideas—both ancient Greek and modern American—that is very much to the point of the present remarks: "The Ijo man who comes to this play will probably recognize things the Greeks never dreamt of. The idea of sacrifice is a universal one, but the theme of impotence is something that doesn't have the same kind of cultural significance for you as it has for me. The business of reproduction, of fertility, is a life and death matter in my home area. If a man doesn't bear, he has not lived. And when he is dead, nobody will think of him. Whereas here, you have other interests and preoccupations which have made you less concerned with the issue of procreation, and the sense of survival after death that we derive from it" (*Palaver: Interviews with Five African Writers in Texas*, ed. Bernth Lindfors et al. [Austin: African and Afro-American Research Institute of the Univ. of Texas at Austin, 1971], p. 16).

196

tive" to have gone bad. Obi is destroyed utterly according to the notions of either Africa or the West: on the one hand childless for eternity, on the other hand loveless and incomplete.

In an essay titled "The Role of the Writer in a New Nation," Achebe discusses what he calls "the crisis in our culture" which, he says, is both a cause and a consequence of disorder, both the origin and the result of split and contradictory opinions. He concludes the essay by declaring, "The village code of conduct has been violated but a more embracing and a bigger one has not been found."[26] Of the writer's role in such a situation he says, "The writer in our society should be able to think of these things and bring them out in a form that is dramatic and memorable." This is clearly what Achebe himself has intended and, I think, has accomplished in *No Longer at Ease*, where the "village code of conduct" is rapidly disappearing, and in *A Man of the People*, where that code is gone almost entirely and none bigger or more embracing is yet in sight. At the present end of this historic process of cultural disintegration the hero of *A Man of the People* is forced to attempt his own individual solution, his own personal reintegration, because the village can no longer offer him, as it could his grandfather and even to a large extent his father, a coherent identity or a defined role. In a different essay, but on a similar subject ("The Black Writer's Burden"),[27] Achebe says that the necessary act for the black African writer today is to assert his humanity in its fullness and to assert it not with pleas nor with *négritude*, not with meaningless boasts nor with inferior whimperings, but, especially since independence, to assert it as one who is fully intelligent, fully critical, fully aware, as one who neither requires nor demands special considerations or favors or criteria merely because he is

[26] "The Role of the Writer in a New Nation," *Nigeria Magazine*, No. 81 (June 1964), p. 159.

[27] *Présence Africaine*, Eng. ed., No. 59 (3d Quarter 1966), pp. 135-40.

197

African. If this assertion of humanity should happen to imply criticism of his own people, culture, or nation, so be it; but in any case, Achebe says, the requirement in an African writer, the burden he assumes in writing, is to show intelligence, alertness, responsibility. *A Man of the People*, which is a very fine achievement and the climax, for the present, of Achebe's career as Ibo novelist, demonstrates his possession of all these strengths; it shows Achebe practicing in his fiction what he preaches in his essay.

"Je ne peux pas comprendre," Achebe told the interviewer from *Afrique*, "pourquoi un grand nombre d'écrivains africains, d'expression française notamment, ont une telle nostalgie pour le passé" (p. 42). This may seem an odd remark coming from the author of *Things Fall Apart* and *Arrow of God*, yet what I assume Achebe means, and what he meant when he said he felt a compulsion to celebrate the ancestors, is that we return to the past and should return to it, as he sees things, not because (like Camara Laye) we are nostalgic, but because there we will discover the roots of the present. *Things Fall Apart* and *Arrow of God* are thus essential sources for the experience of *No Longer at Ease* and *A Man of the People*. "For our knowledge of the past," as Dilim Okafor-Omali says, "will illuminate our present path to a greater future. Our culture is our heritage and our pride" (p. 159). True, in *A Man of the People* Odili Samalu sees that culture as being largely impossible to the present-day Nigerian; but he would place the same value on it were it accessible, and he unquestionably feels the need, along with his creator and Okafor-Omali, to establish some kind of morality in the present, for the future, out of the past. *A Man of the People* depicts Ibo society at the fourth stage of development as described by Okafor-Omali (when, as Achebe seems to suggest, only a personal reintegration can repair the tragedy of cultural disintegration), and it is an example of African fiction of the third stage of evolution as defined by O. R. Dathorne ("a concern in depth with the person, his private predicament"). Achebe's tale is one of

198

certain loss and possible gain, of a hollowness and emptiness where there was before something of great value, and
of a felt need to construct or reconstruct a new kind of ethic
to replace the one that is now impossible.

In *A Man of the People* Achebe takes up his African/
European subject again, this time with new characters and
in a new tone and with a decidedly different resolution. The
theme is now worked out almost entirely in terms of character and character development. Instead of culturally representative, static figures set in conflict, we have one character of various desires and divided loyalties who changes
and grows in understanding in the course of the novel and
who comes to a happy end, even though it is qualified with
considerable irony, in the final pages of the book. The time
of the novel is 1964-1965—that is, after full Nigerian independence but before the military coup of 1966. Odili
Samalu, a secondary-school teacher and the hero of the
novel, re-encounters, after some sixteen years, his one-time
schoolmaster, who, though an almost illiterate vulgarian,
has in the meantime become a member of parliament, the
minister of culture, a "man of the people," and an exceed-
ingly corrupt politician—M. A. Nanga, or, as he prefers to
be called, "Chief the Honourable Dr. M. A. Nanga, M.P.
LL.D." (p. 18). Odili receives favor from Nanga, goes to
stay with him in the capital city, and is outraged to learn,
in a fine comic scene, that Nanga has stolen his mistress
Elsie for a one-night affair. Odili leaves Nanga's house determined to get revenge, first by contesting Nanga's seat in
parliament, second by alienating the affections of the pretty
young girl (Edna) whom Nanga intends to take as his second or "parlor" wife. In the end, Odili is seized at a political
rally for Nanga, is beaten and hospitalized, and Nanga is
elected without opposition. But then a military coup turns
everything around: Nanga is jailed and Odili marries Edna,
whom he now loves with a true and deep, specifically Western passion.

The most notable thing about *A Man of the People* that

199

distinguishes it from the other novels is that it is told in the
first-person by Odili. There is no overview in the novel of
a culture or cultures. Everything is seen from within the
categories. What this means, in practical terms, is that we
receive a full picture of Odili's character-in-change, his rea-
sonings, his motives, and his ideals; it means also that we
experience the conflict, between political aggrandizement
and moral rectitude, along with Odili right from inside. By
the time of A Man of the People, everyone has his individualized character, the conflict is entirely internal, sexual relations involve either "romantic love" or "being loving to,"
and there is no effective community voice, speaking ancient
and ancestral wisdom, to guide actions. To indicate the
moral distance traveled from Things Fall Apart, one might
point to the remark of a married white American woman
with whom Odili has a brief and casual affair. As they chat
together, with a sort of inane mindlessness on her part and
a restrained hostility on his, she says, "Sex means much
more to a woman than to a man." (Her rationale: "It takes
place inside her. The man uses a mere projection of himself," p. 50.) Without either disputing or defending this, one
can still remark that this would never have been said, or
anything like it, in the world of Things Fall Apart. Even
here it rather scandalizes Odili and could probably only
have been said by an American. The remark would be entirely meaningless to, for example, Nwoye's nameless
mother (the American's name, incidentally, is Jean, her husband is John, and they insist immediately on first names)—
Wife No. 1, who lived only in the role of bearer of children
for husband and ancestors. Hers could never have been a
life determined by a search for personal satisfaction or
pleasure, by a yearning for individual fulfillment or
completion.

The novel concludes with Odili's reflection that there is
no longer such a thing as community spirit or will or voice.
In his world the only possibility lies in personal fidelity and
individual loyalty, a recapture of individual wholeness and

perfection through love. This is how Achebe, through Odili, says it in the fine conclusion to his novel (Odili's friend Max has been killed by Chief Koko, a corrupt politician whom Max opposed in the election; Max's lover Eunice shot Koko dead on the spot—and all for love of Max):

"Max was avenged not by the people's collective will but by one solitary woman who loved him. Had his spirit waited for the people to demand redress it would have been waiting still, in the rain and out in the sun. But he was lucky. And I don't mean it to shock or to sound clever. For I do honestly believe that in the fat-dripping, gummy, eat-and-let-eat regime just ended . . . —in such a regime, I say, you died a good death if your life had inspired someone to come forward and shoot your murderer in the chest—without asking to be paid." (pp. 140-41)

Love, in the view of the individualist Odili, love Western, romantic, and sentimental, love is great—and might conceivably, barely prevail. Sex, according to this cautiously optimistic ethic, has little or nothing to do with procreation and ancestral continuation (the traditional African view); rather, it appears either in the guise of romantic love (the Western view, perhaps the modern African also) or as "being loving to" (amalgamation and confusion of traditional African and modern Western: polygamy for pleasure rather than procreation).[28] A society that conceives thus of

[28] One finds this confusion nicely illustrated in "Home and Marriage Counselling" columns which are popular features of many West African newspapers. Correspondents frequently begin their request for counsel with such remarks as, "Dear Counsellor: I am loving to four women. . . ." The following is drawn at random from one of these columns: "Mr. Counsellor: I am a young man of middle age (24) and loving to a lady of 32 years. She is loving to another man who supports her financially. I am also loving to another lady who has a child for me and further lives with me. When this woman glances at this girl who has the baby, she becomes angry to the point of harming her. This girl doesn't bother to get in the woman's way. Secondly, the same woman loves for the sake of money; that is to say, when I

love and sex will also exalt the individual, and so it is with Achebe's latest novel.

A *Man of the People* is very likely a slighter thing than the sturdy, plodding, much better-known *Things Fall Apart*; but what it lacks in massive solidity of structure, A *Man of the People* more than makes up in technical refinement: in flexibility of characterization and subtlety and delicate assurance of tone. The nature of Achebe's achievement might be made clearer if one imagined a new generic name for such a work as *Things Fall Apart*: an historical/ cultural fiction, perhaps, or a sociological presentation, or a ritual, anthropological drama. (This novel, for good reason, is most popular with ethnologists and anthropologists, with social scientists in general, and with "African studies" experts.) A *Man of the People*, on the other hand, is preeminently a "novel," with all the dramatized complexity of human relations implied by the tradition of the novel. While the satire of A *Man of the People* rejects, there is a

---

take pay and give her a sum of money, you can see the last tooth in her jaw, but . . ." etc. This particular counsellor usually gives highly moralistic and Christian advice, inclining toward a confused but Western view of love. In response to a request for a definition of love, we get this: "Your question 'What is Love' and 'How can one know when one is really in love' is a very timely one when a multitude of people do not know what real love is because they have never experienced it. I personally believe that Love is the most wonderful and most satisfying emotion the Creator has put into men, however it will be impossible to give you an adequate answer within the limits of this column. Perhaps I might just tell you that love is that spark which leaps from one heart to another and creates this being drawn to one another. Of course this is only a very vague and complete insufficient statement and I hope you will realize that this column cannot afford the vast space such an answer would need. Sincerely. . . ." It may be that this 'counsellor' does not take his profession with quite the same seriousness as Nathanael West's "Miss Lonelyhearts," but he (I think it is safe to speculate that the writer of this column, in Africa today, would still be a "he") is a neat, if shallow, representative of the kind of moral confusion consequent upon the mixing of African and Western love ethics.

parallel movement, focussing on Odili and his moral growth, that makes discoveries and accepts, that integrates experience around a new personal center and asserts this individual personality as a replacement for the village code of conduct that has been violated and destroyed. *A Man of the People* takes place in a world much worse off, much more corrupt and cynical and generally nasty, than the world of *Things Fall Apart*; yet Achebe, or at least his hero, finds in this wretched world a life that is both meaningful and possible. *A Man of the People* does not merely show that a certain world of grace is lost forever—of course it is —but takes that loss for granted and attempts to say what there may be of value in this world without innocence that lies about us. This latest novel of Achebe's—and this will suggest how very different it is, and how far he has come, in theme and technique, from *Things Fall Apart*—reminds the reader, by its tone, its theme, and its conclusion, of no one so much as E. M. Forster: in its very slightness and un- pretentiousness, in its humanistic spirit, in its sensitive and unheroic hero, in its humor—a light play of irony over a subject often heavy with solemnity—in its dramatic sud- denness of plot action, in its emphasis on the worth of per- sonal relations as against anything else the world can offer. Where Forster, however, ordinarily keeps to the private world of individuals, Achebe carries his theme into the pub- lic realm of political involvement—to have his hero discover in the end that it is only, after all, in the private realm that there is anything meaningful at all, specifically that the only valuable pursuit and possession is the whole self, to be found through the love of one individual person. There, for the moment at least, on the point of individual fulfillment, Achebe seems to bring the novel from Anglophobe Africa to the same conclusion as the contemporary Western novel.

# CHAPTER V

# Pornography, Philosophy, and African History

THEY ORDER this matter differently in Francophone Africa. Whether one judges that they order it better, as Laurence Sterne declares is the case in France herself, or order it worse, will depend no doubt on the observer's sensibilities; that they order it differently, however, is beyond dispute. The fiction that borders on sociology and anthropology, the novel that describes for us a people, their traditions and their culture, and recreates the traditional, coherent community for us in representative figures—as Chinua Achebe does for the Ibo and James Ngugi for the Gikuyu, even as Ezekiel Mphahlele does for the alienated and exiled South African, though it would be contradictory to call this last a traditional or coherent group—these ethnographic portraits in prose scarcely exist in the literature produced by African writers in French. *Things Fall Apart*, as Davidson Nicol rightly points out, is very specifically oriented and ethnically focussed: Achebe's first novel, he says, is interesting to European readers "because of what is to them its setting in a classic rural African society; but to an African reader the setting does not present itself as African, but specifically, as Ibo."[1] One need not, as Nicol seems to imply, be African to observe that it is crucially important for an understanding of Achebe's fiction to recall that he is Ibo, and the same goes for the "Gikuyuness" of James Ngugi's novels; if we forget that Mphahlele is a *déraciné* from urban South Africa, neither *Down Second Avenue* nor *The Wanderers*

[1] *Africa: A Subjective View* (London: Longmans, Green, & Co., 1964), p. 78.

204

will have much meaning at all for us. But it is of comparatively little consequence that Camara Laye is Malinké or
that he is from Guinée, that Yambo Ouologuem is Dogon
or that he is from Mali, that Cheikh Hamidou Kane is Peul
or that he is from Sénégal. The fact and significance of
blackness, with all the reverberations that that literal and
symbolic condition has produced in history, psychology,
philosophy, religion, and literature, is of infinitely greater
moment in reading the fiction of Camara Laye, Yambo
Ouologuem, and Cheikh Hamidou Kane than either specific
ethnic culture or nationality. Not that these three writers
perceive the same significance in blackness, for indeed they
do not; but they all concentrate their search for meaning on
the question of what it is to be black, or what it is to be African, both in history and in the present, both in Africa and
in Europe, rather than on such questions as what it is to be
Ibo or Nigerian, what it is to be Gikuyu or Kenyan, what it
is to be a forced wanderer from South Africa.

One should hasten to say, however, that by "the fact and
significance of blackness" one does not intend quite the
same thing as "*négritude*." It has become almost a cliché in
the criticism of African literature to observe that writers in
French adhere to the doctrine of *négritude* as an aesthetic
principle and that writers in English, from Wole Soyinka
to Chinua Achebe to Ezekiel Mphahlele, reject *négritude*
as being in no way a valid criterion for judging literature.
Achebe, for example, expressed succinctly the typical negative response to *négritude* of African writers in English, and
incidentally drew the line in linguistic terms, when he declared (in an interview published, ironically, in French)
that for him as a writer the doctrine was simply meaningless: "Je suis contre les slogans. Je ne pense pas que, par
exemple, la 'négritude' ait un sens quelconque. Le panafri-
canisme? Peut-être. La négritude, non. Je ne peux pas comprendre pourquoi un grand nombre d'écrivains africains,
d'expression française notamment, ont une telle nostalgie

205

pour le passé."[2] Achebe's remark is not difficult to under-stand—*négritude has*, for the most part, been proclaimed by writers in French and not by writers in English—but the contrast between French and English writing from Africa goes much deeper than an adherence to or a denial of *négritude*, or it is centered elsewhere. Achebe's last remark, however, may point the way, at least through a back door, to formulating the real distinctions between the two bodies of literature. It is obviously fair comment to say that Camara Laye, especially in *L'enfant noir*, exhibits a nos-talgia for the past. But Achebe's own *Arrow of God* and *Things Fall Apart*, as I have suggested earlier, are not en-tirely free of some nostalgia for the past, tempered though it may be by a hint of flaws in the old society. And again, in fiction in French, no one would suggest that Yambo Ouologuem displays any nostalgia for the past, or for any-thing else, in *Le devoir de violence*: "This novel," according to the Cameroonian writer Simon Mpondo, "more than any-thing ever written, marks . . . the end of Negritude's rosy image of ancestral Africa. . . ."[3] So novelists from Franco-phone Africa do not necessarily or invariably resemble one another in declaring for *négritude* or in yearning for the past, not at this late date anyway, nor can they always be distinguished from their Anglophone counterparts on bases of *négritude* and nostalgia. Yet there are important ways in which Yambo Ouologuem's writing resembles Camara Laye's but differs from Chinua Achebe's, and ways in which Cheikh Hamidou Kane's *L'aventure ambiguë* relates to *Le devoir de violence* and *Le regard du roi* but contrasts with *Things Fall Apart* and *Weep Not, Child* and *The Wanderers*.

To put the contrast in rather stark and exaggerated

[2] "Entretien avec Chinua Achebe," *Afrique*, No. 27 (octobre 1963), p. 42.

[3] "Provisional Notes on Literature and Criticism in Africa," *Pré-sence Africaine*, NS No. 78 (2d Quarter 1971), p. 141.

terms, the novel from French West Africa tends to be abstract and philosophic in its thought, yet concrete and sensuous in its apprehension of the world and in its expression. The West African novel in English, on the other hand, most often comes down midway between these poles of abstraction and sensuousness to discover its subject and its mode not in any philosophical dialectics but in social structures and social conflicts. As a description of their apprehension and presentation of reality, it would be legitimate to call *Le regard du roi*, *L'aventure ambiguë*, and *Le devoir de violence* "philosophical" novels, but it is very near impossible to think of a single African novel in English, whether from West Africa, East Africa, or South Africa, for which "philosophical" would be an appropriate adjective. Likewise, no Anglophone fiction expresses itself in the highly colored prose of African fiction in French—the deliberately repulsive images and revolting language of, for example, *The Beautyful Ones Are Not Yet Born* (by the Ghanaian Ayi Kwei Armah) not being at all the sort of thing one has in mind in describing the vision and the expression of Camara Laye, Cheikh Hamidou Kane, and Yambo Ouologuem as highly sensuous. This philosophic-sensory mode issues often in a variety of mysticism—very unlike anything in the hardheaded, realistic, social fiction of African writers in English—and it produces something that one might call the "symbolic" novel as opposed to the "representative" novel written by, say, Achebe. The range of reference or the scope of significance in the three specified novels in French is continental; it is simply African—i.e., pan-African—as against the limited cultural reference (Ibo and ex-British colony) in *Things Fall Apart* or *No Longer at Ease*. The characters and events of French West African literature symbolize experience that is virtually universal in occurrence, at least in the perspective of the writer within Africa; the characters and events of English West African literature, on the other hand, represent something

207

ethnically limited and geographically and politically restricted.

The best current example of all these tendencies in French fiction from West Africa, and a very brilliant novel besides, is Yambo Ouologuem's *Le devoir de violence* (called, in the excellent translation by Ralph Manheim, *Bound to Violence*).[4] Though any philosophy that Ouologuem might profess would no doubt be quite different from Camara Laye's or Cheikh Hamidou Kane's philosophy, yet

[4] *Le devoir de violence* (Paris: Éditions du Seuil, 1968); *Bound to Violence* (New York: Harcourt Brace Jovanovich, 1971). A small scandal blew up, in the pages of the *Times Literary Supplement* and elsewhere, around *Le devoir de violence*. The *TLS* of 5 May 1972 printed, in parallel columns, about one page from Ouologuem's novel and a page from Graham Greene's *It's a Battlefield*, and no doubt the similarity, amounting to identity, between the two texts justifies the tone of smug self-satisfaction in the *TLS* note. Why Ouologuem should have chosen to transfer the passage from Greene's book to his own is hard to explain since it is unremarkable enough in its original context and out of place, out of style, and out of character in Ouologuem's book (though the pornography that immediately follows is strictly in character). However, this is not the only aspect of Ouologuem's practice that is difficult to understand or explain: he is a very peculiar writer and, one gathers, a very peculiar man.

Eric Sellin, in "Ouologuem's Blueprint for *Le Devoir de violence*" (*Research in African Literatures*, 2 [Fall 1971], pp. 117-20), points out structural similarities between Ouologuem's book and André Schwartz-Bart's *Le Dernier des Justes* and calls into question the originality if not the authenticity of Ouologuem's novel. What is more interesting than the structure of Ouologuem's book, however, as I hope to demonstrate in the analysis that follows, is its extraordinary style, and the parallel passages quoted by Sellin to make his point are most remarkable for their stylistic differences—as also Ouologuem's essential style is different throughout from Graham Greene's typical style. I am not at all sure that anyone has got to the bottom of Ouologuem yet, but I feel certain that he is a stranger and more bizarre—and more brilliant—writer than the *TLS* or Eric Sellin understand in their admonitory smugness.

Robert McDonald offers a rehash of the Graham Greene business, but without providing much illumination or any new insights, in "*Bound to Violence*: A Case of Plagiarism," *Transition*, No. 41 (1972), pp. 64-68.

208

their novels are all philosophical in the same sense, and though their varieties of mysticism differ (Camara Laye is a nature mystic, Kane a religious mystic, and Ouologuem a sensual mystic), yet they are all, more or less, mystics. "My novel is not traditional," Ouologuem has said, "and, although it is based in fact and history, it is not autobiographical."[5] In *Bound to Violence*, as also in his intensely ironic *Lettre à la France Nègre*, Ouologuem still is concerned, as any writer of *négritude* literature might be, with his own and his ancestral past—indeed, he is very profoundly concerned with it—but he is far too subtle and complex, not to say too ironic and scornful, to accept, as a sufficient relation to that past, the cultural narcissism offered up by what he calls "les concierges de la négritude."[6] It is true, as Ouologuem says, that his book is not, in any strict sense, "autobiographical": its details are not drawn from nor do they relate only to the author's own life or his private experience. But in another and larger sense, the book might be said to have in it certain autobiographical elements and intentions: it performs an act of symbolic autobiography not, like Achebe, for a specific group of Africans, whether that group be Ibo or Dogon, but for black Africans in general. "My aim," Ouologuem told a correspondent from *West Africa*, "is to do violence to the misconceptions of Africans so that we can realise what the real problems are. This is our 'duty of violence.'"[7] Elsewhere, he refers to "l'image d'une Afrique par trop déformée par ses chantres et ses littérateurs" (*Lettre*, p. 190), and it is precisely this grossly distorted image of Africa and Africans that Ouologuem would destroy, replacing it with a valid portrait based on a revision of history and a redefinition of

[5] Interview with Mel Watkins published in *N.Y. Times Book Review*, 7 March 1971, p. 7.

[6] *Lettre à la France Nègre* (Paris: Éditions Edmond Nalis, 1968), p. 189.

[7] "Malian Prizewinner," *West Africa*, No. 2689 (December 14, 1968), p. 1,474.

personality, a redrawing of the African image. Thus *Le devoir de violence* represents, it seems to me, something that one might take, in a figurative sense, for a reconstituted and epic autobiography of Africa and her people.

History, which plays the same role in the autobiography of a continent as memory does in the autobiography of an individual, is vitally important to Ouologuem's effort. What he sets about doing, primarily in *Devoir de violence* but also in the journalistic-essayistic-satiric mishmash that he calls *Lettre à la France Nègre*, is to revise, essentially and radically, the history of black Africa. "And if you thought that the end of colonialism was the end of the agony, then it is time to wake up," Ezekiel Mphahlele told the participants in the Dakar Conference in 1963.[8] To the sentimentalized history of Africa written by *négritude* historians (African or European), fitted out with the stock characters of the good black man in his primal African paradise and the bad white man who came like Satan to destroy and enslave, both Mphahlele and Ouologuem say "No," because psychologically that image is too simple and historically it is, in part if not entirely, false. Not only did the agony of Africans not end with the end of colonialism, according to Ouologuem, but it also had its beginning long, long before the advent of Europeans in Africa. "Voilà," Ouologuem says, after the Congo and Biafra, "soudain que l'on ne peut plus prétendre devoir cultiver les champs fleuris de l'Afrique gentillette et heureuse, baptisée dans le bonheur idyllique avant l'arrivée de l'Homme blanc . . ." (*Lettre*, p. 190). In Ouologuem's reading of history, there were Africans, both the "Notables" and Arabs, who were past masters in inflicting human agony on what Ouologuem, with bitter irony, chooses to call the "négraille" ("niggertrash") long before the "Flençèssi" (the French) came, with their ridiculous name and their delusions of power, to

[8] Reprinted as "Remarks on Négritude" in *African Writing Today*, ed. Ezekiel Mphahlele (Harmondsworth, Middlesex: Penguin, 1967), p. 252.

exercise their particular but, in comparison with the Saifs, inexpert and "humane" brand of agony. And far from having been baptised in idyllic happiness, the continent, like its population, had been "baptisé dans le supplice: baptised in torture."[9] Though he aims at doing violence to a false image by way of writing an accurate history of black Africa, Ouologuem has no intention, of course, of simply standing the old image on its head—that would be as distorted as the first view that gives all evil to the European, all good to the African. Ouologuem, it is true, finds a great plenty of evil for the white man, but he is too generous with that commodity to deny the black man his share in evil as well; he is more even-handed than either *négritude* historians or colonial apologists in distributing vices among Africans and Europeans. One might quote the remark that Ouologuem uses as an epigraph to Chapter III of *Les milles et une bibles du sexe*—"Qu'est-ce le vice? Un goût qu'on ne partage pas."—[10] and suggest that in his view, a rather cynical one, this would apply to hypocritical African shock before European vices as well as to European horror at so-called African savagery. But that each world has its own vices might well imply that each has its characteristic virtues too.

Again in an ironic tone and cynical voice, Ouologuem, in his *Lettre à la France Nègre*, suggests the probable motive lying behind what he considers the fantasies of *négritude*; at the same time, he hints at what he intends in *Bound to Violence* and what there might be of a positive nature in African history to fill out the largely negative achievement of that novel. "Si la *négritude*, cependant, vaut toujours parce qu'elle est un cadre auquel il reste encore à donner

[9] This, like many other verbal echoes, indicates the intimate relation between *Devoir de violence* and *Lettre à la France Nègre*: on p. 9 of the former, Ouologuem refers to "sa population, baptisée dans le supplice"; on p. 190 of the latter, he describes "ce continent, baptisé dans le supplice."

[10] *Les milles et une bibles du sexe* (Paris: Éditions du Dauphin, 1969), p. 78.

meilleur contenu, ce contenu ne saurait être que s'il n'érige pas des autels et des statues à cent mythes, qui ne répondent et n'ont jamais correspondu à quoi que ce soit de vivant en Afrique: foire aux chimères où s'est exaltée l'imagination de plus d'un marchand d'idéologie, échaffaudant mille impostures dont le mérite—peut-être—est de rassurer, à la Bourse des valeurs de la primitivité, tous les petits rentiers de la tragi-comédie . . ." (p. 191).

So the concept of "Negrohood" (as it is called in one of Senghor's many statements on the subject) may, after all, be worth something, but only if a new painting is fitted to the frame of *négritude*, only if it is redefined, only if the history of black Africa is rewritten and the personality of the black African redrawn. Ouologuem has a new picture to put in the frame, of course, a picture he calls *Le devoir de violence*, which would not only deprive the addict of old-style *négritude* of many of his most cherished illusions, but would also lower the stock-exchange value of the hoked-up primitive arts produced by the happy and noble savage, that phantom that issues from the heated and sentimental imagination of "journalistes, sociologues, ethnologues, africanistes, littérateurs et négrophiles 'spécialisés,'" all of whom have a vested interest in maintaining the image of the simple, noble primitive that they themselves have created and that they sell on the various world markets: "mi *y'a bon, banania*, mi Platon petit nègre," Ouologuem says, with bitterness, of this fantasy creature.[11]

[11] *Lettre*, pp. 191 and 192. It is difficult to be certain what the relation between Ouologuem's *Lettre* and *Devoir de violence* might be, but they were obviously written in close conjunction with one another (and both were published in 1968), so much so that phrases, lines, and paragraphs are virtually repeated in the two books. According to the interview in *West Africa*, *Devoir de violence* was originally a thousand pages long, or about five times the length of the published version. It seems likely that *Lettre* is composed of fragments that would not quite fit the fictional plan of *Devoir* and, rather than lose some choice items, Ouologuem put them together as another book (*Lettre* is notably fragmentary and loose-jointed, extremely various in

For the most part, Ouologuem's historical revisionism is carried out with a kind of violent and grotesque good humor, but even so, insanely comic as it sometimes is, what Ouologuem does is largely a negative thing, a mad, antic dance performed on the grave of *négritude*, and the conclusion to which he comes is pervasively pessimistic and melancholy. "He admits," according to the interviewer in *West Africa* (p. 1475), "that his novel is negative since it provides no solution to the problems posed. . . ." As a satirist—and satire is a very large part of his intention—Ouologuem is an unyieldingly aggressive and destructive artist, attacking and ridiculing, not creating and defending. The satirist's art, as Ouologuem practices it, neither offers solutions of its own nor proposes answers; instead it exposes problems and opposes the too facile solutions of others. What is positive in *Devoir de violence* comes only as an implication, sometimes only as an implication from an implication—which, for the unwary reader, can be a very dangerous exercise in fixing an author's attitude or discovering his meaning. The tone of *Devoir de violence*—and of *Lettre à la France Nègre* and *Les milles et une bibles du sexe*, for that matter —is so consistently and impenetrably ironic, so much a matter of personæ assumed, shifted, and transformed, that the reader almost never knows if he has Ouologuem or if he has simply another leering, grimacing mask hiding whatever (if anything) lies behind it. There are, however, two aspects of *Bound to Violence* that have an implicit positiveness about them and there is, further, an implication, necessarily tenuous and elusive, that one might draw from these two

tone, in technique, and in its effects). On p. 189 of *Devoir*, for example, Ouologuem refers to the "négrophilie philistine, sans obligation ni sanction, homologue des messianismes populaires, qui chantent à l'ame blanche allant à la négraille telle sa main a *Y'a bon, Banania*" and on, coincidentally, the same page (189) in *Lettre*, he describes "ceux-la . . . qui s'insurgeaient en philistins d'une négrophilie sans obligation ni sanction." He refers again to the "philistine négrophiles" in the interview in *West Africa* (p. 1475).

implied positives: first, there is the terrific and compressed energy with which Ouologuem accomplishes his destruction; and, second, there is the texture of Ouologuem's extraordinary and brilliant prose. Both these relate more to the manner of the book than to its matter, and to draw conclusions about the author's positive beliefs, his ideas, his philosophy, from aspects of his stylistic manner can be, as I have suggested, rather dangerous—especially as Ouologuem frequently writes in styles that are confessedly borrowed: the style of the *griots*, of the Arab historians, and of the traditional tales of family and clan (not to mention the style of Graham Greene). Be that as it may, I think that Ouologuem's use of language—an extremely rich, colorful, intense, and sensorily heightened vehicle for whatever his vision may be—implies a good deal about what he takes to be the deepest reality of Africa as "an immense body in quest of its identity" (*Bound to Violence*, p. 167), or what he understands as the essential nature of Africa as a spiritual-sensory experience. In the experience of Ouologuem's Africa, spirit and senses are inextricably joined, as they are also in the language that he uses to render that experience. It is here, in this linguistically implied vision of what Africanness is and what likewise the experience of Africa is—a unified mode of being—that Ouologuem turns most clearly away from African writers in English, from Chinua Achebe and Ezekiel Mphahlele, and approaches writers whom in other ways he hardly resembles at all: Cheikh Hamidou Kane and Camara Laye.

If one omits his remark about "tendresse" (though in context it is a legitimate observation), what Robert Pageard has to say about *L'aventure ambiguë* and *Le regard du roi* applies also to *Bound to Violence* and makes of them a novelistic trio characteristic of West African literature in French: "L'audace de la langue, le symbolisme, le glissement vers le fantastique, une tendresse tout à fait contraire aux tendances européennes actuelles, apparentent *L'aven-*

*ture ambiguë* au *Regard du roi* de Laye Camara."[12] If we were to change that "tendresse"—for Ouologuem only—to eroticism or sensuality, then we would have an adequate description of *Bound to Violence*, which, like the other two novels, mediates, by means of symbolism, between the poles of philosophic abstraction and sensory experience. *Ambiguous Adventure*, for which the reader hardly requires an introductory note to recognize that there is an "autobiographical savour"[13] about it, tells the story of Samba Diallo, educated in a traditional Islamic school, then in a French school in Africa, and finally in Paris, until, drawn apart by the diverse philosophies of Islamic Africa and Christian Europe, he feels that he has lost that unity of being which he enjoyed when he was able to concentrate his existence entirely in his religious belief. The autobiographical element in *Ambiguous Adventure* has little to do with the traditional customs and the ceremonial observances of a social group (as in Achebe and Ngugi). Here the autobiography is of the mind and the spirit, of thoughts and beliefs and attitudes; it is a philosophical autobiography, and the characters represent various philosophic possibilities and influences. Samba Diallo, when he talks of his study of philosophy in France, refers to it as an "adventure" and thinks of that adventure as dangerous: "It may be that we shall be captured at the end of our itinerary, vanquished by our adventure itself" (p. 104). Indeed, he suggests that he may well have chosen philosophy as a subject because of its dangerousness. For Samba Diallo, as for his creator, it is not material prosperity or technical learning or women or anything so gross that seduces the African to lose his identity to Europe. The real enemy is a foreign philosophy, attractive, seductive, beguiling: sinuous lines of thought and

[12] Robert Pageard, *Littérature négro-africaine* (Paris: Le livre africain, 1966), p. 87.

[13] *Ambiguous Adventure*, trans. Katherine Woods, preface by Vincent Monteil (New York: Collier-Macmillan, 1969), p. ix.

chains of pure logic, intimate intercourse of abstract ideas and the copulation of disembodied concepts. This separation of thought from total being, or transformation of being into abstract, acting and interacting ideas, is a dangerous game, as Samba Diallo's fate demonstrates, for one whose being has heretofore been entirely absorbed in his belief. Before going to France, under the influence of his father and the guidance of his Islamic teacher, Samba Diallo participated in a union, not of abstractions in the head, but of full being with divine spirit—a mystic union, identity of the believer and his belief, the worshipper and his worship.

Though Samba Diallo may succumb to the wiles of Western abstraction so that he ends up, in his person as in his philosophic practice, an example of Cartesian dualism, divided in being and ambiguous in will, his creator, as author of the novel, does not follow him. Kane says, among other things, that the implicit philosophic assumptions of Africa and France are very different and that, in the case of Samba Diallo anyway, it is not possible to reconcile them. Yet *Ambiguous Adventure,* as a dramatization of contrasting philosophies, as an embodiment of differing attitudes, as an autobiographical fiction, does include, comprehend, and reconcile the opposed assumptions. It is a novel based on ideas, in the abstract manner of France and the West, but it is also, simultaneously, a novel that dramatizes what Kane indicates is a peculiarly African—specifically Islamic African—philosophy. Perhaps one should simply observe that it proves possible for the artist to reconcile the conflicting assumptions in a way that would not be possible for any man in life.

This reconciliation within the frame of the art work is effected, for example, at the beginning of Chapter Seven when the Frenchman, Paul Lacroix, and Samba Diallo's father, "the knight," watch a typically African sunset— which may or may not also signify the end of the world. "On the horizon, it seemed as if the earth were poised on

216

the edge of an abyss. Above the abyss the sun was suspended, dangerously. The liquid silver of its heat had been reabsorbed, without any loss of its light's splendor. Only, the air was tinted with red, and under this illumination the little town seemed suddenly to belong to a strange planet" (p. 68). The Frenchman is frightened by this "cosmic drama being played out outside" because it seems to him a portent "that we are closer to the end of the world than we are to nightfall" (pp. 68-69), and he is incapable of believing in the apocalypse: he can imagine the end of the world only as an atomic blast, as some horrible, human-produced accident, not as the culmination and climax of human-divine spiritual intercourse, a consummation, the knight suggests, devoutly to be wished. But as to the atomic blast, the knight says, "Our most simple-minded peasant does not believe in such an end as that, episodic and accidental. His universe does not admit of accident. In spite of appearances, his concept is more reassuring than yours" (p. 69). The two men, living embodiments of opposed philosophies—the abstract, mental, materialistic Westerner who sees history as chance and accident versus the unified sensory-spiritual African, with his immediate knowledge of being, who sees history as providence and as a movement toward a fated end—continue their characteristically intellectual dialogue (characteristic of fiction from French West Africa), reflecting in everything they say what they are and what they mean. "Then from the bottom of my heart," the knight tells Lacroix, for whom, as a spiritually underdeveloped person, he feels more pity than anything else, "I wish for you to rediscover the feeling of anguish in the face of the dying sun. I ardently wish that for the West. When the sun dies, no scientific certainty should keep us from weeping for it, no rational evidence should keep us from asking that it be reborn. You are slowly dying under the weight of evidence. I wish you that anguish—like a resurrection" (p. 71). Like two symbolic men, which is what they are, the

217

African and the European conclude their dialogue with the end of the day, or the end of the world, or both. "There was a moment of silence. Outside, the vesperal drama had come to an end. The sun had set. Behind it, an imposing mass of bright red cloud had come crumbling down like a monstrous stream of clotted blood. The red splendor of the air had been progressively softened under the impact of the slow invasion of the evening shade" (pp. 71-72).

This mingling of intense intellectuality with brilliant, exotic sensuousness, or this deployment of sensuous effects to an intellectual end, would be hard to match in any novel in English from Africa, but in Ouologuem's writing, where the sensuousness takes an erotic-pornographic turn as against Kane's religious-natural inclination, one finds a similar prose expressing, in one sense, a similar sensibility. Nor is the apocalyptic sunset an isolated passage. It is appropriate, given the philosophic mode of Kane's novel, that at the end, after "the fool" has stabbed Samba Diallo and he is dying, the reader should be reminded of a European philosopher who was surpassingly intellectual (and later on inclined to the mystical) but who had no touch with Africa: Ludwig Wittgenstein. It is appropriate because Kane's great triumph is to combine Western abstraction with African mysticism. "So too at death," Wittgenstein says, "the world does not alter, but comes to an end." And, in a dependent corollary to that observation: "If we take eternity to mean not infinite temporal duration but timelessness, then eternal life belongs to those who live in the present. Our life has no end in just the way our visual field has no limits."[14] In the subjectively apocalyptic end to his life, a parallel to the sun dying and the day ending, Samba Diallo rejoins abstract thought to sensuous feeling, concentrating his entire being in the moment and on the divine, to achieve again the mystic union from which, in France, he had fallen away into ambiguity. At the moment of his death, when the

[14] *Tractatus Logico-Philosophicus*, 6.431 and 6.4311.

218

world ends and time is replaced by the eternity of the present, two voices speak in dialogue, one of them Samba Diallo's consciousness, the other apparently the voice of universal consciousness:

"But it returns to you. Toward whatever side you turn, it is your own countenance that you see, nothing but that. You alone fill the closed circle. You are king. . . ."

"I am two simultaneous voices. One draws back and the other increases. I am alone. The river is rising. I am in its overflow. . . . Where are you? Who are you?"

"You are entering the place where there is no ambiguity. Be attentive, for here, now, you are arriving. You are arriving."

"Hail! I have found again the taste of my mother's milk; my brother who has dwelt in the land of the shadows and of peace, I recognize you. Announcer of the end of exile, I salute you."

"I am bringing your kingdom back to you. Behold the moment, over which you reign." (pp. 163-65)

The last lines of the novel are given over to the two voices, blended now, however, into one, as Samba Diallo's consciousness merges with universal consciousness; and that end of the world, foreseen, anticipated, and desirable, yet unknown and dreaded, that the knight spoke of to Lacroix and that Samba Diallo himself has long contemplated and with which he has been rather more than half in love, is finally achieved. Kane says at one point (p. 47) that "the profound truth" of his story "is wholly sad"; rather than contradict him with the observation that it has a happy ending, it would perhaps be safer to say that the ending is triumphant and simply, entirely mystical.

"The moment is the bed of the river of my thought. The pulsations of the moments have the pulsations of thought; the breath of thought glides into the blow-pipe of the moment. In the sea of time, the moment bears the image of the

219

profile of man. . . . In the fortress of the moment, man in truth is king, for his thought is all-powerful, when it is. Where it has passed, the pure azure crystallizes in forms. Life of the moment, life without age of the moment which endures, in the flight of your élan man creates himself indefinitely. At the heart of the moment, behold man as immortal, for the moment is made from the absence of time. Life of the moment, life without age of the moment which reigns, in the luminous arena of your duration man unfurls himself to infinity. The sea! Here is the sea! Hail to you, rediscovered wisdom, my victory! The limpidness of your wave is awaiting my gaze. I fix my eyes upon you, and you harden into Being. I am without limit. Sea, the limpidity of your wave is awaiting my gaze. I fix my eyes upon you, and you glitter, without limit. I wish for you, through all eternity." (pp. 165-66)

So the subjective world explodes at death, as the philosopher would have it, into merger with objective consciousness.

What this grand, mystic climax recalls in other African literature is, of course—leaving Ouologuem's fiction aside for the moment—the end of Camara Laye's *Radiance of the King*, where Clarence's individual separateness is conclusively dissolved in the embrace of the child King. Kane in his finale, impressive as it is and though his metaphor of the river flowing into the sea is more conventional than the metaphor of the *enfant noir* in *Radiance of the King*, does not quite succeed, as Camara Laye does, in overcoming the obvious problems inherent in an attempt to translate mystical experience into images and language. There remains something of the vague and the inapprehensible in Kane's account of mystical transport, while in Laye's novel the child King is immediate and present, tangible and apprehensible as a symbol of the transcendent and the divine. This condition of being that he symbolizes is hinted at earlier when Clarence, impatiently waiting for the King to arrive at some unspecified time in the future, is advised to call on an old woman named Dioki, who lives with her pet snakes and charms them, and, it is suggested, does some other, less mentionable, things with them as well. When Clarence finally goes to Dioki she refuses to tell him anything about when the King will come, shouting, "I am not the king! I am not the king!" Indeed she is not, but when she throws herself on the ground amidst the hissing serpents an odd thing happens: "They were embracing her, enfolding her: and she—she was crying out. But what sort of embrace was this? Clarence could hardly believe what he saw. These were the passionate convulsions of love itself!" (p. 220). When Clarence looks away from this scene of quasi-bestiality ("quasi" because there is something suspiciously human, not altogether unconnected with Clarence himself, about those serpents), he has a glorious vision of the king, present to him somehow as a consequence of the grossly sensual lovemaking of Dioki and her serpents. Later Clarence feels "strangely shattered, strangely torn" (p. 225), as if he were . . . or as if he had . . . , "But the comparison was so unthinkable that Clarence dismissed it at once" (p. 225), and Camara Laye never quite says whether or not the vision of the King's radiance is connected with bestiality, or with voyeurism, or perhaps with a combination of the two. The two boys who brought Clarence to Dioki and then watched him with her are, however, happy to tell him that "We saw the old woman coming towards you. . . . She put her arms round your shoulders and pressed you against her. She. . . ." But Clarence, who is not sure whether he has dreamed all this and who prefers not to consider what he, the snakes, and the old woman may have done together, cuts the boys off, and the rest, which is silence, is left to the reader's imagination.

One thing, however, is certain, and that is that in going south (Dioki is of the South), in searching for the King and for the mystical union that he signifies, Clarence must open his senses and surrender them, and through them his spirit,

221

to the lavish, exotic richness of the African forest that presses on him all around; opening himself to sensory experience specifically includes sexuality. "The perfumes, the remains of all those perfumes steal into his lungs," as he goes southward through the womb-like, suffocating, enervating forest, "like the vapours of a poisonous bloom; they creep even lower, into his belly: and lower still, a burning, glowing, and already far from innocent commotion . . ." (p. 98), which makes Clarence ask the beggar, his guide, if this is the South, where he anticipates seeing the King. " 'The South is everywhere,' the beggar said softly" (p. 98). It is indeed everywhere, Clarence finds, including his loins. "Yes, perhaps this inferno of the senses is everywhere. . . . He dozes; and in spite of himself the perfumes of the forest are working within him, the poisonous bloom is opening slowly . . . and again the green tunnel of the forest opens and swallows him up. And the sea stretches away, the musty smells of earth and the poisonous smells of flowers roll endlessly towards him, and he feels the unthinkable fire stirring again in his loins . . ." (pp. 98-99). The insidiously attractive and vaguely exciting, but also overripe and nauseating putrescence of the forest—and of the South— eventually smothers and crushes and splits Clarence's senses wide, making of them open wounds that fear and desire and finally require more and more of the thing that has so satiated them, numbed them, and rubbed them raw.

If taken step by step, the transition by which one passes from the religio-natural mysticism of Cheikh Hamidou Kane to the religio-natural-sexual mysticism of Camara Laye to the natural-erotic-pornographic mysticism of Yambo Ouologuem is very regular and very slight, though, reverting to an earlier matter, the first two writers might be said to subscribe more or less to the notions of *négritude*, while Ouologuem certainly does not. Differ as they may on *négritude*, however, there is an undercurrent of agreement, for the most part implicit, unstated, dramatized, among these three writers in French about the peculiar, special

nature of the African experience, about how it contrasts
with the European or French experience, and about what
happens when the two come in contact with one another.
In the "Avertissement" to *Les milles et une bibles du sexe*,
which is a frankly pornographic book (or "érotique" as
Ouologuem prefers to call it), having explained how "Utto
Rodolph"[15] came to him with a manuscript of sex exploits
to edit because Rodolph had imagined from reading *Devoir
de violence* that Ouologuem would make an appropriate
editor for that sort of material, Ouologuem says he agreed
but that this would be his first and last excursion into this
kind of literature—a kind of literature that, as practiced in
its pure form by Ouologuem, is, in the language of the
courts, possessed of little redeeming social value. "Et, si j'ai
pris sur moi de présenter *Les Mille et Une Bibles du Sexe*,
c'est également parce que, en raison de certains aspects
érotiques de mon premier roman, divers pays africains ont
rejeté de leurs frontières *Le Devoir de Violence*. J'étais, aux
yeux de chefs d'Etats irresponsables ou incultes, j'étais,
pour avoir osé dire du Nègre qu'il faisait l'amour, un
cartiériste vendu à une France raciste, laquelle s'amusait de
voir dénigrer par un Noir les mœurs des peuples noirs.
Soit," Ouologuem says, turning on his irresponsible and un-
cultivated critics. But if those critics thought *Le devoir de
violence* was raunchy and constituted a betrayal of the
black man's cause, then—so Ouologuem seems to say—let
them try *Les milles et une bibles du sexe*. The vices of the
white man as lovingly detailed in that book would, except
for one fact pointed out in *Lettre à la France Nègre*, make

[15] The book claims to be by "Utto Rodolph" (the name, in an apparent fit of forgetfulness, is spelled "Rudolf" throughout the "Avertissement"), who is described as "un grand aristocrate parisien" and
a "personnalité fort connue" (p. 13). In their *Bibliography of Creative
African Writing*, Janheinz Jahn and Claus Peter Dressler list "Utto
Rodolph" simply as a pseudonym for Ouologuem, which is no doubt
the real relation obtaining between the two; at any rate, in my discussion of the book, and in relating it to *Bound to Violence*, I have
assumed that "Utto Rodolph" is one of Ouologuem's many masks.

his critics blush ("Quel danger? Un Nègre saurait-il rougir?" *Lettre*, p. 11). Measuring his words carefully and venomously, Ouologuem delivers his tense counterattack: "Il est bon d'être primitif, certes, mais impardonnable d'être primaire. Tant pis pour les primaires qui se revent censeurs" (pp. 17-18). Someone somewhere might consider Ouologuem a "primitif" (in fact he ironically adopts that mask in his poem called "Quand parlent les dents nègres")[16] but no one anywhere could imagine him, on the evidence of his three books, to be a "primaire," especially not in matters of "l'érotisme."

The erotic adventures in *Mille et une bibles du sexe*—and this fact of setting reflects, I think, significantly on actions in *Devoir de violence*, which is located almost entirely in Africa—take place for the most part in France and the participants, again for the most part (when they are not dogs or other dumb beasts), are French. When the four sensualists, who momentarily sort themselves out from the swarming background of group sex and mass inter-excitation that occupies a good part of the book—Régis, Harry, Vive, and Emmanuelle ("artistes du sexe de l'érotisme," p. 286)—set out on a safari in Africa, Ouologuem ("naïvement") declares himself, apropos of the new setting, "désolé de voir l'Afrique mêlée à cette affaire" (p. 275). One might well discount some of Ouologuem's distress at finding Mother Africa mixed up in all this (after all, the "confessions-poker" that make up Utto Rodolph's manuscript are supposed to have been "triées, revues, corrigées et editée par Yambo Ouologuem," which is to say he should have had a pretty free hand to do as he liked in the way of including and

[16] "Quand parlent les dents nègres" was first published under the title "1901" in *Présence Africaine*, NS No. 51 (3e trimestre 1964), pp. 99-100; under the revised title it was published with five other poems by Ouologuem in *Nouvelle somme de poésie du monde noire*, a special number of *Présence Africaine*, NS No. 57 (1er trimestre 1966), pp. 88-95. The poem is also in *Modern Poetry from Africa*, ed. Gerald Moore and Ulli Beier, rev. ed. (Harmondsworth, Middlesex: Penguin, 1968), pp. 75-76, with the title "When Negro Teeth Speak."

excluding material), but the interesting fact is that the descriptions of the sensual, the exotic, and the erotic take a rather new turn—more natural, less strained, less grotesque, and less pornographic—in Africa from what they were in France. Ouologuem goes on to give a partial explanation of his dismay and in his explanation hints at what Africa is like, in contrast to the cold climate of, for example, France:[17] "J'aurais voulu qu'Utto Rodolph choisît pour décor un cadre autre—d'un exotisme moins collectif. . . ." Without further complaint, however, the "editor" says he set about trying to rewrite the first of the African-safari confessions, but on reading over the effort he was dissatisfied: "il manquait la dimension de la psychologie de cet érotisme là" (p. 275). Ouologuem's distress seems to come down to this lament: what is a poor pornographer to do if, in the very setting and atmosphere of his story, he discovers a super-powerful, sensual-sexual energy omnipresently flowing in the universe and expressing itself naturally in a collective exoticism-eroticism? Where is his art gone, if that which he would whip up artificially is there all the time in nature? Who, in that situation, needs the pornographer's art? To describe such a natural phenomenon is to describe something relatively normal and sane, bursting at the sensory seams perhaps, but all the same more or less robust and healthy in its expression; in short, it is to describe, or to try to describe, the African experience according to Ouologuem.

Comparatively, the forms of sex in Africa, as Ouologuem

[17] England and the English, naturally, are even further removed than France and the French from the "exotisme . . . collectif" of Africa. Golda, after she has been drawn out of her frigidity and has been introduced to almost every known variety of sensual experience (and to a few varieties heretofore unknown), takes on many lovers but prefers to avoid the sensually dead English: "Elle fut courtisée, aimée et prise par divers amis de rencontre, elle évita systématiquement les Anglais—parce qu'ils se lavaient les mains avant de faire l'amour, frappaient à la porte, toussotaient, ouvraient, entraient, la pénétraient à peine, et satisfaits, rentraient chez eux" (p. 230).

renders them in *Mille et une bibles*, are natural—one to
one, man and woman, the ordinary appendages and orifices,
no foreign instruments such as smoking guns, telephone
receivers, whips, fragile crystal flutes, switch-blade knives,
"godemichets," etc. True, a lion does get into the act in
Kenya, but even then the beast carries some of his nobility
with him, and the passage is nothing like as depraved as the
one that deals with the massive dog, the woman on a block
of ice, and a crowd of voyeurists back in Paris, or the scene
of Golda, Harry, the motorcycle policeman, and a hot
Maserati automobile beside a French superhighway. The
atmosphere of Africa that embraces the figures the moment
they step from the plane seems somehow to offer promise
in itself of a kind of fulfillment—the individual in relation
to the surrounding, enveloping sensory universe—denied
to the human creatures in the thin air of France, with their
restless and frenzied, perpetually unsatisfied sensuality and
their eternal greed for something new and different to revive the over-teased and weary senses. The immense age,
yet tremendous richness, hence continual freshness, of
everything in Africa makes unnecessary the itching search
for something ever new. When the characters first arrive in
Africa (Liberia), "c'était l'époque de la mousson, féconde
en nuits d'apocalypse. . . . Or le paysage était luxuriant de
baroque, avec son folklore exubérant de carmins, de bou-
gainvilliers, d'hibiscus, d'amaryllis de vermeille, d'orchidées
de formes étranges, de couleur diabolique" (p. 284). Immediately they drown themselves in the abundant fruits of
nature that in their variety and plenitude render any less
natural satisfaction for the senses irrelevant: "Ananas,
oranges, pamplemousses, citrons, noix de cocos, fraîches ou
traitées en coprah, mangues sucrées, papayes fondantes,
corossols aux protubérances poilues, au goût suave et
acidulé, kakis, jackfruit aux formes de courge, tout cela, ils
le goûtèrent, découvrant des arbres magnifiques, l'hévéa,
le plaque-minier, l'ébène, le raphia, les bambous géants, et,
plus loin, le baobab et ses fruits—pain de singe au goût

aigrelet" (p. 284). This is the same Africa—an enveloping sensory experience inducing a state of mind, a condition of spirit—that Clarence discovers in *Radiance of the King*; the same Africa, where "everything took me into the very essence of itself, as if nothing could exist except through me," that Samba Diallo felt he had lost in coming to France in *Ambiguous Adventure* (p. 139). And when Ouologuem comes to describe the women of Africa—"ses femmes noires aux seins insolents, avec ses joliesses en boubous lamés et sans corsage, leur démarche canaille de nonchalance, leurs silhouettes agrémentées de laisser-aller"—he significantly does so in purely natural terms as if the women were an overflow of nature, as if nature had poured into them all her sensuous variety, her heavy, ripe vitality, her endless, rich, luscious luxuriance: "leurs fesses qui bombent au bas de leurs reins cambrés, leur sexe: crépu et électrique quand le frotte le pubis masculin, leurs poitrines: redondantes sous le soleil lourd, le robuste ouvrage de leur sensualité, née comme du climat, débordant les corps comme la volupté de cieux autres" (p. 286). With nature thus lavish, expressing herself in a superabundance of ripe fruits, human and otherwise, Africa has little need of those "parties" so frantically sought out in France: "allant de réunions d'amis (trois à six couples) au gigantisme (trois cents couples) en passant par les messes noires, les ballets roses ou bleus, les scènes de pendaison, les inventions insolites en Ardèche . . ." (p. 15).

Régis, who eventually comes to the fore as the central character of *Bibles du sexe*, and who may or may not be the same person as the fabulous "homme sans race ni contrée" (who in turn may or may not be rather closely identified with Ouologuem himself), at a certain point in the book has an odd perception of a more than personified nature while driving in the countryside: "Régis buvait le vent empli de senteurs amollisantes. Les effluves flattaient inégalement les roches aux genêts herbus et la garrigue. Le regard de la nature était à chaque virage une découverte, avec, ici un

227

décor d'humus bleui, là un tunnel rougeoyant de ruines éventrées en entonnoir, lequel s'agrandissait, rocailleux ou étoilé de floraisons, étonnamment brun de puissance, et préhistorique. D'un coup, tout devenait démence. Féerie. Surnaturel. Vrai vagin d'air d'herbes d'algues et de roches" (p. 306). A momentary aberration of Régis' senses, one should imagine, this perception of the countryside as an immense vagina, caused no doubt by his mind's being concerned with the upcoming "party" to which he is driving. This reading of Régis' mad vision of the landscape receives some confirmation in *Bound to Violence* when Sankolo, who has been drugged so that his senses are entirely disordered and aberrant and who, like Clarence, has been sent on a journey ever deeper into the South, finds the experience of himself inseparable from that of nature and begins to perceive both of them in demented ways: "I ask the earth to stop moving, to let me rest without anguish, my body no longer a clenched fist in the gaping wound of the sunset. . . . The path turns into an immense vagina."[18] This is essentially the same mystic union, the same merger of subject and object—in Sankolo's case drug-induced—as Clarence experiences on his journey southward in *Radiance of the King* and again during his forest stupor and hallucinatory dreamnightmare after he reaches the South (pp. 197-205). It is also, though differently caused, essentially the same merger of subjective and objective consciousness that Samba Diallo experiences at the moment of his death in *Ambiguous Adventure*. In *Bibles du sexe* preeminently, but also here and there in *Bound to Violence*, the union of interior and exterior, the joining, "beyond fear and death," of the individual with nature, realizes itself in highly erotic sexual per-

---

[18] *Bound to Violence*, p. 105. In the original "the gaping wound" is "la plaie béante." In *Bibles du sexe*, Ouologuem's strange imagination often conceives of the vagina as a wound, gaping, sweet, or pulpy—"la plaie pulpeuse" (p. 227), for example—a conception that is made graphic in certain of the drawings illustrating the text.

228

formances. Different as lovemaking may seem from dying or rendering homage to the King, when successful it points, in Yambo Ouologuem, to the one same end as the mystic dissolution and natural reunion in Cheikh Hamidou Kane and Camara Laye—for instance, in *Bibles du sexe*, Harry teaching Golda, in a natural setting, the terrors of death and, beyond that, the ecstasies of erotic pleasure: "Alors, comprenant que l'homme a voulu lui façonner, par-delà la peur et la mort, l'amour du plaisir—elle laissa ses lèvres confier à la nature le délire où l'homme et la femme, à l'image du rituel des messes druidiques, se fondent dans la nature pour devenir herbe, arbre, terre ou oiseau, et en porter le nom" (p. 218).

Most readers of *Bound to Violence* are no doubt first and most forcibly struck not by Ouologuem's peculiar variety of mysticism but by the extremity of his expression, by the syntactic insanity and the mad brilliance of his language. From the first line ("Our eyes drink the brightness of the sun and, overcome, marvel at their tears. *Mashallah! wa bismillah!*"), Ouologuem seldom offers the reader any respite from the intensity of his expression, or from the intensity of his relation to the language and the relation of that language to what it describes; the reader consequently finds himself going back again and again in an effort, which usually proves vain, to discover some logical sense in Ouologuem's images, his similes and his metaphors. One might expect to encounter such difficulties of image and syntax in reading, let us say, Hopkins or Rimbaud or the Surrealist poets (with all of whom Ouologuem shows interesting similarities), but one does not expect to encounter such problems in a book that proclaims itself a prose fiction, a novel. Like Van Gogh with his paint, Ouologuem seems to want to get right inside his medium and merge with it in a kind of hot frenzy; he seems to have a need to smear himself with it, to touch and caress and violate it. Like Rimbaud and Hopkins, Ouologuem is unwilling to allow a separation of himself or his

229

experience from the language that describes it. For a good part of *Bound to Violence* (especially up to the last, short chapter) language is hardly a conceptual thing at all, but rather a voluptuously and violently sensuous creature that Ouologuem treats as a living thing: he makes love to it, both tenderly and violently, he caresses and tortures and rapes it, and he often surprises the reader into sharing the same sort of relation to it.

Operating with a kind of delirious passion from within his medium, Ouologuem distorts, distends, explodes the ordinary limits of language into a succession of irrational similes, metaphors, and hyperboles. His words are related one to another not by their dictionary definitions (and the reader who goes to a dictionary to understand Ouologuem will soon find his head spinning) but in their capacity as images or as sounds or as colored, sensual things in themselves. Especially this technique, or this relation, obtains in scenes involving either eroticism or violence—or, frequently, both. The logic behind this linguistic illogic would seem to be that for either of these experiences the language of reason or of ordinary discourse is entirely inadequate, since the experiences themselves, like the mystic's vision, are neither rational nor discursive. The scene involving the Frenchman Chevalier and his black, Baudelairian mistress Awa (it is certain that Ouologuem is as thoroughly versed in Baudelaire's special blend of exotic, voluptuous sex and luxurious, repulsive-attractive putrescence as he is in Rimbaud's derangement of senses and language)—"her breasts, warm and soft as two doves of living wool"—is a nice example, and exact, of sex rearing its head (ugly or not as one likes) right through and out of the language. After Chevalier's two dogs, Dick and Médor, have done their bestial best (or worst—at any rate their most) on Awa, Chevalier takes over and, in the event, is himself taken over: "A slap from him made her bark [the proximity of the dogs perhaps?], she coiled up with pleasure, panting under his cruel caress, manipulating him like a queen or a skillful whore. Her mouth was still hungry for this man's pink, plump mollusk, and the tongue in her mouth itched to suck at the pearl of sumptuous orient that flowed, foaming as though regretfully, from the stem . . ." (p. 57). There is, no doubt, method in this verbal madness—which does not, however, alter the fact that it *is* madness. Effective though Ouologuem's pornographic description may be, it is not, one might point out, altogether realistic, neither here nor in *Bibles du sexe*, nor is it linguistically rational, and all that his ellipsis points serve to do is to suggest that the reader, his imagination heated up by the descriptive extravagance, should carry the scene on to that erotic end most pleasing to himself. "A flowing cup—Awa—a lavish board!" She becomes for Chevalier virtually what his medium, his language, is for Ouologuem: "An Eve with frantic loins, she cajoled the man, kissed him, bit him, scratched him, whipped him, sucked his nose ears throat, armpits navel and member so voluptuously that the administrator, discovering [like Baudelaire?] the ardent landscape of this feminine kingdom, kept her there day after day, and, his soul in ecstasy, lived a fanatical, panting, frenzied passion" (p. 57). There may be, as at least one reviewer has suggested (John Thompson in the *New York Review of Books*, 23 September 1971), a considerable admixture of irony here in Ouologuem's pornography, but there is also, somewhere behind the irony, a straight face: if Ouologuem were *only* ironic, we should not have been given *Les milles et une bibles du sexe*—though admittedly it is most difficult to know, in reading *Bound to Violence*, when we are looking on a straight (albeit leering) face and when only on another mask.

The paradigm of this technique of doing deliberate violence to the language, of distorting syntax and disordering the senses, of jamming together images that, once coupled, result in the most irrational of similes and metaphors, comes in the description by Sankolo of his drugged and delirious hallucinations, his nightmare journey through the forest of deranged senses.

"A lion pants, he has come a long way: he stands before me. He roars, sticks out his tongue, walks away backwards and vanishes over the horizon. He perches on a treetop, turns into a superb pink panther with fiery glowing jaws, licked by flames:
"It is the sun that is setting. . . .
"My eyes aim at the infinite. The sun goes to sleep. It is still far away. It's afraid of falling. It's a timorous pink panther, trembling behind the dunes and the blue valleys. My headache is a barnyard. Ferocious. With its cries, its familiar sights, its sudden flapping of wings, its squawking. At the edge of the barnyard begins a desert of greenery that rasps my mucous membrane." (pp. 104-05)

Under the effect of this surrealistic hypertension, the senses no longer mediate between an external, objective world and interior consciousness: they become the point of frenzied merger rather than of separation, and, assaulted by an excess of sensations, they fuse everything into one indistinguishable mess—or, if one prefers, into a mystic union —of exterior fact and interior consciousness.

"The night crushes me so with its procession of indefinable sensations that I *become* the wind, the silence of nature, its fears, its darkness, its expectation. . . . I pace on springy legs. Spongy legs, my body sinks into them, I struggle to tear myself away from them. . . . My eyes are two round onions. Tears dance in them but never roll down my cheeks. . . .
"The landscape dances. My eyelashes paint it, cut it up into needles, into granite, into spurs eroded by the wind, into masses of foliage. . . . Swarms of twinkling sparks collapse into a hole of aching clouds, jostled and gesticulating, then rigid, stiff with fatigue." (p. 106)

While Sankolo's description provides the paradigm of sensory derangement and of surrealistic intensification to a supersensory level, a number of other descriptive passages operate according to the same technique: for example, the vicious subjugation of the population by the Saifs ("the Crown forced men to swallow life as a boa swallows a stinking antelope," p. 5); the very fine description of the coupling of Kassoumi and Tambira, whose love is seen—and this is almost unique in Ouologuem—as something more tender than violent (pp. 36-43); the account of "the practice of infibulation (the sewing up of the vagina)," carried out with sadistic delight and designed to insure virginity (pp. 47-48); the description of the Saif exercising his "right of the first night" by blasting "the barrier of stitches which, luckily for Tambira, had rotted" (p. 49); Sankolo's address to his member as he delightedly, slaveringly watches a couple making love ("yes, there, taste her flesh, her real flesh, make me vomit the delight of her orgasm," p. 91); etc., etc. It has been suggested by a number of commentators (most prominently and most often by Léopold Senghor) that African literary art is more often surrealistic than realistic, and Ouologuem implies, by the very fact and nature of his bizarre, intense, highly colored prose, that there is an emotional surrealism inherent in encounters of sex and violence to which language, if it would be adequately descriptive, must accommodate itself. We see the surrealism associated with violence for example when Wampoulo and Kratonga murder the French governor Vandame:

"Suddenly Wampoulo clasped his shoulders and shook them so frantically that Vandame's neck swung and broke.

"Quicker than speech, his arms waltzed above him, then rowed him softlier home, to the Artful Creator.

"Blood spurted from the nape of his neck like reluctant rubies grasped by a beetle. His eyeballs like frightened beads, Vandame drank a dewdrop from a blade of grass. He was a righteous man."[19]

The duty of violence that provides the motive and title for Ouologuem's book is not, in passages like this, limited to false images of Africa and Africans—his subject and substance—but extends itself to include style and language as well and set ways of seeing and saying things. Only by this radical verbal and perceptual revising, Ouologuem implies, will we escape from the myths and falsifications that have

[19] P. 115. The account of Vandame's death is entirely different in the French original. After playing a game of William Tell, shooting at a crumpled-up paper on Vandame's head, Kratonga finishes him: "Kratonga visa de nouveau. Le pistolet aboya. Un petit trou, rond, apparut sur le front du gouverneur, près du sourcil droit, à la naissance de la racine nasale. Ses yeux s'entrouvrirent, le rapport glissa à terre, il fit un pas pour se relever, comme s'il voulait tenter de s'enfuir. Puis il s'affala doucement, et, un instant raide, tournoya sur lui-même, bavant contre le sable et tombant à la renverse, sur le ventre. Ses pieds raclèrent le roc, on entendit des borborygmes sortir du fond de sa gorge, puis ses poumons se vidèrent en un long rale saccadé. C'était un juste" (p. 133). (This change in the way in which Vandame dies leads to a minor discrepancy in the English version: the pistol that is placed near Vandame's body in both versions to explain his death works well enough in the French but could hardly account for the broken neck in the English.) I am assured that Ouologuem himself rewrote the passage after the translation was done and that he made several other small changes after reading the translation. This is the justification for doing a stylistic analysis of writing in translation: Ouologuem satisfied himself as much with the version in English as with the version in French.

In this same general passage—but only in the English, not in the French—Ouologuem introduced into the translation a number of apparent allusions to English and American literature (some of which remain as inexplicable as his borrowing from Graham Greene): "the awful daring of a moment's surrender. . . . Then blood shook his heart" (Waste Land); "There was no end, only addition" (Four Quartets); "because he could not stop for death" (Emily Dickinson). These make little sense in Ouologuem's text—especially the Emily Dickinson—but they provide another instance of the oddity and inexplicability of his writing practice.

arisen to surround and obscure the experience of Africa over the centuries.

This stylistic vitality in *Bound to Violence*, like the book's thematic insistence, is regularly achieved at the expense of both plot and characterization. Few novels are quite so poor in sequential plot (i.e., a pattern of logically and thematically consecutive events) as *Bound to Violence*: in so far as plot exists at all in the book it is insignificant, and this is also more or less the case with characterization. The reviewer who said of *Le devoir de violence* that the "characters live and suffer and are like real living people"[20] could hardly have offered a more misplaced observation. Ouologuem's figures suffer all right—a suffering that is described in the most resplendent, the most astonishing, and the most baroque of language and imagery—but they are not the kind of living and lovable Dickensian characters implied by the reviewer's formulation. To return to a point made earlier, *Bound to Violence* is arranged to satiric ends and is largely a negative achievement, destructive and corrective; this accounts not only for the scarcity of positive, human characterization but for the disjointed and episodic organization of the book as well. What structure there is in the novel is built on repetitions, designed to show, for the "négraille" in particular, that "plus ça change, plus c'est la même chose," and the figures who act these repetitions out in their lives assume, as a result of treading the same paths again and again, a certain generalized, symbolic character.

The story that Ouologuem tells in a series of significant, symbolic episodes as a compressed history of Africa—each episode a repeat in essence of those which have gone before—is a tale of slavery in many and various guises, an omnipresent fact in human history: women in *Bound to Violence* are enslaved by men and men by their passion for women; Africans are enslaved by the false images con-

[20] Hans Maes-Jelinek, in *African Literature Today*, No. 4 (1970), p. 55.

cocted by European anthropologists and the guardians of "négritude"; Sankolo is enslaved by drugs and sex and by a pair of masters who shunt him back and forth between them as a living corpse, a "zombi"; Raymond Spartacus is enslaved by Saif ben Isaac al-Heit, who gives him the mere show of a political power that is really manipulated by Saif; and the "négraille" are enslaved by everyone—African notables and Arab traders, German ethnologists and French administrators. It is in the succession of Saifs (from the consolidation of their empire in 1202 right down to 1947) and in the relation of Saifs to the "négraille" that Ouologuem gives us his paradigm of slavery which he proceeds to conjugate and dramatize in all the separate, historical instances of the condition. Though there are other slavemasters in *Bound to Violence*, it is the Saifs (Ouologuem's name for the rulers of the "ancient Nakem Empire," identified on the book-flap as "the great medieval empire of Mali," though in details it resembles Mali less than it does the Songhay Empire—i.e., the empire around Gao that succeeded Mali) who most fully embody and express the lust to define the lives and to control the destinies of other men, as, in reverse, the "négraille" epitomize those who are defined and controlled and enslaved. In the hereditary line of manipulative, cynical, ingeniously cruel Saifs Ouologuem shows us the complete tyrant, the politician perfected, the epitome of the slavemaster, and the people on either side of this wretched story, the "négraille" or the Saifs, come to be not so much uniquely themselves as they are figures in a shared and representative destiny: they are all, psychologically and socially, symbolically and literally, either slaves or enslavers; and that, Ouologuem implies, has been the timeless division of human life in African history.

In his first two chapters, both of them short and tightly compacted ("The Legend of the Saifs" and "Ecstasy and Agony"), Ouologuem presents the grand sweep in time (1202-1901) and in space (symbolically all of Africa) that will provide the historical background and the thematic roots for the twentieth-century story that occupies the remainder of his book. "Against this background of horror," Ouologuem says, in the *griot* voice he assumes in recounting the Saif's legend, "the destiny of Saif Isaac al-Heit stands out most illustriously; rising far above the common lot, it endowed the legend of the Saifs with the splendor in which the dreamers of African unity sun themselves to this day" (p. 5). But whether the story of this first and greatest of the Saifs "(God refresh his couch)" is "truth or invention" cannot now be certainly determined because "the memory of this past—glorious as it was—has survived . . . solely thanks to the Arab historians and to the oral tradition of the Africans" (p. 8)—all of which is legend and much of which may be myth and fantasy as well. It is to this question—the authenticity of traditional African history—that *Devoir de violence* addresses itself; it is an important question since "the legend of Saif Isaac al-Heit still haunts Black romanticism and the political thinking of the notables in a good many republics" (p. 8). The ingenious method in which Ouologuem probes the authenticity of the legend is to rewrite history in the voice, in the tone, and in the language of the *griots* and the Arab historians themselves, but of course he adopts these masks, and others, ironically so that events are seen with a twist—or two or three twists—given to their significance.

The profession of the *griot* is unknown in the Western world with its profusion of written documents. "En Afrique Noire," D. T. Niane explains in *Recherches sur l'empire du Mali au moyen âge*,[21] "il faut faire la distinction entre la tradition populaire, véhicule des légendes historiques, et ce que nous appellerons 'la tradition-archives': celle-ci pour l'Ouest Africain est détenue par ceux que l'on appelle communément 'Griots.' . . . le Griot a été le livre vivant des souverains de l'Ouest Africain." When Ouologuem refers to

[21] Djibril Tamsir Niane, *Recherches sur l'empire du Mali au moyen âge* (Conakry: République de Guinée, Ministère de l'Information et du Tourisme, 1962), p. 5.

"the oral tradition of the Africans," and when he orally re-
constructs the history of Africa, it is in both these traditions,
popular and archivist, that he is working. An excellent example of the popular tradition, too long to reproduce here
but stunningly like what Ouologuem describes at the beginning of *Devoir de violence*, is to be found in Boubou
Hama's three-volume autobiography called *Kotia-Nima*.[22]
Boubou Hama says that in the evenings he and the other
children of the family listened, "suspendus à ses lèvres," to
their grandmother—not a *griot* in any professional sense,
but a family elder—as she told the stories of their people.
"Elle nous exposait le système de l'univers sonraï [i.e.,
Songhay]. Elle nous enseignait la mystique africaine" (1,
13). More particularly, however, "Diollo Birma nous enseignait aussi l'histoire du village" (p. 14), and it is this account, covering seven pages of text, that resembles so strikingly, in spirit and in detail, the history in "The Legend of
the Saifs" and "Ecstasy and Agony" (in fact, Diollo Birma's
story refers several times to warriors from Bandiagara,
Ouologuem's home village, to whom she gives the title
"Sofa"—cf. Ouologuem's "Saif"). On the evidence of *Devoir
de violence*, it seems more than likely that as a child Ouologuem, like Boubou Hama, heard such stories as he tells
(and perhaps heightens a bit) in his novel—stories that
would have been, again as with Boubou Hama, presented
as family history, as village history, as the history of the
people, Songhay or Dogon, and that the child when grown
up might imagine as the symbolic history of Africa.

In addition to this popular tradition, there is much also
of the professional *griot* in *Bound to Violence*. The history
of Saif Isaac al-Heit, for example, is apparently modelled
on the life of Sundiata Keita,[23] the ruler who first unified
and solidified the Empire of Mali, as that life is recorded in

[22] Boubou Hama, *Kotia-Nima*, 3 vols. (Paris: Présence Africaine,
1968-1969), 1, 13-20.

[23] D. T. Niane, *Sundiata: An Epic of Old Mali*, trans. G. D. Pickett
(London: Longmans, 1965).

238

*Sundiata* by D. T. Niane from the lips of a present-day *griot*, Mamoudou Kouyaté, who begins his story with pride: "I am a griot. It is I, Djeli Mamoudou Kouyaté, son of Bintou Kouyaté and Djeli Kedian Kouyaté, master in the art of eloquence" (p. 1). Robert Pageard's praise of Niane's achievement in the *Sundiata*—he has, Pageard says, reproduced "l'autorité, la superbe, la fertilité imaginative du griot"—fits Ouologuem's achievement equally well, and what Pageard goes on to say seems more applicable to what Ouologuem does in *Devoir de violence* than to Niane in *Sundiata*: "D. T. Niane ne se contente pas de traduit fidèlement . . . le récit, plein de merveilleux, du griot traditionalist: il l'illustre, de sa connaissance intime de l'Afrique contemporaine, utilise les données de l'histoire et de la géographie, enrichit la légende de ses observations personnelles. Il fait ainsi œuvre d'historien autant que d'artiste."[24] Ouologuem's fidelity to the *griot* tradition is, of course, heavily qualified since, in adopting the *griot* mask, he shows an ironic attitude both toward the manner of the *griot* and toward his subject; but then there is more than one traditional tone for the *griot*, and Ouologuem might be seen, even in his grotesque humor and his mad mockery, to be following one of those traditions. "On appelle du terme générique de griots," according to Bokar N'Diayé in his discussion of the *griot* caste, "les musiciens, chroniqueurs, généalogistes et pitres [i.e., clowns, buffoons] qu'on rencontre dans toutes les sociétés africains et en particulier au Mali."[25] That Ouologuem is speaking through the masks of musician, chronicler, genealogist, and buffoon, of historian, poet, and story-teller ("les *Griots* . . . sont, en même temps, historiologues, poètes et conteurs"),[26] does not make it any

[24] Robert Pageard, "Soundiata Keita et la tradition orale," *Présence Africaine*, NS No. 35 (1er trimestre 1961), p. 51.

[25] Bokar N'Diayé, *Les castes au Mali* (Bamako: Éditions Populaires, 1970), p. 87.

[26] Léopold Senghor, *Liberté I* (Paris: Éditions du Seuil, 1964), p. 207.

easier for the reader to pin down the historic reality behind the fabulous myth or even to determine exactly what Ouologuem, as a revisionist historian, takes to be the reality.

To complete the sources for his legendary history of Nakem, and to confuse somewhat more the reader bewildered already by the many different masks and the various possible reconstructions of history, Ouologuem turns to the histories of the Songhay Empire written by Arab historians, with their overlay of Islamic fatalism, in the sixteenth and seventeenth centuries. The *Tarikh el-Fettach* and the *Tarikh es-Soudan*,[27] both mentioned in *Devoir de violence* —these too are versions of African history, constructs rising out of the African experience, and it is in the confluence of the Arab histories, the extended-family and village traditions, and the *griot* legends that *Devoir de violence* finds its complex and distinctive voice, always, because Ouologuem is primarily a satirist, exercised at an ironic pitch. "Parmi ceux qui firent cette déclaration à son sujet," we are told in the *Tarikh el-Fettach*, "il convient de citer le cheikh Abderrahman Es-Soyoûti, le cheikh Mohammed ben Abdelkerîm El-Meghîli, le cheikh Chamharoûch de la race des génies et le chérif hassanide Moulaï El-Abbâs, prince de la Mecque: Dieu leur fasse miséricorde à tous!" (p. 15). Ouologuem too, looking momentarily out from the mask of Arab historian, invokes the same god in the same terms, though not, perhaps, with quite the same sincerity, in his description of Isaac al-Heit's triumphs in *Devoir de violence*, and he incidentally helps himself at the same time to

[27] These are both available in French translations from the turn of the century: *Tarikh el-Fettach, ou Chronique du chercheur*. . . , "par Mahmoûd Kâti ben El-Hadj El-Motaouakkel Kâti et l'un de ses petit-fils," traduction française par O. Houdas et M. Delafosse (Paris: Librairie d'Amérique et d'Orient, Adrien-Maisonneuve, 1964 [photographic reproduction "de l'édition originale datée de 1913-1914"]); and *Tarikh es-Soudan*, "par Abderrahman ben Abdallah ben 'Imran ben 'Amir es-Sa'di," traduit de l'Arabe par O. Houdas (Paris: Librairie d'Amérique et d'Orient, Adrien-Maisonneuve, 1964 ["reproduction photographique de l'édition original datée de 1898-1900"]).

every one of the exotic and colorful names preceding the invocation: "Tour à tour, redoutable, il défit les Berbères, les Maures et les Touareg, reconnut le cheikh Abderrahman Es Soyoûti, secourut le cheikh Mohammed ben Abdelkerîm El-Meghîli, le cheikh Chamharoûch de la race des Génies, et le chérif hassanide Moulaï El-Abbâs, prince de la Mecque: Dieu leur fasse miséricorde à tous" (p. 13).

This stylistic pastiche, which combines elements from the historical traditions of family and village, from *griot* "archives," and from Arab chronicles, is matched in *Bound to Violence* by a geographical and cultural pastiche, the elements of which Ouologuem draws from all over Africa; here again he freely mixes the real with the imaginary and the historic with the mythic to produce a new historic amalgam with a new interpretation. The population of the Nakem Empire, Ouologuem says, near the beginning of the book, was formed into "groups of varying sizes, separated from one another by all manner of tribes—Radingues, Fulani, Gonda, nomadic Berbers, Ngodo" (p. 4); later these people, "scattered over the savannas bordering on Equatorial Africa," suffered, he tells us, from "the raids of the Masai, the Zulus, the Jaga" (p. 13). The "savannas bordering on Equatorial Africa" are inhabited by many different peoples—but not by the Zulus, who are in South Africa, and if Ouologuem's savannas are in West Africa, as I assume they are, then not by the Masai or the Jaga either (both are situated in Kenya); nor does any place in Africa know the Radingues, the Gonda, or the Ngodo. The Fulani, however, and the nomadic Berbers, like the Tukulör and the Tuareg, mentioned elsewhere (pp. 9 and 10), are real peoples and do, in fact, inhabit the savannas in West Africa (with the Berbers going farther north into the "bitter deserts" and into North Africa). Moreover, the name "Gonda" is not far removed from "Donga," and "Ngodo" looks like a rearrangement of the letters in "Dogon"—which brings us back to the author of the book, who, according to the book-flap, is "the descendant of a Dogon family." Mixing together

241

the real, the imaginary that carries an echo of the real, and the purely imaginary, Ouologuem brings the reader step by step from a verifiable history that no one can deny to an acceptance of Ouologuem's personal vision, or revision, of the African experience. Just as he takes names from the *Tarikh el-Fettach* and throws them together with names of his own fabrication, so Ouologuem mixes historic fact, imaginative fiction, and apocalyptic vision into a maddening blend that calls up echoes from African history in the reader's mind, tantalizing half-identifications that tempt him to find all this on a map and in ancient chronicles, and that lead him in the end to accept, more or less, Ouologuem's drastic and imaginative revision of history. And by bringing peoples from South Africa, from East Africa, from North Africa, from West Africa, and from imaginary Africa to play a part in his drama, Ouologuem expands the significance of local history to a continental circumference. *Le devoir de violence* is thus not the private autobiography of an individual, nor the representative autobiography of a people, but the symbolic autobiography of a continent.

The history of Africa, according to Ouologuem, as far back as the historian can see and right up to the present moment of independence, has been dominated by the fact of slavery—blacks enslaving blacks, Arabs enslaving blacks, whites enslaving blacks—nor will the African future produce anything different, he suggests, until those involved acknowledge the unpleasant realities of the past. "Après tout," Ouologuem asks rhetorically in his *Lettre à la France Nègre*, "quel Africain ignore qu'avant l'Homme Blanc, il y eut également le colonialisme des Notables noirs et celui de la Conquête arabe?" (p. 90). And to simplify the subject matter of his "Lettre aux non-racistes" in the same book, he undertakes to describe the interior of Africa "avant l'Homme Blanc." In those distant times, he says (and the situation is not much different now: it has only taken on a new color), there were no French around, there was no middle class and no working class, there was only the Saif and the "négraille," only the enslaver and the enslaved, only "les intelligents" and "les crétins": "il n'y avait que des empires et des empereurs, et point de prolétaires à l'horizon. Ça et là se dressaient quelques hommes, des individus. . . . Le reste était une forêt vierge de peuplades enchevetrées et indéfrisables: les crétins. A coté de ces crétins, il y avait les intelligents qui vendaient les crétins—grassement—sur les côtes" (p. 61). Ouologuem would have his reader recognize, as his *Lettre* and *Bound to Violence* demonstrate, that there are many kinds of slavery—economic, literary, philosophical, and, especially, psychological—besides the relatively vulgar form of slavery that is physical. The African today, according to Ouologuem, is more likely to be enslaved by false images and by economics than by chains; his freedom will come only in destroying those images and in seeing that slavery has less to do with color than with exploitation.

Fritz Shrobenius, the German anthropologist in *Bound to Violence*, an idiot but also crafty in his own way, cranks out, with the connivance of Saif and his son, a load of false philosophical and artistic images of Africa that prove immensely profitable to him (thus the economics) if not to the Africans, who are betrayed more deeply into slavery by these very images of their own lavishly proclaimed past glory. "The true face of Africa," Shrobenius tells his dupes in Europe, is to be found in the ancient Empire of Nakem, "a society marked by wisdom, beauty, prosperity, order, nonviolence, and humanism, and it is here that we must seek the true cradle of Egyptian civilization."[28] Saif and his

---

[28] P. 94. Shrobenius, as various reviewers have pointed out, is obviously based on Leo Frobenius, the German Africanist of the beginning of this century (Shrobenius arrives in Nakem in 1910). The phrasing of this quotation, however, suggests that Ouologuem is stalking some black game in addition to Frobenius. Cheikh Anta Diop, the Senegalese anthropologist-cum-historian-cum-philosopher, in *L'unité culturelle de l'Afrique Noire*, divides all human history and culture into the "southern cradle" and the "northern cradle," "le berceau Méridional" and "le berceau Nordique," and ancient Egypt, he says, was the direct

243

son, "reeling off spirituality by the yard" (p. 87), keep
Shrobenius supplied with the fake artifacts and the equally
fake "magico-religious, cosmological, and mythical symbolism" (p. 95) that will simultaneously astound Europe
and delight the "négraille" while plunging the latter ever
deeper into misery. "Thus drooling, Shrobenius . . . mysti-
fied the people of his own country who in their enthusiasm
raised him to a lofty Sorbonnical chair, while on the other
hand he exploited the sentimentality of the coons, only too
pleased to hear from the mouth of a white man that Africa
was 'the womb of the world and the cradle of civilization.'
. . . O Lord, a tear for the childlike good nature of the niggertrash! Have pity, O Lord! . . . *Makari! makari!*" (pp. 94-
95). This is only one of the false images of Africa—there are
more, many more—that, Ouologuem claims, enslave the
African and to which the African, Ouologuem, and his reader all owe a duty of violence. In his novel Ouologuem performs his duty by rubbing the noses of these fantasies in the
dirt of historic reality so that the African nation may know
itself: what it has really been and who has really made it as
it is. The new image, ironically, shows a pan-African unity

---

ancestor of black African culture. "Dans le domaine moral," Diop says
of his southern and Egyptian cradle, there is "un idéal de paix, de
justice, de bonté, un optimisme que élimine toute notion de culpabilité
ou de péché originel dans les créations et métaphysique" (*L'unité
culturelle de l'Afrique Noire* [Paris: Présence Africaine, 1959], p. 185).
In the northern cradle, on the other hand, a simple and total opposite
reigns: "Un idéal de guerre, de violence, de crime, de conquête hé-
rité de la vie nomade avec comme corollaire un sentiment de culpabilité ou de péché originel qui fait batir des systèmes religieux ou
métaphysique pessimistes . . ." (*ibid.*). Ouologuem might agree about
the vices of the northern cradle, but he makes deliberate mockery of
Diop and others like him who, as he feels, delude themselves, and try
to delude others, with *négritude* nonsense about a perfect African past
of peace, justice, goodness, wisdom, beauty, etc. They all, Ouologuem
implies, like Shrobenius, have private reasons for serving up this glorious foolishness.

244

too, not, however, a unity, as Cheikh Anta Diop and Kwame Nkrumah would have it, born of brotherhood and compassion and family love extended to the limits of the continent, but one born of greed and political guile, of hypocrisy and violence, of the relation between the man enslaved and the man who enslaves.

In "Dawn," the final section of *Bound to Violence*, Ouologuem once more changes his mask, his style and literary form, to give his reader a philosophic overview of the symbolic history enacted in the seven hundred and fifty years of the Nakem Empire. From the *griot* epic of the first two sections, passing through the novelistic treatment of the present in the long third section ("The Night of the Giants"), Ouologuem finally arrives at the philosophic dialogue that constitutes the final section and that provides commentary on the drama that has transpired in the preceding pages. Before Bishop Henry, the Christian apologist, and Saif ben Isaac al-Heit, Saif of Saifs, the most cunning, cynical, and tyrannical in the whole line of Saifs, settle down to their game of chess, which sums up Nakem history, and to their philosophic dialogue, which comments on that history, Bishop Henry tells Saif a story that is like a compressed image of the entire book. He says he wandered into a movie house where they were showing a picture based on the history of Nakem. At first he could not grasp what was going on, except that there was some plot or some plan and also much violence. Then he came to see that if he could understand the nature of violence itself, if he could understand the principle animating all this action, he would not need to follow any consecutive plot, for every act would be, in its own way, a manifestation of the one same principle. And so in *Bound to Violence*, once the reader has the key, the understanding of slavery everywhere and always, the history of Nakem, an epitome of the history of all Africa, falls into place, allowing the reader to enter the history anywhere—beginning, middle, or end—and still comprehend its significance, just as Bishop Henry comes in in the middle of the picture but picks out the principle that explains.

The philosophic contest between Bishop Henry, the man of religion, and Saif, the man of politics, assumes the form, as Gerald Moore has pointed out,[29] of a dialogue about freedom, taking, for historical text and as the symbolic case, the seven-hundred-and-fifty-year experience of Nakem-Ziuko: freedom—what it is, who has it, how it is won and how it is limited or lost. In their dialogue as in their chess game, and as also in this whole novel, they play out the history of Nakem, in which the reader, like Ouologuem, tries to see the face of the future of Africa: "the legend of the Saifs, a legend in which the future seems to seek itself in the night of time . . ." (p. 167). It is a profoundly sad conclusion to which Ouologuem comes—relieved only by the intensity, the energy, the brilliance of his coming to that conclusion— since the future finds itself in history and the history of Africa is synonymous with the legend of the Saifs. In the *Sundiata* Mamoudou Kouyaté says, "We griots are depositaries of the knowledge of the past. But whoever knows the history of a country can read its future" (p. 41), and Ouologuem agrees that that is all too true. "Often," he says, as Bishop Henry and Saif continue into the African night their game inspired by love and politics, "the soul desires to dream the echo of happiness, an echo that has no past" (p. 181). The soul desires to and it does, deluding itself with visions of glory because it has not wanted to look into history, has not been willing to understand what the past is, or that the past continues to live in the present; it deludes itself, Ouologuem says scornfully, with a mere echo, a sound reverberating with such phrases as "Pan-Africa" and "African unity" (p. 5). "But projected into the world," Ouologuem goes on, "one cannot help recalling that Saif, mourned three million times, is forever reborn to history beneath the hot ashes of more than thirty African repub-

[29] "Action and Freedom in Two African Novels," *The Conch*, 2 (March 1970), pp. 21-28.

246

lics" (pp. 181-82). With that reflection, both ironic and melancholy, Ouologuem brings to a close his symbolic autobiography of the African people and the African continent, where, according to his vision, a history of continuous and surpassing human cruelty has been enacted in a setting of almost infinite natural sensuality.

# CHAPTER VI

# Politics, Creativity, and Exile

AUTOBIOGRAPHY, as a number of observers have remarked, has been, over the past twenty years, the finest literature to come from creative writers of South Africa. For various reasons—social, political, and psychological—South African writers of our time have found autobiography to be the form best adapted to expressing, recreating, or reacting to their experience. In what is no doubt a corollary to this preeminence of autobiography as a literary form in South Africa, "African" and "Colored" writers from that nation have produced a body of autobiographical writing that is the most vital, the most intense and energetic that we have from any part of Africa. Autobiography has served these writers well, and they, in turn, have made a remarkable literature out of the accounts of their lives. If we hold autobiography from South Africa up against Gikuyu or Ibo or autobiography from elsewhere in Africa, we shall, I think, discover something of similarity but much more of difference, and this difference is determined very largely by the different quality of experience, the different texture of life, the different forms of living possible in South Africa. In other words, the shape of autobiography here, as everywhere, is determined by the shape of the life that informs it (forms it, as it were, from within); life, for the black South African, has a particular and peculiar shape, a very distinctive shape indeed.

Gikuyu autobiographers, as I have suggested in Chapter II, all seem to write the same autobiography: for them there is one archetypal Gikuyu life lived in turn by each successive embodiment of Gikuyu spirit; to describe one embodiment is to describe them all. Likewise in the case of South

African writers, a single pattern, naturally with individual variations, emerges from the autobiographies of Ezekiel Mphahlele, Peter Abrahams, Naboth Mokgatle, Alfred Hutchinson, Todd Matshikiza, and Bloke Modisane.[1] Almost as if they were following a single blueprint for writing autobiography, these men all describe variations on a single plan; no doubt this is so because something very like a blueprint was imposed on their lives in South Africa. Moreover, the autobiographical writings of Lewis Nkosi, Dugmore Boetie, Gerard Sekoto, Noni Jabavu, Chief Albert Luthuli, Clements Kadalie, and "Dora Thizwilondi Magidi"[2]—all of them in other ways quite unlike the mono-patterned autobiographies of Mphahlele et al.—serve to confirm and reinforce the notion that the repeated pattern in South African autobiography is the result of an omnipresent pattern in South African life. But at this point the comparison between Gikuyu autobiography, with its one great story of the children of Gikuyu and Mumbi, and South African autobiog-

[1] Ezekiel Mphahlele, *Down Second Avenue* (London: Faber & Faber, 1959); Peter Abrahams, *Tell Freedom: Memories of Africa* (New York: Alfred A. Knopf, 1954); Naboth Mokgatle, *The Autobiography of an Unknown South African* (Berkeley and Los Angeles: Univ. of California Press, 1971); Alfred Hutchinson, *Road to Ghana* (New York: John Day Co., 1960); Todd Matshikiza, *Chocolates for My Wife* (London: Hodder & Stoughton, 1961); Bloke (William) Modisane, *Blame Me on History* (London: Thames & Hudson, 1963). References hereafter in the text will be to these editions.

[2] Lewis Nkosi, *Home and Exile* (London: Longmans, Green & Co., 1965); Dugmore Boetie, *Familiarity is the Kingdom of the Lost* (New York: E. P. Dutton & Co., 1969); Gerard Sekoto, "Autobiography," *Présence Africaine*, NS No. 69 (1st Quarter 1969), pp. 188-94; Noni Jabavu, *Drawn in Colour: African Contrasts* (London: John Murray, 1960) and *The Ochre People: Scenes from a South African Life* (New York: St. Martin's Press, 1963); Albert Luthuli, *Let My People Go* (New York: McGraw-Hill, 1962); Clements Kadalie, *My Life and the ICU: The Autobiography of a Black Trade Unionist in South Africa* (New York: Humanities Press, 1970); John Blacking, *Black Background: The Childhood of a South African Girl; Based on the Autobiography of Dora Thizwilondi Magidi* [pseud.] (New York: Abelard-Schuman, 1964). References in the text are to these editions.

raphy, with its single pattern of exile and recollection, breaks down entirely, for the pattern of South African autobiography is not determined by any internal social cohesion or social logic, not by what I have called social synecdoche, nor by a cultural heritage that extends from the present individual back through legendary ancestors to a divine source. Rather the pattern is determined by precisely the opposite—by a social disunion, by a cultural and political dichotomy. The classic pattern of South African autobiography describes a progressive alienation that, forced to the extreme, becomes spiritual and physical exile.

Looking back at South Africa from just over the horizon of exile in London or Accra or Lagos, Abrahams, Mokgatle, Matshikiza, Modisane, Hutchinson, and Mphahlele all tell the story of their alienation from the land of their birth—one story, one pattern, one climax. That climax figures both as a structural element in the work of art and as a logical conclusion to life in South Africa: with the same structural inevitability, exile ends the one and the other, the autobiography and the South African existence. Any of these writers could be taken as typical, but the most typical would have to be Ezekiel Mphahlele, for whom exile provides not only the structural element but also the thematic content in his autobiography and in several of his other books as well, most notably *The African Image* and *The Wanderers*. Exile, as a literal fact and a spiritual condition, has been at the center of Mphahlele's work in autobiography, in literary-social criticism, in fiction, and even in one poem. While the other writers have gone on to different themes or have fallen silent because exile has deprived them of their natural subject matter, Mphahlele has made exile and wandering his subject and has returned to it again and again in a variety of forms. He has produced a literature that has about it very little sense of place or setting; it is not set in South Africa nor in Nigeria nor in Kenya nor in England but in the mind of the man forced out of his homeland to wander, forever and aimlessly, as an alien. Mphahlele's

250

focus falls on the internal and the psychological, on the condition of rootlessness: its causes, its significance, its effects on the individual, its possible benefits and its inevitable cost. Though he pursues this theme more exhaustively than the other South African writers, however, Mphahlele is doing something different from them only in degree, not in kind: he fixes almost entirely on an experience that they all knew and that they all, at least once, described.

On the last page of *Tell Freedom*, in the culmination of a pattern that was to become standard and classic in the life stories of South Africans, Peter Abrahams says, "For me, personally, life in South Africa had come to an end. . . . I had to go or be forever lost. I needed, not friends, not gestures, but my manhood. And the need was desperate" (p. 370). Whether they escaped from South Africa by boat as Abrahams did, or by train as Modisane did, or by plane as Mphahlele, Mokgatle, and Matshikiza did, or by all three as Hutchinson did, the writers who, in the next ten and twenty years, followed Abrahams in getting out, invariably echoed his account of the departure and the political-personal circumstances that forced it. "Then the train entered and puffed its way out of Mafeking," Bloke Modisane says on the final page of *Blame Me on History*, describing the same overland journey to Rhodesia and Tanganyika, in March 1959, that Alfred Hutchinson had taken some five months earlier; "and South Africa and everything I had known, loved and hated remained behind me. I was out of South Africa" (p. 311). At the railway station in Johannesburg, Modisane, who was forced by the political environment of South Africa "to choose permanent exile from the country of my birth" (p. 191), was seen off by Lewis Nkosi, the playwright and *Drum* journalist, who was soon to be in exile himself. In a collection of autobiographical and critical essays published in 1965, *Home and Exile*, Nkosi not only commented on but gave a name to the corporate experience of so many South African writers, including himself and Modisane.

251

Naboth Mokgatle, temperamentally more inclined to politics than to creative literature, nevertheless found himself forced into exile (in 1954), just as his more literary compatriots had been before him and were to be after him. Flying out of South Africa with no passport and no visa and with only the most tenuous of reasons to be going to a trades union conference in Rumania, Mokgatle could hardly believe his good luck in being released by the police at the airport, and once in Europe he had to fight long and hard to maintain that luck. Getting out, as he describes the experience—as indeed Peter Abrahams, Bloke Modisane, Ezekiel Mphahlele, and Todd Matshikiza describe it—was the single thing of greatest importance. "I followed the other passengers into the plane," Mokgatle says, showing the same apprehension that Modisane and Hutchinson felt that the Special Branch Police might any moment pluck them off the train or plane; "but I did not feel sure that I was leaving South Africa, my country, my home, the soil which gave birth to me and all my ancestors before me, the country in which I was deprived of dignity, human rights and all respect" (*Autobiography of an Unknown South African*, p. 330). Because he records the details of his life chronologically and without the artist's eye for significant detail or the philosopher's need to find a meaning in his experience, Mokgatle's book is largely lacking in structure and pattern. While it is true that his autobiography does lead up to exile and to political asylum in London, there is no reason why it should be London rather than Paris or Moscow. Mokgatle describes the human need for escape from oppression, but it is not escape to anything in particular. His escape *from* rather than *to* is not the artist's escape, motivated by a search for conditions in which he can not only live but create.

Todd Matshikiza, the composer responsible for the music of *King Kong*, which Mphahlele calls "a great jazz opera,"[3]

[3] Ezekiel Mphahlele, *The African Image* (New York: Frederick A. Praeger, 1962), p. 34.

turns the pattern of South African autobiography inside out in *Chocolates for My Wife*, but his subject still remains, in spite of the book's many differences, the typical "home and exile" of Nkosi's title and of the other autobiographies. Instead of concluding his book with a climactic departure from South Africa, Matshikiza reverses the order to begin with his arrival in London: "Arrival. The English Channel dressed up in the most beautiful blue and white, the most gorgeous of satins as my family and I flew across towards London Airport. I kissed her, the English Channel. I kissed her each time the jet plane dipped a wing, a nose, a dive to give us a glimpse of great London where we were heading" (p. 7). Matshikiza continues in the same manner with a series of impressions and sketches of London and England and of English and South Africans, both black and white, in England; he reverts in memory to scenes from South Africa and ends, after a comparatively long section about police and jail in Johannesburg, with a brief return to London. In all this there is little apparent structural logic—simply a scene here and a memory there, an impression of this and an idle recall of that, riffs and improvisations blown on a variety of momentary subjects but composing nothing very coherent.

In another way, too, Matshikiza's little book differs from *Down Second Avenue* or *Tell Freedom*, from *Road to Ghana* or *Blame Me on History*: it is not written as an account of and an exercise in finding oneself or as an account of the circumstances that required leaving South Africa (though those circumstances are doubtless implied by some of the experiences narrated in the "home" part of the book); and *Chocolates for My Wife* is not written to himself or to an outside world with little knowledge of South Africa. Beginning in London and mostly concentrated there, it appears to be directed back to South Africans, as if to say, "Look at what London is like," and "See how too clever I am moving in cosmopolitan circles—especially cosmopolitan white circles." It is like a dream of glory, retailed to the folks back home. "Dreaming away like this in Kensington, London, I looked into Esmé's soft brown eyes and said, 'London, baby.' She smiled softly, tenderly, sipping leisurely at iced orange, and said, 'Have a drink.' I poured a long one and put it out there to look all mine" (p. 32). It is not precisely an exercise in keeping the faith, but what Matshikiza's tone seems to say to those still in South Africa is, "Read it and admire and eat your hearts out that it is not you." Living in an elegant flat in Queen's Court or walking in "the heart of Kensington High Street, surrounded by white, genuine white people" (p. 33), Matshikiza seems capable of savoring the pleasures of exile, so unlike the pains of home, more completely than any of the other South African *déracinés*, while disregarding any disadvantages there might be in that same exile. Not that home never enters his thoughts, but when it does it is usually in a very special Matshikiza way: "This will be a proud day for me when I write back home to tell them I have been practising piano near Kensington Palace" (p. 45).

Alfred Hutchinson also works an individual variation on the pattern of exile from South Africa, though his rearrangement of the elements is not so extreme as Matshikiza's. Hutchinson was one of the defendants in the infamous treason trial that dragged on for two years, from 1956 to 1958, and he seized the opportunity of an adjournment of the trial to make his escape over the long "road" that took him by train, by automobile, by boat, and by plane through Bechuanaland, Rhodesia, Nyasaland, Tanganyika, Nairobi, Entebbe, and Leopoldville and eventually to Ghana. Hutchinson's book is structured, somewhat like a picaresque novel, on his flight and subsequent journey, and so it concerns events on the way rather than the comforts that come after travel is concluded. In Tanganyika, for example, less than halfway to Ghana, Hutchinson was very differently situated from Matshikiza with his feet up and a drink in his hand in Kensington: "Two white men and a woman sit drinking, and an African drops ice-cubes into their glasses. The lake water is warm and greenish. But I drink it, sieving the greenish threads with my teeth, my heart full of envy of the people with the ice-cubes in their drinks" (p. 127). Hutchinson probably had sufficient ice in his drinks after reaching England, but that is not what *Road to Ghana* is about; consequently in that book we have only the greenish threads sieved with the teeth near a lake in Tanganyika. Hutchinson's book focusses on that period of exile between departure and arrival, between Abrahams, Modisane, and Mokgatle on the one hand and Matshikiza on the other. Thus, on the last page of *Road to Ghana*, Hutchinson does not tell of leaving South Africa (which is on p. 69), but of arriving at the airport of Accra, the culmination of his journey. "The plane hits the tarmac and rises like a half-startled bird and settles down. . . . This is the end of the road, the very end of the road to Ghana" (p. 190). *Road to Ghana*, partly because of Hutchinson's skill in description and his eye for characterization, partly because the book is leading to a definite place and displays a clear thematic structure, reads rather like a novel: it conveys not just experience, but experience with meaning—a meaning for Hutchinson personally and, through his artistry, for all men who share his feeling for freedom.

Exile and freedom, freedom and exile—for the black South African, and especially if he happens to be an artist, these two are eventually, and often tragically, variations on a theme. Chief Albert Luthuli, who would never go into exile and was therefore forced by the government into isolation, shows very clearly in his own life history why younger men—men who in age might be Luthuli's children—have found it necessary to leave their homeland permanently. "We pray very hard about our children," Luthuli says, "most of all because of the South Africa in which they are growing up. In the days when Professor Matthews and I were young teachers at Adams the world seemed to be opening out for Africans. It seemed mainly a matter of proving our ability and worth as citizens, and that did not seem impossible" (*Let My People Go*, p. 46). Those halycon days are no more, as witness Luthuli's autobiography and all the others under consideration. For Abrahams, Mphahlele, Modisane, and Hutchinson the world was not opening out but—and one feels it all through their autobiographies —closing in on them, stifling any instinct or motive to free response and natural creativity. From the days when Luthuli was a young man in South Africa until now, laws have been systematically passed that, in their cumulative effect, exclude the black South African from any share in determining how he will live his own life. Subject to police raids at home and to inspection of passes in the street, forbidden the city or enclosed in a "location," denied the right to brew beer and to hold any but menial jobs (and then at wages far below the level for Europeans), forbidden to congregate in groups of blacks and to socialize with whites, he is forced into exile if he would choose at all how he wants to live. If he does not go into exile abroad, then—as the autobiographies of Albert Luthuli and "Dora Thizwilondi Magidi" demonstrate, and, in another way, the autobiographical fiction of Dugmore Boetie—he is exiled in his own country, alienated from himself and from the realities that determine his life. This special horror, ever present in the political life of South Africa, explains why South African autobiography, which occasionally is somewhat less than literature (for example, Modisane's shrill incoherence in spots), also seems sometimes to be more than literature (for example, Hutchinson sieving the greenish threads and the implications of that scene). Politics and literature seldom make comfortable bed companions, but this is especially true when the writer is a victim of a simple and vicious political oppression.

In a survey of the history of South Africa that runs parallel to the account of his own life, Albert Luthuli demonstrates clearly how and why the existence of a black South African is inextricably entangled in politics. As a result of all the laws of exclusion—in education, in commerce, in residency, in sports, in cultural affairs, in land tenure, in voting rights, in the most trivial and ordinary details of daily existence as in the most momentous decisions of a man's life—merely for the black South African to continue to live, to cope as he best can, to survive at all is a political gesture: not because he chooses to be political—Mphahlele, Abrahams, Modisane, and Matshikiza preferred not to be— but because all the efforts of a huge and crushing political machine are directed at using, exploiting, and destroying his humanity. Thus any attempt to retain that humanity, to realize or protect or exercise it, must inevitably be political. Bloke Modisane, disillusioned, as many men have been, with the self-serving acts of political leaders, in reaction burned his Youth League card and determined to have nothing more to do with politics: "I was disillusioned beyond reconciliation, and decided to separate my life and interests from politics. . . . I assumed a mask of political innocence and established a reputation for being apolitical" (p. 139). It was not to be very long, however, before Modisane realized that what may be all very well for a writer elsewhere could not go in South Africa: "But I am black . . . [and] because I am black I was forced to become a piece of the decisions, a part of black resistance. . . . A non-committed African is the same black as a committed Native. . . . There was no choice, during riots the police shot their rifles and sten guns at anything which was black" (p. 140). Todd Matshikiza too learned that "there was no choice" so long as he was in South Africa. In jail because he was caught having a drink in the apartment of a white friend, Matshikiza says he was taunted by an African policeman at the Special Branch, who sang a protest song about Luthuli: "I object, quietly, at his mercy, 'I have nothing to do with politics'" (p. 101). Matshikiza may not have wanted to have anything to do with politics, but as Eric Hopland, the white man who supplied the drinks, had already told Matshikiza two pages before, "Yes, the lawyers aren't allowed to see any of us. We're political suspects" (p. 99). For Matshikiza

257

to have had a drink, with or without ice-cubes, with a white man was already to have committed a political crime, however little Matshikiza wanted to have to do with politics.

There are, of course, variant forms of political activity as there are variant forms of exile. The possibilities of political response are not restricted to such public gestures as Mokgatle's speechmaking and Luthuli's leadership of the African National Congress. The apolitical pose assumed by Modisane—because in South Africa it was only a pose without substance—was as much a political gesture as his burning his Youth League card or his throwing stones at the police as they moved through Sophiatown. Alfred Hutchinson, fleeing from the treason trial to meet his English fiancée in Ghana, was performing a doubly political act, for even love, if it is between a white and a black (or a "Colored," which is how Hutchinson was finally classified), is politicized in South Africa. Peter Abrahams suggests a way of responding to the ubiquitous political pressure without seeming to—a way that Ezekiel Mphahlele also knew and that caused both of the writers to leave South Africa so that they might escape the growing, destructive bitterness within themselves and might regain, as Abrahams calls it, their "manhood." The way of responding that Abrahams suggests has, of course, been known to many men besides Abrahams and Mphahlele, and so also have its consequences: "A man can submit today in order to resist tomorrow. My submission had been such. And because I had not been free to show my real feeling, to voice my true thoughts, my submission had bred bitterness and anger. And there were nearly ten million others who had submitted with equal anger and bitterness" (*Tell Freedom*, pp. 369-70). The tragedy of South Africa is that everyone, but most especially the black man, is caught in a dance where no one is free to act but only to react, and in this dance of death there is no creation but only destruction. Only by whirling out of the dance itself could Abrahams and Mphahlele, Modisane and Hutchinson free themselves to live rather than committing them-

258

selves to the death that Modisane saw, felt, and described all about him in Sophiatown.

Had these men not succeeded in freeing themselves from the *Totentanz* of South Africa, their fate would very likely have been the same as the fate of Dugmore Boetie, or perhaps their deaths would have been more violent and sudden than his; in either case, the outcome could not have been a happy one. Boetie's slow death from cancer, as Barney Simon describes it in his epilogue to *Familiarity is the Kingdom of the Lost*, had a horrible symbolic appropriateness about it, as if the South African social and political disease had been turned in on his physical body and manifested there: the effects of apartheid, like a cancer, living and growing and killing the individual from within as from without. Although Boetie's *Familiarity is the Kingdom of the Lost* purports to be an autobiography, one must confess that it does not always have a tone of verisimilitude about it. But that much of his narrative is apparently untrue is only secondarily important, for what Boetie gives us is precisely the fantasy life we might expect from someone crushed utterly by what South Africa is. Boetie did not have the option of exile, and the fantasies of *Familiarity is the Kingdom of the Lost* were the only responses available to him. In the end, Boetie was alienated by South Africa from nothing less than reality. The insane violence that he describes in his harsh, powerful prose (the opening scene, for example) may never have happened literally, but it did happen in other, equally important, ways—there the violence is, manifest on the surface of the book as in the grotesquely deformed personality of the man. Likewise, the fantasies about war heroics in North Africa or the ingenious but improbable con games that Boetie claims to have worked on society do not, on one level, ring true, but on another and deeper level they are the very essence of the truth of a mutilated psyche. It may well be that Boetie tells us more about the grim truth of South Africa unconsciously, in his style and in his untruths, than he does consciously.

259

In the light of the fate of Dugmore Boetie, and of millions of others who have doubtless lived the same life as he did but have never written out the truth of South Africa either consciously or unconsciously, Lewis Nkosi's remark that "the total effect of the apartheid laws in South Africa is to make it almost illegal to live" (*Home and Exile*, p. 35) is scarcely even hyperbolical. For the novelist like Mphahlele or Abrahams the problem is intensified: not only must he try in some way to stay alive under the apartheid laws but also, beyond that human struggle for mere survival, professionally he is debarred by the rigid, inhuman classifications of apartheid from touching his very subject. Apartheid forces groups together and apart and it forbids the members of any one group to consider themselves as individuals in relation to members of other groups. This non-human, non-individual division and classification may suit the purposes of the political tyrant, but the novelist who is thereby deprived of the opportunity to analyze the motives and the meaning of individual behavior is without a subject. Thus Timi Tabane, the central and obviously autobiographical character in Mphahlele's *The Wanderers*, before he leaves South Africa for exile in Nigeria and Kenya, speculates on why a character named Rampa should have left his wife behind in the village to go to work in the city, and he realizes that "to say simply 'migrant labor and its evils,' would be merely to talk sociology and politics."[4] To use such a phrase, which provides no human or individual answer to the question, is to talk the language of politics and apartheid. "And yet," Timi goes on in his thought, "in a society in which every hour of waking and sleeping, in which every meal, every area of work, in which every facet of life is governed, dictated by politics, was it a blameworthy act to diagnose social relationships in such terms?" For the common man, the answer to Timi's rhetorical question may be "no"; for the novelist (like Mphahlele) it has to be "yes," it is blame-

[4] Ezekiel Mphahlele, *The Wanderers* (New York: Macmillan, 1971), pp. 102-03.

worthy. And so the novelist has to get out of the society that dictates life in such terms or lose his profession.

Noni Jabavu, who is not a novelist but a sensitive memoirist of her family and her people (and who, married to an Englishman, lives safely outside of South Africa), nevertheless develops a novelist's theme in *The Ochre People* and, though less extensively, in *Drawn in Colour*. In these two memoirs of the life of the old and distinguished Jabavu family in South Africa, Noni Jabavu stresses repeatedly how complex, how subtle, how delicate, and how centrally important human relationships are in Xosa society and Xosa linguistic structure, and indeed in indigenous South African and African civilizations generally. *The Ochre People*, which tells the story of Noni Jabavu's difficult and prolonged adjustment to a new human, family relationship—her father's remarriage—is a dramatization of her theme through her own experience. As a subsidiary and parallel theme, Noni Jabavu returns several times to this new thing of apartheid and to the way in which, through brutal and inhuman legislation, it cuts right across all the traditional relationships and in effect returns South African society to a primitive and starkly dehumanizing set of laws in place of the rich, varied, and complex set of relations growing out of families and extended families. "The language seems to have been almost invented to handle situations that involve personal relationships and the imponderables that intensify emotions" (*The Ochre People*, p. 94). Noni Jabavu, like the Xosa language she extols, is herself extraordinarily sensitive to the nuances of human relationships, to the individual in relation to a refined network of human ties and contacts. Her language resembles the novelist's medium, but it is not the language that politics talks, and it is most especially not the language of apartheid.

In *Drawn in Colour* Noni Jabavu tells how she returned from England to South Africa to attend the funeral of her brother, murdered by *tsotsis* in Johannesburg, and how the prevailing political climate struck her. Stepping from the

261

plane, she says, "I could feel the racial atmosphere congeal and freeze round me. The old South African hostility, cruelty, harshness; it was all there, somehow harsher than ever because Afrikaans was now the language. You heard nothing but those glottal stops, staccato tones; saw only hard, alert, pale blue eyes set in craggy suntanned faces" (p. 3). Their language, Noni Jabavu implies, with its peculiar structure and its special sounds, its "glottal stops" and "staccato tones," is deeply rooted in the Afrikaners' personality and it expresses and reveals them, as also does their policy of apartheid, better than they might understand. That personality and its attendant doctrine, whether expressed in Afrikaans or in English, was a pervasive and oppressive reality for the black or "Colored" South African like Peter Abrahams: "All my life had been dominated by a sign, often invisible but no less real for that, which said: RESERVED FOR EUROPEANS ONLY" (*Tell Freedom*, p. 369). That sign, as Abrahams goes on to say, was responsible for the quality of his life in South Africa—"the filth and squalor of the slums," the death all about him, "the marks of rickets on my body"—and hence was responsible also for the escape from South Africa that enabled him to stay alive and write and "tell freedom."

Ezekiel Mphahlele, telling that freedom from his own experience, found that not even exile was a powerful enough medicine to remove the marks of rickets on the body or the effects of apartheid on the psyche. In exile in Nigeria, the effects of oppression, as Mphahlele describes it in *The African Image*, linger on in his personality, in his responses, and in his relationships, especially with whites: "And so I realize now something I was never aware of when I was in South Africa: that the white man has poisoned my life at the spring; it goes against me all the time, this anger, in my dealings with white people" (p. 224). Though Mphahlele has broken free from the dance, it is as if the movement of the dance were continuing in his head, upsetting his sense of balance, breaking the rhythm of the deli-

262

cate adjustments necessary between people. Yet this is the same Mphahlele who, according to Bloke Modisane in *Blame Me on History*, "had been writing me sane letters [from Nigeria] which implied that he was on the road to a human recovery" (p. 250), and who encouraged Modisane to follow him into exile—no doubt because a vague imbalance seemed better to him, and to Modisane, than destruction back in the violence and chaos of a racially divided and categorized South Africa at war with itself. That was no country for old men or for young men, but especially no country for a black or a "Colored" novelist. Apropos of racial categories, Peter Abrahams tells of a young friend smacking his chest and declaring proudly, "Joseph! Zulu!" but when Abrahams wanted to announce his own name and identity he had to go to his aunt, who explained to him thus: "You are Coloured. There are three kinds of people: white people, Coloured people, and black people. The white people come first, then the Coloured people, then the black people" (*Tell Freedom*, p. 46). That rough and ready, white-fabricated system of classifying people might suffice for a childish relationship—in fact, the next day Abrahams says he went back to his friend, "smacked my chest and said: 'Lee! Coloured!' "—but it is far too crude for the requirements of the novelist.

The world of South African autobiography and fiction, divided so starkly into "white people, Coloured people, and black people," is very different from the Gikuyu or the Ibo world, very different also from the world that we find in the fiction of Camara Laye, Cheikh Hamidou Kane, and Yambo Ouologuem. The Gikuyu are united in their "Gikuyuness," the Ibo in their "Iboness," but, as Mphahlele says of South Africa in *The African Image* (p. 30), "5,000,000 Africans are urbanized and therefore detribalized." Crowded together in urban "locations," they have neither the unity of a common heritage (the most dramatic illustration is the setting of "Coloureds" against blacks) nor the unity of a natural mysticism. About the only possible unity is a nega-

263

tive one, which is what Alfred Hutchinson meant when he told a European on the plane to Ghana—who had said, "The trouble with Africa is that there is no unity—no common language or religious bonds"—that "Africa is united— united against white oppression, in her rejection of the white man" (*Road to Ghana*, p. 186). This unity born of oppression has, across Africa, proved only momentarily effective even in the political realm: Kenyatta, for example, has found it desirable since independence to stress *Harambee* (unity, especially internal, national unity) rather than *Uhuru* (freedom, especially freedom from foreign, English rule) which was the great cry before independence. A nation, as Kenyatta has realized, cannot be built, nor can Africa be long unified, only by acts of rejection, necessary as they may be as a first step. This is much truer for the artist than for the politician. How much art can be created out of rejection and reaction? A certain amount of satire no doubt, but except for satire, mere reaction will not carry the novelist very far. Moreover, satire is not a common mode, nor often well managed, anywhere, and, whatever the reason, effective satire is relatively less frequent in African writing than in European or American literature. In South Africa Bloke Modisane squeezed a rather good satiric short story, "The Dignity of Begging," out of the bitterness of reaction, but otherwise the potential for this genre is seen most clearly and most unhappily in *Familiarity is the Kingdom of the Lost* (which could well be retitled "The Dignity of Thieving and Conning"), where satire manifests itself not in an attack on the vices of the powerful but unconsciously in the grim tragedy of the author's own life. Satire is a dangerous weapon, and particularly in South Africa it is capable of cutting the wrong way.

When Yambo Ouologuem—who happens, conveniently, to be one of the few effective satirists from Africa—tells us that "les Nègres ont jusqu'ici vécu en esclaves, dans la mesure même où ils se définissaient toujours (non par rapport à eux-mêmes) mais d'abord et avant tout par rapport

264

au Blanc,"[5] he is thinking more of ex-French West Africa
and problems there of "assimilation" than of South Africa
and problems of apartheid; he also has reference more to
a psychological-literary slavery, accepted if not created by
the victim, than to an economic-political slavery designed
and imposed by the state. What Ouologuem says, however,
here and elsewhere, has considerable potential relevance
for a discussion of the kind of literature that has been and
can be produced in South Africa. In the same vein, Ouologuem told Mel Watkins from the *New York Times*, "Until
now African history has been shown only as a conflict between blacks and whites; all African novels deal with this
colonial conflict. However, actions taken only in opposition
to whites create an atmosphere of paranoia—one does not
deal with reality but with the proclamations of others. The
problem with this is that it is ineffective in changing the attitude of the slave . . . [which] consists of defining oneself
only in relationship to others."[6] If Ouologuem is right in his
psychology, and he undoubtedly is, then his observation
suggests that the South African writer is in a terrible and
tragic bind before he even begins to put words on the page.
For the black South African there is no choice between (in
Ouologuem's phrase) "reality" and the "proclamations of
others" because there is no difference between them: for
him, so long as he remains in South Africa, "reality" *is* the
"proclamations of others." The choice of the black novelist
from South Africa is not between these two identical things
but between dealing with reality or evading it; it is the
choice, as the cases of both Modisane and Mphahlele demonstrate, between writing "protest" literature and writing
"escape" literature. In *The African Image*, Mphahlele tells
us that the short story in South Africa "moves between
escapist and protest types" (p. 186), and in *Down Second
Avenue* (p. 217), looking back from the perspective of Ni-

[5] *Lettre à la France Nègre* (Paris: Éditions Edmond Nalis, 1968),
p. 10.
[6] *Times Book Review*, 7 March 1971, pp. 7 and 34.

geria, he says that the fiction he himself produced in South Africa was caught in this same vicious trap of protest or escape.

A misguided article signed "A.B." that appeared some years ago in *Présence Africaine*[7] attacking Camara Laye as a "fantasist" and escapist writer has considerably more pertinence for South African fiction than for Camara Laye's books, though its prescriptive attitude toward writing fiction is, I think, as wrongheaded in the one case as in the other. A.B.'s argument, which constitutes a major critical statement about African literature, goes thus: literature can follow either the mode of realism or the mode of fantasy, but any work "de qualité"—which A.B. looks for in African writing and does not find—must, by the definition and the premises of the article, be realistic; if it is not socially and politically realistic it gives up, ipso facto, any attempt at greatness. There is, according to A.B., one, and only one, reality in black Africa: "Car, la réalité actuelle de l'Afrique Noire, sa seule réalité profonde, c'est avant tout la colonisation et ses méfaits" (p. 137). Enough African writers of the first importance—from Chinua Achebe to Yambo Ouologuem and from Camara Laye and Léopold Senghor[8] to Wole Soyinka and Ezekiel Mphahlele—have implicitly dis-

[7] A.B., "Afrique Noire, littérature rose," *Présence Africaine*, NS Nos. 1-2 (avril-juillet 1955), pp. 133-45. "A.B." presumably refers to Alexandre Biyidi, i.e., the Cameroonian novelist who usually writes under the pseudonym "Mongo Beti."

[8] Senghor's response to this criticism of Camara Laye and his attitude in general can be taken as representative: "Lui [Camara Laye] reprocher de n'avoir pas fait le procès du Colonialisme, c'est lui reprocher de n'avoir pas fait un roman à thèse, ce qui est le contraire du romanesque, c'est lui reprocher d'être resté fidèle à sa race, à sa mission d'écrivain. Mais, à la reflexion, on decouvrira qu'en ne faisant pas le procès du Colonialisme, il l'a fait de la façon la plus efficace. Car peindre le monde négro-africain sous les couleurs de l'enfance, c'était la façon la plus suggestive de condamner le monde capitaliste de l'Occident européen" ("Laye Camara et Lamine Diakhaté ou l'art n'est pas d'un parti," *Liberté I* [Paris: Éditions du Seuil, 1964], p. 157).

agreed with this idea of what constitutes "the" African reality to make one safe in saying that A.B. does not speak for
a consensus of creative African writers; but he speaks very
clearly all the same, and his idea is an important one to consider in the context of South African reality and South African fiction. "Pour nous," he goes on to declare, "la première
réalité de l'Afrique Noire, je dirais même sa seule réalité
profonde, c'est la colonisation et ce qui s'ensuit. La colonisation qui imprègne aujourd'hui la moindre parcelle du corps
africain, qui empoisonne tout son sang, renvoyant à l'arrière
plan tout ce qui est susceptible de s'opposer a son action"
(pp. 137-38). This sounds like telling the African novelist
what his experience has been—what it *must* have been and
in every case—which hardly seems a valid procedure, but
the thrust of A.B.'s remarks is as clear as the protest writing
on the wall: "Il s'en suit qu'écrire sur l'Afrique Noire, c'est
prendre parti pour ou contre la colonisation. Impossible de
sortir de là" (p. 138). For or against: "Under which King,
Besonian? Speak, or die." Faced with that bullying threat,
the serious African writer, so far as A.B. is concerned, has
neither a choice of subject nor an option as to the stance he
shall assume in regard to that imposed subject. A.B.'s argument, which sounds like a dissertation on the literary-politi-
cal world of South Africa, puts the African writer in a pre-
made and prescriptive straightjacket—the same one for
every writer.

Protest literature—the kind of literature that would invariably be produced by an Africa united only "in her rejection of the white man"—is, in Ouologuem's terms, a literature of slavery: "actions taken only in opposition to whites."
But South Africa forces reaction and protest on the black
writer as a necessary mode. Ironically, A.B.'s prescriptions
for content and tone in African fiction have the same effect
as the South African political machine: both drive the writer into a corner from which he can escape only by fighting
back against a foreign politics, only by a negative reaction.
Mphahlele, like the other South African writers who found

267

a different kind of escape in exile, felt himself, so long as he was in South Africa, bound on that wheel of fire, that political torture machine that would dictate his subject and force him to write not his own but another man's book—Mongo Beti's or Ferdinand Oyono's. To stay or to go, to fight back or to seek a place to create, to write protest fiction or to attempt "something of a higher order" (*Down Second Avenue*, p. 217)—the dilemma came down to this for Mphahlele and for his alter ego Timi in *The Wanderers*, as it did also for Peter Abrahams and Bloke Modisane. "Eventually," Timi thinks, in a reprise of the tormented song of *Down Second Avenue*, "I would have to decide whether to stay and try to survive; or stay and pit my heroism against the machine and bear the consequences if I remained alive; or stay and shrivel up with bitterness; or face up to my cowardice, reason with it and leave. . . . The issue kept coming to the single conscience, like the endless ticking of a clock. . . . I knew I would sooner or later be driven full tilt against the machine. Then again, my intellect would not let me be; it kept hankering after the outer worlds where it imagined it could function in peace . . ." (*The Wanderers*, p. 59). Timi, imitating his creator—or Mphahlele, imitating his own life in the gestures of his fiction as in the events of his autobiography—chooses the intellect and exile against the bitter consequences of staying: he departs South Africa to become one of the wanderers of the title, a man who is a stranger and an alien in all nations.

"To seem the stranger lies my lot, my life/ Among strangers": Hopkins, whom Mphahlele twice cites in *Down Second Avenue* as the literary companion of his moods of loneliness and anguish, described many times and well the special sorrows reserved for the alien. Mphahlele, one can guess from *Down Second Avenue, The African Image, The Wanderers,* and "Exile in Nigeria," has known those sorrows intimately enough. Yet there was an inevitability about his going into exile that makes one sure that today or any time Mphahlele would reaffirm his decision as the necessary and right one. Lewis Nkosi, commenting on his predicament as a writer in South Africa—a predicament shared by all the other black writers who tried to treat the realities of South African life, the realities of home that drove them into exile—says, "I have often thought many times afterwards how difficult it must be to try and reclaim some of this bitter reality for imaginative literature. Words seem to break under the strain" (*Home and Exile*, p. 22). Peter Abrahams, similarly frustrated, found there was no subject for him in South Africa because there was no audience: whites did not want a picture of reality, blacks were too busy living it to read about it, and propaganda, which would oversimplify the reality, was not Abrahams' mode (*Tell Freedom*, p. 312). Mphahlele points to the same intractableness in South African reality as material for the artist when, in *Down Second Avenue*, he says, "our South African situation has become a terrible cliché as literary material" (p. 210). Elsewhere, Lewis Nkosi, both in his practice and in his rationale, suggests how the South African situation can provide material for one kind of literature —the literature most immediately and directly related to lived experience—and he simultaneously indicates why autobiography has been such a vital and effective form in South Africa. "So I am wondering if this is worth it," he says in an essay on the nature of apartheid: "how does one begin to write about apartheid in a way that would be meaningful to people who have not experienced it? I don't know. So instead of writing a political essay, I thought I would simply set down some of the experiences that I and my contemporaries have been through in South Africa. I don't think there is any need to strive for effect; the situation is surrealistic enough as it is" (*Home and Exile*, p. 35). In an autobiographical essay on apartheid, there is no need for the black South African either to "strive for effect" or to emphasize his political stance: the subject itself is so utterly self-satirizing and self-condemning and so thoroughly politicized, or in its inhumanity it goes so far beyond the merely political, that simply to describe its operation as experienced will have—at least should have—an overwhelming, total effect on the reader, including an effect on his political sensibilities.

It seems at first vaguely paradoxical that no writer has been successful who has tried to make the racial situation in South Africa the subject for his fiction, but that a number of creative writers have produced memorable autobiographical works revolving about that same subject. Without considering the matter very deeply, we might think it likely that the novelist or short story writer would do well, having been once hurt already, not to expose himself so personally as autobiography requires and should choose the less direct form of fiction, which would put a distance between himself and the tremendous emotionalism of his subject. But this is not how things have turned out, for fiction from South Africa has often been negligible if not trivial and autobiography has been of great and convincing significance. The fortunes of these two literary forms in South Africa prove the lesson that the nightmare that occurs as waking reality in the broad light of day and in the streets of Johannesburg or Pretoria demands the realistic and interior, first-person voice of autobiography to achieve its fullest effect. What is intractable to the imagination—what *can* the imagination do with something as horrendous as apartheid?—can have an overwhelming effect if simply narrated by the victim. When the writer casts his experience of surpassing violence and inhumanity in the forms of fiction, the reader is virtually invited to feel that this is "only fiction," is merely the product of the writer's imagination.[9] It is much easier to go

[9] Arthur Maimane, who has been for a number of years in exile in Ghana and England, tells a relevant story of a publisher's reaction to his first novel: though it was well-written, the publisher rejected the novel "Because, he told me, they [the publisher's readers] believed that I had exaggerated the treatment Africans received from white people in South Africa. We know *apartheid* is terrible, they were telling me, but we can't believe that it's as bad as you say it is." Maimane's article, entitled "Can't You Write About Anyting [sic] Else,"

away, with a feeling of indifference and clean hands, from fiction about the horrors of South Africa (say, for example, *Quartet*) than it is from *Tell Freedom* or *Road to Ghana* or *Down Second Avenue*. The reality of South Africa, in effect, robs the novelist of his vocation.

The artist, sometimes in fiction, sometimes in autobiography (and frequently the two are indistinguishable; indeed in one sense they are identical efforts), seeks, as if by a temperamental necessity, to find an order in his experience that he can imitate in the order of his work and that, once discovered and imitated, will yield a meaning both in his life and in his art. It is this discovered and imposed order, leading to meaning, that we call the artist's "vision": his special, unique way of seeing, understanding, and creating. This desire to discover an order and meaning in experience is also what one might call the essential autobiographic motive: the sifting of memories and the recreation of events to see how they relate, where they connect, what pattern they establish. This tendency to think autobiographically, to comb experience for meaning, is clearly discernible in *Tell Freedom*, in *Blame Me on History*, in *Road to Ghana*, especially in *Down Second Avenue*. But the tragic irony for the black man born and living in South Africa—if like Abrahams, Modisane, Hutchinson, and Mphahlele he should be particularly given to searching for the thread, the clue to the mystery—is that there is no meaning in life in South Africa. The suffering that that life entails, as the autobiog-

---

was originally delivered as an address to a symposium, "Cultural Days on South Africa," organized in Paris in March 1971 by La Société Africaine de Culture. Various other South African writers, artists, and cinema people addressed the symposium in quasi-autobiographical terms and all their remarks were published in *Présence Africaine*, NS No. 80 (4th Quarter 1971), pp. 111-36.

On the realities of apartheid, whether or not a picture is worth a thousand words, Ernest Cole's book of photographs of South African life—*House of Bondage* (New York: Random House, 1967)—is dramatic confirmation of the autobiographies of black South Africans. Cole is a Bapedi—now in exile, naturally.

raphies of these men prove, the suffering that it *is*, is simply meaningless. Because of this, as artists and as men, they all had to escape; it was only after they were out that they wrote their autobiographies. The arbitrary, artificial, and sterile order imposed by a political, racist dictatorship—the categories and classifications of apartheid: white, Indian, Coloured, African—produces, because it is a man-made scheme, no meaning. "Perhaps," Peter Abrahams says of his reason for leaving South Africa, "Perhaps life had a meaning that transcended race and colour. If it had, I could not find it in South Africa" (*Tell Freedom*, p. 370). The fate of the black South African has been a deliberately designed and political one, arranged by men with no justifiable right to determine the destinies of men. The political rulers of South Africa, though they have assumed a godlike role, are not superior to the human order—quite the contrary: their actions prove them less than human rather than more than human. It is more than coincidental that Mphahlele, Modisane, and Hutchinson all reject Christianity (and Abrahams hardly even mentions it in *Tell Freedom*) as a possible way to meaning for the black South African, because that too in South Africa is man-made, designed by the politics and the patterns of apartheid.

In *Tell Freedom*, Peter Abrahams dramatizes this arbitrary ordering of a man's life in the story of Jim, a coworker for a brief period in a hotel. Because Jim was an "African," according to the categories designed by apartheid, he had to carry a large variety of passes that he obligingly lists for Abrahams: a Trek Pass, an Identification Pass, a Six-Day Special Pass, a Monthly Pass, a Travelling Pass, a Day Special Pass, a Location Visitor's Pass, a Lodger's Permit, a Night Special Pass. Jim concludes his listing "with a crooked smile" and the melancholy reflection that "A man's life is controlled by pieces of paper" (pp. 208-10); when the pattern that determines a man's life has no more logic than that, when it is as capricious as pieces of paper issued or withheld at the will of a vicious and foreign political overlord, then Peter Abrahams' own earlier feeling about South African life is the only one possible: "I went back to the pavement edge. Sitting there, piddling, it seemed to me there was no sense in life. Things happened and no one seemed to know why" (p. 79). How could they? There is no explanation where there is no meaning, no meaning where there is no order except the arbitrary and the political. "Nothing in my life seemed to have any meaning," Bloke Modisane says, as he evokes his own figurative and potentially literal death in the death of Sophiatown; "all around me there was the futility and the apathy, the dying of the children, the empty gestures of the life reflected in the seemingly meaningless destruction of that life, the demolition of Sophiatown . . ." (*Blame Me on History*, p. 117). South Africa, for Modisane and Abrahams, was a meaningless life hurried on to a meaningless end; there, in the end that concludes nothing comprehensible and climaxes nothing explicable, the meaninglessness of the foregoing life is especially apparent. Earlier, Modisane demonstrates how, if not why, life came to that in South Africa: "Our lives were the pieces on the board being manipulated by a man-made fate, children born into a social position and playing out a patterned destiny; I seemed to see us all, black and white, on the draughtboard, manœuvred into a trap, and devoured by South Africa, one colour against the other" (p. 70).

Merely because a man does not receive answers to his questions does not mean, however, even in South Africa, where the gameboard is fixed, that he ceases to search his experience or ask the questions. "Who can say," Ezekiel Mphahlele asks in a review of Dennis Brutus' poems of exile, "what the *meaning* of it all is beyond the desire for freedom? I don't know any exile who ever stopped searching."[10] Mphahlele is himself a prime example of the man

[10] "Debris, Driftwood and Purpose," *Africa Today*, 18, No. 2 (April 1971), 70. Mphahlele's article reviews Dugmore Boetie's *Familiarity is the Kingdom of the Lost* as well as Brutus' *Poems from Algiers*.

who, first in his life and subsequently in his writing, disregards the constant frustration of meaningless results to obey the autobiographic impulse of his personality. The conclusion Mphahlele comes to, and in this he is most typical, is that coherent answers, if they exist, will be found only in exile, where life can be determined by some logic other than the logic of politics. Mphahlele tells of the political meetings he attended in the hope that there he might be offered the explanation that would provide a significant pattern for his life, but even right-minded politics, as he discovered, could only demonstrate for him a negative fact: that the pattern of life in South Africa was without meaning. "Gradually, as I listened" to the political debates, he says, "I was beginning to put into their proper places the scattered experiences of my life in Pretoria. Poverty; my mother's resignation; Aunt Dora's toughness; grandmother, whose ways bridged the past with the present, sticking to neither at any one time; police raids; the ten-to-ten curfew bell; encounters with whites; humiliations. But I only succeeded in reconstructing the nightmare which in turn harassed my powers of understanding" (*Down Second Avenue*, pp. 127-28). When, from his own experience, a man can reconstruct no more than the pattern of apartheid and, as an artist, can imitate nothing more than political fact, he is at a dead-end; if he would act rather than react, if he would make the creative rather than the negative gesture, he must turn elsewhere. Leaving South Africa was, for Mphahlele, a way not only of freeing himself to live and to create, but a way also of providing the element of significance in an otherwise insignificant chain of events, the equivalent of giving all the details of an autobiography significance by the climactic gesture to which, after the gesture has been made and described, all those details are seen inevitably to lead. By that act, performed in life, imitated in autobiography, everything falls into place and acquires meaning precisely by relation to this climax.

As Mphahlele, from the perspective of Nigeria, tells the

story of his pre-exilic life, he was temperamentally given to incessant "autobiographing" even before he came to write *Down Second Avenue* or any of his stories or his novel; that is, he was forever recalling, through memory, into consciousness, all the various experiences he had passed through and all the various selves he had been in an attempt, invariably frustrated, to discover some kind of pattern, some possible design or direction, that, when questioned, would yield an answer and suggest a meaning for those experiences, those selves, that life. Mphahlele tried countless times as he grew up, and in *Down Second Avenue* he tries once again, as he has gone on trying since *Down Second Avenue*, to discover, through the creative power of present consciousness, a pattern in the shards thrown up into awareness by memory. The man was psychologically made with the necessity to do this; consequently this is the way his books read. That pattern, which was negative and confusing until transformed by exile, began to emerge only after the first thirteen years of Mphahlele's life—before that, just random, unrelated images in memory: "Looking back to those first thirteen years of my life . . . I cannot help thinking that it was time wasted. I had nobody to shape them into a definite pattern. Searching through the confused threads," he says, various images reassert themselves, but to no purpose and in no discernible pattern (p. 18). When Mphahlele was thirteen the event occurred—Mphahlele's father threw the contents of a boiling pot over his mother's head and then hit her in the skull with the iron pot —that started the pattern of violence and oppression in his life that was to continue and accumulate until he broke it by his departure from South Africa: "My mother screamed with a voice I have never forgotten till this day. Hot gravy and meat and potatoes had got into her blouse and she was trying to shake them down. . . . That was the last time I ever saw my father, that summer of 1932. The strong smell of burning paraffin gas from a stove often reminds me of that Sunday" (p. 28). From that time on, for the duration of his

275

life in South Africa, this central, traumatic, and symbolic experience drew to it events and images that established a pattern of nightmare, as Mphahlele calls it, a pattern of violence and destruction.

As Mphahlele grows older, as his book progresses, the images, the shards and traces of memory, naturally accumulate and increase. This continual recurrence to the past, this drawing up in sum of the memorable, emotion-heavy experiences of a lifetime—again and again, so that each drawing up becomes in itself another of the memorable, emotional experiences for the next time—is what I have called elsewhere, in the context of a discussion of the artistic autobiography, the technique of recall and recapitulation.[11] The eventual intention and effect of recall and recapitulation is to wind all the experiences up into a compressed pattern where the whole is concentrated into a moment of the whole—which is another way of describing autobiography itself. Thus Mphahlele structures *Down Second Avenue* on a narrative account of his life, studded here and there with what he calls "interludes," passages of revery and reflection that draw up the accumulated images into a tight representation of his experience to that moment, renewing once more, and with an increase of details, the emergent pattern from earlier interludes. As a boy, lying and thinking about the past, Mphahlele says, "No use trying to put the pieces together. Pieces of my life. They are a jumble. My father's image . . . that brutal limp of his. The smell of the paraffin from the stove and the smell of boiling potatoes and curry. An incident on a Sunday morning" (pp. 74-75). But neither memory nor the desire to find order can be so easily denied, and the pieces kept returning, demanding to be explained: "I had seldom thought about my father, but when my mother sued for divorce it seemed old wounds had revived. The smell of paraffin gas from a pressure stove; the smell

[11] *Metaphors of Self: The Meaning of Autobiography* (Princeton: Princeton Univ. Press, 1972), pp. 261-65 and 273-75.

276

of boiling potatoes and meat and gravy and curry; the sound of my mother's screaming . . . ; the sight of a man with a brutal limp. . . . Sensations that had lain dormant for nine years, why were they rekindled? . . . Suddenly I felt as if my life had been one huge broken purpose" (p. 149). And so, in spite of all his efforts to find the meaningful design, his life was a broken purpose as long as Mphahlele remained in South Africa, the details in the pattern accumulating to force that climax that would—but at the cost of uprooting himself—repair the broken purpose, invest the life and the book with meaning, and transform insignificance into significance.

In the "Epilogue" to *Down Second Avenue*, which stands to the whole book as an interlude after the fact, a recall and recapitulation from outside the experience of South Africa and from beyond the break of exile, Mphahlele says of his temperament, which is characteristic for the artist, "It is the lingering melody of a song that moves me more than the initial experience itself; it is the lingering pain of a past insult that rankles and hurts me more than the insult itself. Too dumb to tell you how immensely this music or that play or this film moves me, I wait for the memory of the event" (p. 219). This is the rationale for his book and for autobiography in general, but with something of a difference: because he was born black in South Africa, Mphahlele had to achieve in his life the event that he could place as keystone for all the rest; otherwise, the memories would lead nowhere, would provide the structure for no book. No matter how many memories Mphahlele accumulated, no matter how many "lingering melodies" or "lingering pains," they would not have added up to anything, as the constituents of a meaningful and creative life, until South Africa herself became only a memory. The pattern that Mphahlele eventually discovered and realized in his life and that his autobiography formally imitates is the classic, archetypal pattern of South African autobiography: a pattern of racial encounter, oppression, and violence; of sterile, meaningless division, separation, apartheid; of inevitable political involvement because for a black man to exist at all in South Africa as a human being is a political act; of escape and exile and freedom, freedom that is political, that is human, and that is, in Mphahlele's case, as in Abrahams', Hutchinson's, Modisane's, and Matshikiza's, creative—the freedom of the creative artist from the constricting, destructive necessity to make political gestures, to write political literature, to play the opponent's game, to breathe only the thin, acrid, and poisonous air of political existence and opposition.

"To be a black South African," Lewis Nkosi says in a discussion of Mphahlele's *African Image*, "means to live in perpetual exile from oneself . . . " (*Home and Exile*, p. 123). That which is figurative in Nkosi's remark was made literal in the destiny of Albert Luthuli, who, for his political activities, suffered something that one can only call exile within, alienation while on his own soil. Luthuli refers exactly to South African policy as "our exclusion from our own country" (*Let My People Go*, p. 89), and in one sense it matters little whether the person excluded takes up exile in London or Accra or Lagos or Jamaica or the United States or whether he is banned and forced to live a life of isolation and exile in Groutville like Luthuli himself: it is still exile, alienation, exclusion. In another sense, however, and this is especially so for the artist, it makes all the difference which sort of exile he shall suffer. Speaking not of an exile from himself but of a physical exile from South Africa designed to reintegrate that individual self, Mphahlele once described to Nkosi, during an interview that took place in Paris, the great capital of exile, what he saw as the advantages and disadvantages of being in exile. "You get into the habit of confronting people as people," Mphahlele claimed, "and no more just as political oppressors; and you also find that your experience of life broadens and you have a sense of freedom which you never enjoyed when you were back in . . . back home."[12] No longer is he made to feel, as Mphahlele says was the case back in South Africa

that
anger and bitterness
and running fighting running
were man's vital accessories.[13]

Yet exile has its disadvantages too and these, as Mphahlele feels, "outweigh the advantages in the sense that you are uprooted. . . . For a creative writer, particularly, this is shattering because you have to keep projecting your mind into a situation you have left behind" ("Conversation," p. 8). Of all the difficulties, of all the oppressions, of all the ironies that South Africa works on the black creative writer, this may be the bitterest and the most tragic: that even as he escapes South Africa to live as a man, he is simultaneously deprived both of an immediate impulse to write and of a close sense of his subject surrounding him and impelling him to record it, order it, and give it meaning.

One can see this bitter irony at work in the careers of those writers who have remained silent since freeing themselves of South Africa, except for producing an account of their escape. One can also see it, and perhaps more clearly, in a comparison of Mphahlele's novel *The Wanderers* with his earlier *Down Second Avenue*. *The Wanderers* is a book that gives the sense of having been willed into being by the author's determination to produce a novel. No longer goaded by what he one place calls "the paralyzing spur" (*The African Image*, p. 190) of South African oppression and now without the "psychotic panic" that drove him to response of one kind or another back home, Mphahlele says in "Exile in Nigeria," "I feel a certain void/ now my enemies are out of sight," and this same void becomes a lack of sub-

[12] "Conversation with Ezekiel Mphahlele," *Africa Report*, 9, No. 7 (July 1964), 8.
[13] Mphahlele, "Exile in Nigeria," in *Poems from Black Africa*, ed. Langston Hughes (Bloomington: Indiana Univ. Press, 1963), p. 119.

ject, an emptiness at the emotional center, in *The Wanderers*. Unlike *Down Second Avenue*, with its emotional tension, its cumulative structure, and its overwhelming sense of inevitability, *The Wanderers* might very well go any number of different ways, to any number of different conclusions. His life, Mphahlele implies in "Exile in Nigeria," had become adjusted in South Africa to the ever-present enemy, had adapted itself to a continual defensiveness, had structured itself around the negative response; in Nigeria that structure, negative as it was, exists no longer because the oppressor is no longer in his life. Mphahlele is thrown off balance by thrusting at something and expecting resistance but finding nothing there. This accounts for what he calls the "void" and also for the notable lack of tension and of energy-directing vitality, and for the virtual absence of subject in *The Wanderers*.

Another reason that *Down Second Avenue* is the better of the two books is that, paradoxically, life, as described in the earlier book, presented a necessary pattern that art, in *The Wanderers*, never comes up with. Or perhaps it would be fairer to say that Mphahlele is a finer artist as an autobiographer than he is as a novelist. Everything in *Down Second Avenue* is drawn up behind the author to show the way inevitably to exile; it is an account of the calculus of exile and as such the book achieves meaning for itself and for the life it describes. *The Wanderers*, on the other hand, is aimless, disjointed, an account of a simple, inert, mass wandering. The people are wandering into further exile, but now the exile has no goal and no meaning; it is the conclusion of nothing and a part of no pattern; it is merely moving on with neither desire nor regret—both of which were strong on departure from South Africa. So Timi and his family (for which read "Mphahlele and his family") trail from Nigeria to Kenya and, as one knows from Mphahlele's history, to the United States. But what is it leading to? The book does not conclude, it peters out, just as throughout it goes nowhere but merely goes on, because the truth is that a writer cannot give a logical and necessary conclusion to a subject that does not exist. To the reader's question that would be directed to many episodes in the novel—"Why is this in here? Why at this spot?"—the answer that this happened to the author and so to the central character is insufficient. A novel may be an imitation of reality but the reality should be one fashioned by imagination. Mphahlele shows more imagination in dealing with his experience in *Down Second Avenue* than he does in *The Wanderers,* and he is a better essayist and autobiographer than novelist because he lacks the kind of imagination—the novelist's imagination, one would say—that can create its reality from whole cloth and make it more real than the reality of literal experience; deprived by exile of his natural subject, Mphahlele fails to come up with another.

Mphahlele's case is both typical and symptomatic. Forced to it by South Africa, he produced a moving and intelligent artistic autobiography culminating in exile. Of his own journey into exile, Alfred Hutchinson says, "I would stumble over Africa but eventually I would get to Ghana. Cruel Africa. Kind Africa" (*Road to Ghana,* p. 136). For himself Hutchinson made a vow that was more than his alone, about an Africa that had been made by other people than Africans, though partly by them too of course: Africa the paradox and contradiction, the mother that is cruel and kind, the land that is receptive and that is hostile, and especially South Africa that is one thing to the white man, quite another to the African or to the "Coloured." At the end of it all is Ghana, the promised land. That the Ghana imagined by Hutchinson might never have existed matters not at all in his autobiography, which takes its direction, its structure, and its meaning from that exilic goal shimmering in the distance. On the other hand, it matters everything for the literature produced after exile whether or not the promised land exists. When Mphahlele demonstrates in *The Wanderers* that neither his Nigeria nor Hutchinson's Ghana ever existed (in his thinly veiled version of the Ghana coup of

281

1966 and in his allusions to Nigerian politics), then he implies that they have both become perpetual exiles without
a goal, wanderers on a road that does not lead to Ghana or
to anywhere.

In *Let My People Go* Chief Luthuli quotes a song sung,
he says, around 1913 that says much about exile and, though
it refers specifically to alienation and wandering within
South Africa, carries tragic overtones only too applicable
elsewhere on the continent.

> Where are we Africans
> (We seem to be nowhere),
> We shall wander, and wander, and wander.
> How far shall we go?
> Behold, people of Africa, what a burden we bear!
> We shall wander, and wander, and wander.
> The Englishman this side, the Afrikaner this side,
> The German this side, the German this side,
> We shall wander, and wander, and wander.
> How far shall we go?
> Behold, people of Africa, what a burden we bear!
>
> (p. 199)

Timi likewise, near the end of *The Wanderers*, considers
the remark of a white man that Africa is "no more for us
whites" (p. 339) and goes on to think that, however it is for
the white man, Africa is not for the black exile, wandering
without a home or a community across the vast continent
that gave him birth. A few pages later Timi is prepared to
leave Africa, knows he must leave Africa, but for a destination that is left unimagined. South Africa has often been
said to be a very beautiful land, but it is also, for the black
writer, a land infinitely resourceful in creating tragedies, in
producing many-layered ironies that seem expressly designed to trap and destroy the creative writer one way if
not another. But out of South Africa and in spite of it have
come a number of excellent autobiographies, the documents
of men alienated at home, driven into exile abroad, and now
forced to "wander, and wander, and wander."

282

# Anti-Conclusion

A few weeks ago (as I write these words in December 1972), Heinemann published a book of essays in London called *Homecoming* by a writer named Ngugi wa Thiong'o, and from this simple event in the publishing world, which in itself was not very important, can be drawn some implications of considerable· significance for a book about African literature. The writer of *Homecoming* is not, of course, someone new on the scene but the same Gikuyu novelist whom we have encountered as James Ngugi, now writing under a name that, while different, is less new than it is old: a reversion to a traditional, as it were pre-colonial and pre-Christian, African name—Ngugi-son-of-Thiong'o. This little event, though unremarkable in itself, requires us to see, for one thing, that in African literature we are dealing with a living and changing literature and with writers who are very much alive; this should warn us to be cautious about advancing conclusions on a subject that shows no signs of being prepared to conclude itself or to be concluded. Or a more striking way to make the same point is to observe that every one of the writers given major consideration in this study is alive and writing; each is, like the author of *Homecoming*, changing and developing as his personality and his vision impel him to. Most of them, moreover, have probably not even reached their full maturity as writers: Ezekiel Mphahlele was born in 1919, Camara Laye in 1928, Chinua Achebe in 1930, Ngugi wa Thiong'o in 1938, Yambo Ouologuem in 1940, which means that they range in age from thirty-two to fifty-three years old and that the average age for the five writers is only forty-one. This is very different from the literary situation in the West, where, when we speak academically of modern British and American literature (and today modern African literature is as much an academic subject as modern British and American literature), we are likely to have in mind such poets as T. S. Eliot, W. B. Yeats, and Wallace Stevens and such novelists as D. H. Lawrence, James Joyce, E. M. Forster, Ernest Hemingway, and William Faulkner. African literature, made up of all those "new-born infants" mentioned by Chinua Achebe, is properly much more a subject for speculation than for conclusion.

Besides providing this kind of salutary warning for impatient critics, Ngugi's name-change indicates that he personally intends henceforth to refuse the Western identity that is implied by a baptismal name and will choose instead to refer himself, by way of a more traditionally African identity, to his father, his family, and his ancestors. Likewise, the Marxism that Ngugi proclaims throughout his book, carrying African Socialism one step further in logical rigor to African Marxism, points to the same tendency and desire to merge individual achievement and identity with communal effort and existence. With his name-change and his Marxism, Ngugi raises a question that inevitably recurs in any discussion of African literature and that can be taken to be the basic issue, so far at least as the African writer himself is concerned, of African literature: that is, the twofold yet single question of the writer's relation to his past and to his community, which involves a definition both of his own and his community's identity.

This is not to say that Ngugi's notions are typical and that other African writers are doing or thinking the same. On the contrary, most other novelists would, to one extent or another, disagree with him in his paradoxical politics of reactionary revolution. Ngugi seems to want to make his past his future: he would revive social and cultural structures of the past as a reality of the future, and what he calls for to accomplish this is a present revolution not to achieve something new but to restore an ideal pre-colonial state that he, at least, takes to have been one of original peace, harmony, justice, and goodness. Put in this way, it is clear that not only Yambo Ouologuem but also Chinua Achebe, Wole

284

Soyinka, Ezekiel Mphahlele, and many other African writers would disagree with Ngugi's solution, though they would doubtless concur with one another and with Ngugi in saying that the question he raises is an essential one. In the conclusion to a recent review of Kofi Awoonor's *This Earth, My Brother. . .* , Chinua Achebe says, "The question that one must ask at the end of Awoonor's book is 'What then?' He hasn't given any answer, and doesn't have to. But of late many writers have been asking such questions: What then? What does Africa do? A return journey womb-wards to a rendezvous with golden age innocence is clearly inadequate. . . . The future is unavoidable. It has to be met. What is not inevitable is malingering purposelessness."[1] Another question that African writers have asked themselves time and again—and it is still the same essential question as the one that concerns the writer's relation to his past and to his community—is: "What is the role of the writer in African society and in the future of Africa?" The question of the artist's role in society has infinitely more life in it when asked in Africa than it would have in the Western world precisely because of the writer's and the individual's relation to community and to past in African society.

The creative writers we have considered would appear to be moving away, in their thought and practice, in their attitudes and fictional techniques, from the traditional African concept of the individual and his relation to his community, both immediate and extended—away from the feeling, at least in its strictest form, that (as Noni Jabavu says) "a person is a person (is what he is) because of and through

[1] *Transition*, No. 41 (1972), p. 70. Cf. Soyinka's remark about what he sees as the African writer's tendency to evade the present by glorying in the past: "Of course, the past exists, the real African consciousness establishes this—the past exists now, this moment, it is co-existent in present awareness. It clarifies the present and explains the future, but it is not a fleshpot for escapist indulgence, and it is vitally dependent on the sensibility that recalls it" (*The Writer in Modern Africa*, ed. Per Wästberg [Uppsala: Scandinavian Institute of African Studies, 1968], p. 19).

other people" (*Ochre People*, p. 69). This individualizing tendency on the part of the writers, however, might be accounted for by the simple fact that, as their writing demonstrates, the old community no longer exists, at least not with the coherence and integrity that it had, or is presumed to have had, fifty and one hundred years ago. To an interviewer who remarked that "the contemporary Nigerian Society from which you spring must have preserved the patterns of African traditional life to a large degree, if not in the cities, at least in the villages," Chinua Achebe responded: "Yes, I think it is true to a large extent; certainly it was true when I was growing up. *I think it's not quite so true today because the change is sort of accelerating*, but when I was growing up in my village, it was still possible to catch glimpses of what the complete traditional society must have looked like."[2] The breakup of the old is certain: we can view it in the performances of autobiography and fiction. The Gikuyu autobiographers, whose techniques imply a spiritual and historical continuity of being, are now nonetheless the chroniclers of a dispersed and separated people, so that the picture of internal coherence, stability, and continuity that we get in *Facing Mount Kenya* seems more like a memory or an evocation of an ideal existence than a description of present reality. Camara Laye has reenacted from his own experience the breakup in his generation of the traditional Malinké community, and Achebe has been the historian of that accelerating change which he describes as occurring in his time. Thus there is no longer a traditional community with which or by which the African

[2] Interview in *African Writers Talking*, ed. Dennis Duerden and Cosmo Pieterse (London: Heinemann, 1972), p. 9. The italics are mine and reinforce the analysis of Chapter IV above where it is pointed out that the worlds of *Things Fall Apart* and *Arrow of God*, though a generation apart, are very similar; but that in *A Man of the People* social disintegration is noticeably more advanced than in *No Longer at Ease*, though only a few years separates the action of these two novels, because, as Achebe says, "the change is sort of accelerating."

writer can identify himself and so, if for no other reason, he has been left to seek a more individual, personal way.

With this disintegration of "the complete traditional society" as his cultural *donnée*, the African writer is faced with a host of very basic questions—philosophic, aesthetic, and moral—that he must answer for himself before he can even begin to produce a work that answers to the ethical demands of his situation. The questions that the African writer is asking himself are not, it seems to me, unique to African literature, but his answers may be and, given recent cultural and political developments there, the questions have for him a special poignancy and immediacy. Consider *A Man of the People* and the questions that that novel implies in action and in setting (I choose Achebe's novel for convenience, but the same questions are implicit in *Bound to Violence, A Grain of Wheat, The Wanderers,* and in Soyinka's recently published prison journal, *The Man Died*): How much can individual action do in the face of social disintegration? Are personal relations any answer at all? To what extent is the individual justified in seeking personal fulfillment, or in sharpening and refining his individual consciousness, pushing it as far as it will go, more or less in disregard of the community and of social obligations? How much freedom of action does the individual possess? How much meaning is there in individual existence when it is separated from community existence? Or, if one considers the artist himself rather than his creations—if one turns from the case of Odili Samalu to that of Chinua Achebe—is it possible for the writer (and if possible, is it morally desirable for him to make the attempt) to repair the ruins in his own private world simply by the strength of his creative imagination? Can the work of art, in itself and alone, compensate for and rectify the disintegration and chaos in a man's life and his society? Can order in the realm of art—as the work of Western writers like Pound and Eliot and Yeats and Joyce and Proust and Virginia Woolf implies—effec-

287

tively annul for the individual disorder and disintegration in the social realm? I doubt very much that Achebe—or, as nearly as I can tell, any other African writer—would subscribe to this essentially romantic, Western, and non-social doctrine of art and the artist. Achebe has recently said that he is not now working on a novel because (apparently) he finds the current realities of Nigerian life not amenable to a novelistic presentation; this may well be seen, especially from the retrospect of the future, to say something of considerable significance about the novelist, his subject, and his role in African society. If the breakup of the old is assured, however, the composition of the new is very much under debate; this is true equally of literature (what shall the novelist write about and to whom or to what ought he be committed?) and of society (how much should be retained from traditional Africa and how much should be imported of Western materialism and individualism?). African writers are very far from speaking with a single voice on these matters, and writing, as they do, in such a fluid situation, they do not offer the critic much of a hook on which he can hang confident or firm conclusions.

Moreover, if the African writer seems to us to be developing fictional techniques and psychological attitudes that have more in them of Western individualism than traditional African communalism would ordinarily allow, it is still not altogether clear what the general significance of this fact might be. If, for whatever reason, he is more individualistic than others in his society, does this mean that the writer is the avant-garde and the harbinger of something that we can expect to see occurring generally in African social structure and African attitudes toward human existence? Does he, that is, presage a change in African thought or African philosophy or the African world-view (and *is* there such a thing)? Or is he perhaps just a strange bird (which, after all, artists tend to be in any society) whose views are his own and not those which others currently hold or which they will in the future hold? I have remarked

288

(in Chapter III) that Camara Laye's rendering of the African experience as a matter of particularly intense and heightened sensory activation is a brilliant stroke; but one ought now to observe further that when he does this Camara Laye is approaching Africa and the African experience from an essentially exterior and foreign position. It is Camara Laye returning to Africa from Paris who understands the continent as an intensity of sights, smells, sounds, tastes, and touches—not the Camara Laye of *Dark Child*; it is Clarence, the European, not *l'enfant noir*, who is suffused and overwhelmed by the sensory wealth of the forest. Similarly, Yambo Ouologuem wrote his erotic and pornographic exercises with European knowledge behind him. No African, I think, whose entire life had been spent in Africa and within the African milieu would be likely to think of it in these terms because, as also in Cheikh Hamidou Kane's *Ambiguous Adventure*, they are essentially terms of *contrast*: this is what differentiates and distinguishes Africa from Europe. The very fact of writing in English or in French already constitutes a self-determined alienation on the part of the intellectual or "évolué" since the foreign language and his professional use of it can only remove him from the great majority of non-intellectual Africans. One might also observe that the "chosen tongue," as Gerald Moore calls it, whether English or French, seems to have much to do with the sort of literature produced: the African who "chooses" French has found possibilities in the linguistic medium that the African who "chooses" English has not found, and vice versa. But in whichever language he writes, and by the mere fact of writing rather than performing orally,[3] he is producing a literature that will be more widely read in the West than in Africa, and he thus

---

[3] In *Oral Literature in Africa* (Oxford: Clarendon Press, 1970), Ruth Finnegan has dealt very thoroughly with all the various questions of African oral literature: the special conditions attending its performance, its particular linguistic resources and devices, and the different genres of the literature.

sets himself apart from the African community in an apparent individuality.

On the other hand, it is reasonable to observe that the Africans who do read the works produced by African writers are no doubt those who will lead such changes as will occur in African society in the future. Thus the artist, being (as most people would agree that he is) the consciousness of his time, is merely in advance of his society—not totally divorced from it—and he is displaying to that society and others those realities about it of which it was not aware and would otherwise remain unaware. If this is so, then society will be tomorrow, by the effective power of the artist's vision, where he is today; at any given moment it will always be one step behind him. One might suppose, especially given the centrality of social concerns in the vision of the African writer, that he is indeed rehearsing a change that society will itself perform in the future; that his ideas, which may seem strange or extreme now, will be commonplace in a later time. But there still remains the question of how strange or how extreme those views really are, and how far the African writer shows himself prepared to carry them.

Wole Soyinka gives us a clue, I think, when he argues that if the writer will attend to his proper business as an artist, if he will speak "as the record of the mores and experience of his society, *and* as the voice of vision in his time," then he can have an effect—a decisive and appropriate effect—in shaping that better society which should, according to Soyinka, be the artist's and everyone's responsibility. "Any faith," Soyinka told himself when languishing in prison and in order to ward off the seductive notion that he might turn to creation of the isolated self as a proper goal since he was to spend so much time in isolation anyway, "that places the *conscious* quest for the inner self as goal, for which the context of forces are mere battle aids is ultimately destructive of the social potential of that self. Except as source of strength and vision keep inner self out of all expectation, let it remain unconscious beneficiary

290

from experience. Suspect all conscious search for the self's authentic being; this is favourite fodder for the enervating tragic Muse."[4] For Soyinka, the beginning of the artist's effort, but not the end, lies in strength of personality, in cultivation of an individual voice and vision. *But not the end,* for the end is "the social potential of that self"—this is the important point, and this is where Soyinka, whose voice is as individualized and, I should say, as westernized[5] as the voice of any African writer, parts company with the "cult of individualism" of the Western world, where the classic text is John Stuart Mill's "On Liberty" and the most splendid recent performance in literature Yeats's massive creation and expression of individual personality spread throughout a dozen or fifteen volumes; for Yeats, one might point out, the tragic Muse was not enervating but precisely an impetus to creation and thus, transcending it all, to ecstatic joy.[6] In these cases, the end is not "social potential" (a phrase that Yeats, if not Mill, would have detested), nor is it ultimately social transformation, but simply the fullest

[4] *The Man Died* (London: Rex Collings, 1972), p. 87.

[5] Which is one reason for not treating Soyinka's *The Interpreters* in this book. While it might not be quite true to say that that novel offers no problems to a Western reader, yet I think it would be accurate to remark that technically and structurally it is more at home among Western than among African novels and would probably puzzle an African reader more than it would a Western reader. It was not for nothing that Joyce's name was frequently invoked by reviewers of *The Interpreters.*

[6] This is not the place for an extended discussion of tragedy and comedy as literary modes, but it has been pointed out before (for example by Cheikh Anta Diop) that African literature tends to be optimistic and comic as contrasted with the tendency of Western literature to be pessimistic and tragic. This contrast is obviously simplistic and overdrawn, especially as regards Western literature, but there is something to be said for the view that a literature that exalts the existential individual will incline to the tragic (since individual existence cannot but end) and that a literature that is socially oriented and that exalts communal rather than individual existence will incline to the comic (since communal existence does not end and society, at least theoretically, can always be improved).

291

and most various development and expression of individual character. Any social effect that that self might have would be, for the Western individualist, distinctly secondary and incidental. No African writer, I think, has suggested going so far, and it is extremely doubtful that any will soon do so.[7] Thus the African artist's commitment to a code of individualism, while no doubt more highly developed than one would find elsewhere in his community (the artist, we recall, according to Mbonu Ojike, "is the only individualistic personality in Africa"), is still, in comparison with the Western ideal, a partial thing sharply qualified and clearly limited by the traditional African view of what constitutes ultimate social and philosophic reality.

In an "approach to African literature"—which must, after all, approach something that already exists, even though that something may be, as in this case it certainly is, constantly changing and growing—I do not see that one can go much further than this. An approach can lead us to a literature, and critical analyses of individual works can open that literature up to us; but by the very nature of his task the literary critic cannot say what a literature is going to be or how it will develop, and, especially, he cannot say what it should be or how it ought to develop (in spite of the fact that critics—whom one could easily enough name, both African and non-African—have done just this). Nevertheless, it is perfectly legitimate, and as accurate as it is legitimate, to observe that the prevailing tone of the most recent literature from Africa has been one of profound disillusionment, and sometimes, though not invariably, of consequent pessimism. This pervasive sense of disillusionment may well be related, as both cause and effect, to the writers' assump-

---

[7] I hesitate before the case of Yambo Ouologuem, but what he has attempted up to the present time is so largely negative and so bizarre and eccentric that I do not see what one can say about him in the present context. Who knows what he thinks about individualism or about the role of the African writer? Ouologuem may himself know, but I doubt if anyone else does.

292

tion of a more individualistic stance, restricted and qualified though that may be. If the writer becomes disillusioned with the limitations that the community would necessarily impose on his art—which must always be, in part at least, a personal and individual thing—then the natural consequence would be a further isolation or individuation. Likewise, if he already stands apart in a certain isolation, if he holds, in some measure, a non-African ideal of individualism, he may thereby find his disillusionment with the group and the mass of mankind sharpened and increased. Whatever the personal cause and whatever the effect, *The Beautyful Ones Are Not Yet Born*, by Ayi Kwei Armah; *This Earth, My Brother. . .*, by Kofi Awoonor; *A Dream of Africa*, by Camara Laye; *Bound to Violence*, by Yambo Ouologuem; *The Wanderers*, by Ezekiel Mphahlele; *A Man of the People* and the most recent stories in *Girls at War*, by Chinua Achebe; *Homecoming*, by Ngugi wa Thiong'o; and *The Man Died*, by Wole Soyinka—all testify to a spirit of deep disillusion with the way things are now in Africa and with the way they are going. Only *Homecoming*, of all those mentioned, offers any positive solution or hopefulness about African society, and there it is achieved only by the suggestion that revolution is still a possibility and is a consummation devoutly to be wished. Otherwise, the foul disgust and loathing of *The Beautyful Ones Are Not Yet Born* and the poignant contrast between the ideal and the real in *This Earth, My Brother . . .* both speak of dreams of Africa ruined and hopes for her destroyed. Similarly, the contrast between Africa remembered in *Dark Child* and Africa re-observed in *A Dream of Africa* points to the same source of melancholy in the artist's vision. With Yambo Ouologuem, the only possible reason for not saying that he is disillusioned about the present state of African society is that there is no evidence that he ever held any illusions about Africa or anything else, and the picture of Africa that he presents in *Bound to Violence* offers no positive hope at all: Ouologuem may himself have a solution, but his novel, at

293

any rate, suggests no way for Africa to break from the toils of her own history. *The Wanderers*, perhaps in part because of its failure as a novel, has much less hopefulness about it than *Down Second Avenue*—which in turn may partly be due to the structural success of the autobiography. To compare *A Man of the People* or the title story of *Girls at War* with *Things Fall Apart* or *Arrow of God* is to discover in Achebe a deepening bitterness directed not, as sometimes in the earlier novels, against Europeans but against the dominant elements of Nigerian society. Ngugi's discontent in *Homecoming*, likewise, is a consequence of the capitalistic and imperialistic tendency in the ruling African elite that he sees as showing the same brutal disregard for the suffering proletariat as the physically but not spiritually departed missionary and colonial overlords. *The Man Died* is one long and detailed description from within of Soyinka's personal suffering from what he calls "the colossal moral failure within the nation" (p. 19). To say that *The Man Died* is a bitter and disillusioned book would be both over-obvious and under-stated. Elsewhere,[8] turning his contempt from the rulers of Nigeria to African writers themselves, Soyinka has put the matter very strikingly in a paradox: that the South African writer might well come to be an object of envy to writers from elsewhere in Africa because he has not abdicated the artist's responsibility for producing a literature with the voice of vision and has not, as Soyinka believes other African writers have done, surrendered his art, as a vendible craft, to the state or to political movements.

And yet, having noted this apparently ubiquitous disillusion among African writers—a disillusion that seems to come from the writer's being somewhat apart from society and that then, as a consequence of his criticism, produces a further separation—can we say that it is an unhealthy thing? Perhaps (so the argument would go) it is the failure

[8] "The Writer in an African State," *Transition*, No. 31 (June/July 1967), pp. 11-13.

of African literature, since it is so profoundly oriented in social directions, not to have answered the question "What
then?" and not to have solved the problems of the past and
of the community, of the individual and his identity that
this literature has itself raised. I do not quite agree with
this view, and certainly there are few who would not say
that it is healthier for the state of African literature that it
should show disillusion with present corruption rather than
blind celebration of past glories. But to return to the point
of the critical function: the observation that there exists a
tone of disillusionment in contemporary African writing is
a reflection on what there is to reflect on, not a speculation
about something existing only in the critic's proleptic imagination; it seems to me to be stretching the limits of the
critical act unnecessarily far to say that a novel should provide this or that answer or indeed that it should or should
not provide an answer at all. Here, well short of prediction
and prescription, criticism must halt; the most that can be
offered by way of conclusion to such a study as this
approach to African literature is a speculative, descriptive
non-conclusion and a patient, non-prescriptive anti-conclu-
sion. If we only wait, we can be assured that African writers
will themselves show us the way.

# Bibliography

"Abbs, Akosua" (M. E. Nockolds). *Ashanti Boy*. London: Collins, 1959.

Abderrahman es-Sa'di, *see Tarikh es-Soudan*.

Abraham, W. E. *The Mind of Africa*. Chicago: Univ. of Chicago Press, 1962.

Abrahams, Peter. "The Blacks." *Holiday*, 25 (April 1959), pp. 74-75, 112-26.

————. *Tell Freedom: Memories of Africa*. New York: Alfred A. Knopf, 1954.

Achebe, Chinua. *Arrow of God*. London: Heinemann, 1964.

————. *Beware, Soul Brother and Other Poems*. Enugu, Nigeria: Nwankwo-Ifejika & Co., 1971.

————. "The Black Writer's Burden." *Présence Africaine*, Eng. ed., No. 59 (3d Quarter 1966), pp. 135-40.

————. "Chinua Achebe on Biafra." *Transition*, No. 36 (1968), pp. 31-37.

————. "English and the African Writer." *Transition*, No. 18 (1965), pp. 27-30.

————. *Girls at War*. London: Heinemann, 1972.

————. *A Man of the People*. Garden City, N.Y.: Doubleday & Co., 1967. (First published 1966.)

————. Review of *This Earth, My Brother* . . . (Kofi Awoonor). *Transition*, No. 41 (1972), pp. 69-70.

————. *No Longer at Ease*. London: Heinemann, 1963. (First published 1960.)

————. "The Role of the Writer in a New Nation." *Nigeria Magazine*, No. 81 (June 1964), pp. 157-60.

————. *The Sacrificial Egg and Other Stories*. Onitsha: Etudo Ltd., 1962.

————. *Things Fall Apart*. New York: Astor-Honor, n.d. (First published 1958.)

————. "What Do African Intellectuals Read?" *Times Literary Supplement*, 12 May 1972, p. 547.

297

Afrifa, Akwasi Amankwa. *The Ghana Coup, 24th February 1966* (preface by K. A. Busia). London: Cass, 1966.

Ajala, Olabisi. *An African Abroad.* London: Jarrolds, 1963.

Ajao, Aderogba. *On the Tiger's Back.* Cleveland: World Publishing Co., 1962.

Akiga, Benjamin. *Akiga's Story: The Tiv Tribe as Seen by One of Its Members*, trans. and annotated by Rupert East, 2d ed. London: Oxford Univ. Press for the International African Institute, 1965.

———, *see* also Westermann, ed., *Autobiographies d'Africains.*

Akou, Martin, *see* Westermann, ed., *Autobiographies d'Africains.*

Akpabio, Udo, *see* Perham, ed., *Ten Africans.*

Amadasou, Igbinokpoguié, *see* Westermann, ed., *Autobiographies d'Africains.*

Amar, Andrew. *A Student in Moscow.* London: Ampersand, 1961.

Amory, Mark. "The King Who Died in Bermondsey." (London) *Sunday Times Magazine*, 22 October 1972, pp. 22-41.

Anozie, Sunday O. "Le nouveau roman africain." *The Conch*, 2 (March 1970), pp. 29-32. (On *Le devoir de violence* and *The Beautyful Ones Are Not Yet Born*.)

Antera Duke, *see* Forde, Daryll.

Anti-Taylor, William. *Moscow Diary.* London: Robert Hale, 1967.

Armah, Ayi Kwei. *The Beautyful Ones Are Not Yet Born.* London: Heinemann, 1969.

Awolowo, (Chief) Obafemi. *Awo: The Autobiography of Chief Obafemi Awolowo.* Cambridge: Cambridge Univ. Press, 1960.

———. *My Early Life.* Lagos: John West Publications, 1968. (Coincides with first nine chapters of *Awo*.)

Awoonor, Kofi. *This Earth, My Brother. . . : An Allegorical Tale of Africa.* Garden City, N. Y.: Doubleday & Co., 1971.

Awouma, Joseph. "Le conte africain et la société traditionelle." *Présence Africaine*, NS No. 66 (2e trimestre 1968), pp. 137-44.

Azikiwe, Nnamdi. *My Odyssey: An Autobiography*. London: C. Hurst & Co., 1970.

B., A. "Afrique Noire, littérature rose." *Présence Africaine*, NS Nos. 1-2 (avril-juillet 1955), pp. 133-45.

Baba of Karo, *see* Smith, Mary F.

Barnett, Donald L. and Karari Njama. *Mau Mau from Within; Autobiography and Analysis of Kenya's Peasant Revolt*. New York: Monthly Review Press, 1966.

Beier, Ulli. "In Search of an African Personality." *The Twentieth Century*, 165 (April 1959), pp. 343-49.

————, ed. *Introduction to African Literature: An Anthology of Critical Writing from "Black Orpheus."* London: Longmans, 1967.

Bello, Alhaji Sir Ahmadu, Sardauna of Sokoto. *My Life*. Cambridge: Cambridge Univ. Press, 1962.

*Bernard Dadié: écrivain ivoirien*, textes commentés par Roger Mercier et M. et S. Battestini. Paris: Fernand Nathan, 1964.

Beselow, Thomas E. *From the Darkness of Africa to the Light of America*. Boston: Frank Wood, 1891.

Blacking, John. *Black Background: The Childhood of a South African Girl; Based on the Autobiography of Dora Thizwilondi Magidi* (pseud.). New York: Abelard-Schuman, 1964.

Boetie, Dugmore. *Familiarity is the Kingdom of the Lost*, ed. Barney Simon. New York: E. P. Dutton & Co., 1969.

Bonne, *see* Nii Kwabena Bonne III.

Bozeman, Adda B. *The Future of Law in a Multicultural World*. Princeton: Princeton Univ. Press, 1971.

Brench, A. C. "Camara Laye: Idealist and Mystic." *African Literature Today*, No. 2 (January 1969), pp. 11-31.

————. *The Novelist's Inheritance in French Africa*. London: Oxford Univ. Press, 1967.

Burness, Donald. "Six Responses to Apartheid." *Présence Africaine*, NS No. 76 (4th Quarter 1970), pp. 82-95.

Bwembya, *see* Perham, ed., *Ten Africans*.

Camara, Laye, *see* Laye, Camara.

*Camara Laye: écrivain guinéen*, textes commentés par Roger Mercier et M. et S. Battestini. Paris: Fernand Nathan, 1964.

Cartey, Wilfred. *Whispers from a Continent: The Literature of Contemporary Black Africa*. New York: Random House, 1969.

Clark, John Pepper. *America, Their America*. London: Heinemann, 1968. (First published 1964.)

————. *The Example of Shakespeare*. London: Longmans, 1970.

Clark, Leon E., comp. *Through African Eyes: Cultures in Change*, 6 vols. New York: Praeger, 1970-1971.

Coka, Gilbert, *see* Perham, ed., *Ten Africans*.

Cole, Ernest, with Thomas Flaherty. *House of Bondage*. New York: Random House, 1967.

Cole, Robert Wellesley. *Kossoh Town Boy*. Cambridge: Cambridge Univ. Press, 1960.

Conton, William. *The African*. London: Heinemann, 1964. (First published 1960.)

Crowther, Samuel. *Journal of an Expedition up the Niger and Tshadda Rivers Undertaken by Macgregor Laird in connection with the British Government in 1854*, 2d ed. London: Frank Cass & Co., 1970.

————. *Journals of the Rev. James Frederick Schön and Mr. Samuel Crowther who, With the Sanction of Her Majesty's Government, accompanied the Expedition up the Niger in 1841 on behalf of the Church Missionary Society*, 2d ed. London: Frank Cass & Co., 1970. (Includes, as an appendix, the first narrative of Crowther's early life.)

Crozier, Brian. "Six Africans in Search of a Personality." *Encounter*, 16, No. 5 (May 1961), pp. 37-45.

"Cultural Days on South Africa: A Symposium." *Présence Africaine*, NS No. 80 (4th Quarter 1971), pp. 111-36. (Includes Alex La Guma, "The Condition of Culture in South Africa"; Arthur Maimane, "Can't You Write About Anyting [sic] Else?"; Edward Ngaloshe, "Economics and Apartheid"; Lionel Ngakane, "The Cinema in South Africa"; Gerard Sekoto, "The Present Situation of a Non-White Artist in South Africa.")

Curtin, Philip D., ed. *Africa Remembered: Narratives by West Africans from the Era of the Slave Trade*. Madison: Univ. of Wisconsin Press, 1967.

Dadié, Bernard. *Légendes et poèmes*. Paris: Seghers, 1966. (Includes *Climbié*.)

———. *Patron de New York*. Paris: Présence Africaine, 1964.

d'Almeida, Damien. *Le jumeau; ou mon enfance à Agoué*. Cotonu: Les Éditions du Bénin, 1966.

Dathorne, O. R. and Willfried Feuser, eds. *Africa in Prose*. Harmondsworth, Middlesex: Penguin, 1969.

David, Jay and Helise Harrington, eds. *Growing Up African*. New York: William Morrow & Co., 1971.

Davidson, Basil. *Africa in History: Themes and Outlines*. New York: Macmillan, 1969.

———. *The African Past: Chronicles from Antiquity to Modern Times*. Boston: Little, Brown & Co., 1964.

Dei-Anang, Michael. "La culture africaine comme base d'une manière d'écriture originale." *Présence Africaine*, NS Nos. 27-28 (août-novembre 1959), pp. 5-10.

Delf, George. *Jomo Kenyatta: Towards Light about "The Light of Kenya."* Garden City, N.Y.: Doubleday & Co., 1961.

"Diallo, Georges" (le Révérend Père Georges Janssens). *La nuit du destin*. Mulhouse: Éditions Salvator, 1969.

Dinesen, Isak. *Out of Africa*. New York: Random House, 1938.

Diop, Birago. *Les contes d'Amadou-Koumba*, 3d ed. Paris: Présence Africaine, 1969.

————. *Les nouveaux contes d'Amadou Koumba* (préface de Léopold Senghor). Paris: Présence Africaine, 1958.

Diop, Cheikh Anta. *L'unité culturelle de l'Afrique Noire: Domaines du patriarcat et du matriarcat dans l'antiquité classique*. Paris: Présence Africaine, 1959.

Dipoko, Mbella Sonne. "My People." *Présence Africaine*, NS No. 73 (1st Quarter 1970), pp. 148-55.

Dogbeh-David, G. Richard. *Voyage au pays de Lénine. Notes de voyage d'un écrivain africain en URSS.* Yaoundé: Éditions CLE, 1967.

Drachler, Jacob, ed. *African Heritage*. New York: Collier-Macmillan, 1964.

Duerden, Dennis and Cosmo Pieterse, eds. *African Writers Talking: A Collection of Interviews*. London: Heinemann, 1972.

Duke, Antera, *see* Forde, Daryll.


East, Rupert, *see* Akiga, Benjamin.

Edwards, Paul and David R. Carroll. "An Approach to the Novel in West Africa." *Phylon*, 23 (Winter 1962), pp. 319-31.

Emenyonu, Ernest. "African Literature: What does it take to be its critic?" *African Literature Today*, No. 5 (1971), pp. 1-11.

Enahoro, (Chief) Anthony. *Fugitive Offender: The Story of a Political Prisoner*. London: Cassell, 1965.

"Entretien avec Camara Laye." *Afrique*, No. 26 (juillet 1963), pp. 54-57.

"Entretien avec Cheikh Hamidou Kane." *Afrique*, No. 16 (septembre 1962), pp. 64-65.

"Entretien avec Chinua Achebe." *Afrique*, No. 27 (octobre 1963), pp. 41-42.

Equiano, Olaudah. *The Interesting Narrative of the Life of Olaudah Equiano, or Gustavus Vassa, the African. Written by Himself*, 2 vols. London: Printed for and sold by the Author, 1789. (First ed. reprinted with a new introduction by Paul Edwards [London: Dawsons of Pall Mall, 1969].)

Faye, N. G. M. *Le débrouillard.* Paris: Gallimard, 1964.

Feldmann, Susan, ed. *African Myths and Tales,* new ed. New York: Dell Publishing Co., 1970.

Finnegan, Ruth. *Oral Literature in Africa.* Oxford: Clarendon Press, 1970.

Fischer, Stanley L. "Africa: Mother and Muse." *Antioch Review,* 21 (Fall 1961), pp. 305-18.

Foli, Boniface, *see* Westermann, ed., *Autobiographies d'Africains.*

Forde, Daryll and G. I. Jones. *The Ibo and Ibibio-speaking Peoples of South-eastern Nigeria.* London: Oxford Univ. Press for the International African Institute, 1950.

Forde, Daryll, ed. *Efik Traders of Old Calabar, Containing the Diary of Antera Duke, an Efik Slave-Trading Chief of the eighteenth century.* London: Oxford Univ. Press for the International African Institute, 1956.

Fox, Lorene K., ed. *East African Childhood: Three Versions* (written by Joseph A. Lijembe, Anna Apoko, and J. Mutuku Nzioko). Nairobi: Oxford Univ. Press, 1967.

Gabousou, Fritz, *see* Westermann, ed., *Autobiographies d'Africains.*

Gatheru, R. Mugo. *Child of Two Worlds.* London: Routledge & Kegan Paul, 1964.

Gecaga, B. Mareka. *Home Life in Kikuyu-Land, or Kariuki and Muthoni.* Nairobi: The Eagle Press, 1949.

Gicaru, Muga. *Land of Sunshine: Scenes of Life in Kenya before Mau Mau.* London: Lawrence & Wishart, 1958.

Gleason, Judith. *This Africa: Novels by West Africans in English and French.* Evanston, Ill.: Northwestern Univ. Press, 1965.

Greenberg, Joseph. *The Languages of Africa.* Bloomington: Indiana Univ. Press, 1963.

303

Gronniosaw, James Albert Ukawsaw. *A Narrative of the Most Remarkable Particulars in the Life of James Albert Ukawsaw Gronniosaw, An African Prince, Written by Himself.* Bath: S. Southwick, in Queen Street, 1774.

Gueye, Lamine. *Itinéraire africain.* Paris: Présence Africaine, 1966.

Hama, Boubou. *Kotia-Nima,* 3 vols. Paris: Présence Africaine, 1968-1969.

Hassan, Malam (Sarkin Ruwa, Abuja) and Malam Shuaibu (Mukaddamin Makarantar, Bida). *A Chronicle of Abuja,* trans. F. L. Heath. Ibadan: Ibadan Univ. Press for the Abuja Native Administration, 1952.

Hassani, Rashid Bin, *see* Perham, ed., *Ten Africans.*

Hevi, Emmanuel John. *An African Student in China.* New York: Frederick A. Praeger, 1963.

Heywood, Christopher, ed. *Perspectives on African Literature.* London: Heinemann, in association with Univ. of Ife Press, 1971.

Hodgkin, Thomas, ed. *Nigerian Perspectives.* London: Oxford Univ. Press, 1960.

Hughes, Langston, ed. *An African Treasury.* New York: Crown Publishers, 1960.

————, ed. *Poems from Black Africa.* Bloomington: Indiana Univ. Press, 1963.

Hutchinson, Alfred. *Road to Ghana.* New York: John Day Co., 1960.

*The Insider: Stories of War and Peace from Nigeria.* Enugu, Nigeria: Nwankwo-Ifejika & Co., 1971. (Includes "The Madman" by Chinua Achebe.)

Itote, Waruhiu (General China). *"Mau Mau" General.* Nairobi: East African Publishing House, 1967.

Jabavu, Noni. *Drawn in Colour: African Contrasts.* London: John Murray, 1960.

————. *The Ochre People: Scenes from a South African Life*. New York: St. Martin's Press, 1963.

Jahn, Janheinz. *Muntu: An Outline of the New African Culture*. New York: Grove Press, 1961.

————. *Neo-African Literature: A History of Black Writing*. New York: Grove Press, 1968.

———— and Claus Peter Dressler, comps. *Bibliography of Creative African Writing*. Nendeln, Liechtenstein: Kraus-Thomson, 1971.

Jones, Eldred. "Jungle Drums and Wailing Piano: West African Fiction and Poetry in English." *African Forum*, 1, No. 4 (Spring 1966), pp. 93-106.


Kabaka of Buganda, *see* Mutesa II, the Kabaka of Buganda.

Kadalie, Clements. *My Life and the ICU: The Autobiography of a Black Trade Unionist in South Africa*. New York: Humanities Press, 1970.

Kane, Cheikh Hamidou. *Ambiguous Adventure*, trans. Katherine Woods. New York: Collier-Macmillan, 1969. (First published 1962 as *L'aventure ambiguë*.)

Kane, Mohamadou. "The African Writer and His Public." *Présence Africaine*, Eng. ed., No. 58 (2d Quarter 1966), pp. 10-32.

Kariuki, Joseph. *Ode to Mzee*. Nairobi: Chemchemi Cultural Center, 1964.

Kariuki, Josiah Mwangi. *"Mau Mau" Detainee: The Account by a Kenya African of his Experiences in Detention Camps 1953–1960*. London: Oxford Univ. Press, 1963.

Kaunda, Kenneth. *Zambia Shall Be Free: An Autobiography*. London: Heinemann, 1962.

Kayira, Legson (Didimu). *I Will Try*. Garden City, N.Y.: Doubleday & Co., 1965.

————. *The Looming Shadow*. Garden City, N.Y.: Doubleday & Co., 1967.

Kenyatta, Jomo. *Facing Mount Kenya: The Tribal Life of the Gikuyu*. New York: Random House-Vintage, n.d. (First published 1938.)

———. *Harambee: The Prime Minister of Kenya's Speeches 1963–1964*. Nairobi: Oxford Univ. Press, 1964.

———. "Kikuyu Religion, Ancestor-worship, and Sacrificial Practices." *Africa*, 10, No. 3 (July 1937), 308-28.

———. *My People of Kikuyu*. Nairobi: Oxford Univ. Press, 1966. (First published 1942; republished with new introduction 1966.)

———. *Suffering without Bitterness: The Founding of the Kenya Nation*. Nairobi: East African Publishing House, 1968.

Kesteloot, Lilyan. *Les écrivains noirs de langue française: naissance d'une littérature*. Bruxelles: Université Libre de Bruxelles, 1963.

Killam, Gordon D. *The Novels of Chinua Achebe*. London: Heinemann, 1969.

Kirk-Greene, Anthony and Paul Newman, trans. *West African Travels and Adventures: Two Autobiographical Narratives from Northern Nigeria*. New Haven: Yale Univ. Press, 1971. (Autobiographies of Dorugu and Maimaina of Jega, Chief of Askira.)

"Kofi Awoonor: An Interview," conducted by John Goldblatt. *Transition*, No. 41 (1972), pp. 42-44.

Kumalo, Ndansi, *see* Perham, ed., *Ten Africans*.

Kwami, Madame Marthe Aféwélé, *see* Westermann, ed., *Autobiographies d'Africains*.


Larson, Charles R. *The Emergence of African Fiction*, rev. ed. Bloomington: Indiana Univ. Press, 1972.

Laude, Jean. *Les arts de l'Afrique noire*. Paris: Librairie Générale Française, 1966.

Laye, Camara. *The Dark Child*, trans. James Kirkup and Ernest Jones. New York: Noonday Press, 1954.

———. *A Dream of Africa*, trans. James Kirkup. New York:

Collier-Macmillan, 1971. (First published 1966 as *Dramouss.*)

————. *L'enfant noir.* Paris: Presses de la cité, n.d. (First published 1953.)

————. "Et demain?" *Présence Africaine,* Nos. 14-15 (juin-septembre 1957), pp. 290-95.

————. *The Radiance of the King,* trans. James Kirkup. New York: Collier-Macmillan, 1971. (First published 1956 as *Le regard du roi.*)

————. "Les yeux de la statue." *Présence Africaine,* NS No. 13 (avril-mai 1957), pp. 102-10.

Leigh, Ione. *In the Shadow of Mau Mau.* London: W. H. Allen, 1954.

Lindfors, Bernth. "Achebe's African Parable." *Présence Africaine,* NS No. 66 (2d Quarter 1968), pp. 130-36.

———— et al., eds. *Palaver: Interviews with Five African Writers in Texas.* Austin: African and Afro-American Research Institute of The Univ. of Texas at Austin, 1972.

LoBagola, B.K.A. ibn. *LoBagola: An African Savage's Own Story.* New York: Alfred A. Knopf, 1930.

Luthuli, (Chief) Albert. *Let My People Go.* New York: McGraw-Hill, 1962.


Maes-Jelinek, Hans. "Yambo Ouologuem, *Le devoir de violence.*" *African Literature Today,* No. 4 (1970), pp. 54-55.

Magidi, Dora Thizwilondi (pseud.), *see* Blacking, John.

Mahmoûd Kati, *see Tarikh el-Fettach.*

Major, Joseph N. *Forever a Stranger.* New York: Carlton Press, 1969.

"Malian Prizewinner." *West Africa,* No. 2689 (December 14, 1968), pp. 1,474-75.

Maquet, Jacques. *Africanité traditionelle et moderne.* Paris: Présence Africaine, 1967.

Matshikiza, Todd. *Chocolates for My Wife*. London: Hodder & Staughton, 1961.

Maurois, André. *Aspects of Biography*. New York: D. Appleton & Co., 1929.

Mazrui, Ali A. "Africa and the Crisis of Relevance in Modern Culture." *Présence Africaine*, NS No. 72 (4th Quarter 1969), pp. 9-20.

Mbiti, John S. *African Religions and Philosophy*. Garden City, N.Y.: Doubleday & Co., 1970.

Mboya, Tom. *Freedom and After*. Boston: Little, Brown & Co., 1963.

McDonald, Robert. "*Bound to Violence*: A Case of Plagiarism." *Transition*, No. 41 (1972), pp. 64-68.

McHardy, Cécile. "Love in Africa." *Présence Africaine*, NS No. 68 (4th Quarter 1968), pp. 52-60.

Mdumi, Martin Kayamba, *see* Perham, ed., *Ten Africans*.

Melone, Thomas. *De la négritude dans la littérature négro-africaine*. Paris: Présence Africaine, 1962.

Mockerie, Parmenas, *see* Perham, ed., *Ten Africans*.

Modisane, Bloke (William). *Blame Me on History*. London: Thames & Hudson, 1963.

Modupe, Prince. *I Was a Savage*. London: Museum Press, 1958. (Reissued in a revised ed. in the U.S. as *A Royal African* [New York: Frederick A. Praeger, 1969].)

Mohome, Paulus. "Negritude: Evaluation and Elaboration." *Présence Africaine*, NS No. 68 (4th Quarter 1968), pp. 122-40.

Mokgatle, Naboth. *The Autobiography of an Unknown South African*. Berkeley and Los Angeles: Univ. of California Press, 1971.

Moore, Gerald. "Action and Freedom in Two African Novels." *The Conch*, 2 (March 1970), pp. 21-28. (Discussion of *Le devoir de violence* and *The Beautyful Ones Are Not Yet Born*.)

————. *The Chosen Tongue: English Writing in the Tropical World*. London: Longmans, Green & Co., 1969.

308

————. "English Words, African Lives." *Présence Africaine,* Eng. ed., No. 54 (2d Quarter 1965), pp. 90-101.

————. *Seven African Writers.* London: Oxford Univ. Press, 1962.

————. "Time and Experience in African Poetry." *Transition,* No. 26 (1966), pp. 18-22.

————, ed. *African Literature and the Universities.* Ibadan: Ibadan Univ. Press for The Congress for Cultural Freedom, 1965.

———— and Ulli Beier, eds. *Modern Poetry from Africa.* Harmondsworth, Middlesex: Penguin, 1968.

Moore, Kofoworola Aina, *see* Perham, ed., *Ten Africans.*

Mphahlele, Ezekiel. *The African Image.* New York: Frederick A. Praeger, 1962.

————. "African Literature: What Tradition?" *University of Denver Quarterly,* 2, No. 2 (Summer 1967), pp. 36-68.

————. "Debris, Driftwood and Purpose." *Africa Today,* 18, No. 2 (April 1971), pp. 67-71. (Review of Dugmore Boetie's *Familiarity is the Kingdom of the Lost* and Dennis Brutus' *Poems from Algiers.*)

————. *Down Second Avenue.* London: Faber & Faber, 1959.

————. *In Corner B.* Nairobi: East African Publishing House, 1967.

————. "The Language of African Literature." *Harvard Educational Review,* 34, No. 2 (Spring 1964), pp. 298-305.

————. *The Wanderers.* New York: Macmillan, 1971.

————, ed. *African Writing Today.* Harmondsworth, Middlesex: Penguin, 1967.

Mpondo, Simon. "Provisional Notes on Literature and Criticism in Africa." *Présence Africaine,* NS No. 78 (2d Quarter 1971), pp. 118-42.

Mqhayi, Samuel Edward Kgouné, *see* Westermann, ed., *Autobiographies d'Africains.*

309

Mtiva, Christophe, *see* Westermann, ed., *Autobiographies d'Africains.*

Mugo wa Gatheru, *see* Gatheru, Mugo.

Mukasa, Ham. *The Story of Ham Mukasa, told by himself,* trans. by Archdeacon Walker. London: Church Missionary Society, 1904. (Added to *The Wonderful Story of Uganda* by J. D. Mullins.)

————. *Uganda's Katikiro in England: being the official account of his visit to the Coronation of His Majesty King Edward VII,* trans. and ed. by the Rev. E. Millar. London: Hutchinson & Co., 1904.

Murdock, George P. *Africa: Its Peoples and Their Culture History.* New York: McGraw-Hill, 1959.

Murray-Brown, Jeremy. *Kenyatta.* London: George Allen & Unwin, 1972.

Mutesa II, Sir Edward Frederick William Walugembe Mutebi Luwangula Mutesa, Kabaka of Buganda. *Desecration of My Kingdom.* London: Constable, 1967.


N'Diayé, Bokar. *Les castes au Mali.* Bamako: Éditions Populaires, 1970.

Ngugi wa Thiong'o (James Ngugi). *A Grain of Wheat.* London: Heinemann, 1968. (First published 1967.)

————. *Homecoming: Essays on African and Caribbean Literature, Culture and Politics.* London: Heinemann, 1972.

————. *The River Between.* London: Heinemann, 1965.

————. *Weep Not, Child.* New York: Collier-Macmillan, 1969. (First published 1964.)

Niane, Djibril Tamsir. *Recherches sur l'empire du Mali au moyen âge.* Conakry: République de Guinée, Ministère de l'Information et du Tourisme, 1962.

————. *Sundiata: an epic of old Mali,* trans. G. D. Pickett. London: Longmans, 1965.

Nicol, Davidson (Abioseh). *Africa: A Subjective View.* London: Longmans, Green & Co., 1964.

Nii Kwabena Bonne III. *Milestones in the History of the Gold Coast: Autobiography of Nii Kwabena Bonne III, Osu Alata Mantse, also Nana Owusu Akenten III, Oyokohene of Techiman Ashanti.* London: Diplomatist Publications, 1953.

Njama, Karari, *see* Barnett, Donald L.

Njururi, Ngumbu, comp. *Agikuyu Folk Tales.* London: Oxford Univ. Press, 1966.

Nketia, J. H. Kwabena. "The Language Problem and the African Personality." *Présence Africaine*, NS No. 67 (3d Quarter 1968), pp. 157-71.

Nkosi, Lewis. "Conversation with Chinua Achebe." *Africa Report*, 9 No. 7 (July 1964), pp. 19-21.

———. "Conversation with Ezekiel Mphahlele." *Africa Report*, 9, No. 7 (July 1964), pp. 8-9.

———. *Home and Exile.* London: Longmans, Green & Co., 1965.

Nkrumah, Kwame. *Dark Days in Ghana.* New York: International Publishers, 1968.

———. *Ghana: The Autobiography of Kwame Nkrumah.* London: Nelson, 1959. (First published 1957.)

Nolen, Barbara, ed. *Africa Is People: Firsthand Accounts from Contemporary Africa.* New York: Dutton, 1967.

Nosente, *see* Perham, ed., *Ten Africans.*

Nyabongo, Akiki K. *The Story of an African Chief.* New York: Charles Scribner's Sons, 1935. (Published in London by G. Routledge & Sons [1936] as *Africa Answers Back* by H. H. Prince Akiki K. Nyabongo.)

Nyandeni, Mazwimabi, *see* Westermann, ed., *Autobiographies d'Africains.*

Nyerere, Julius K. *Ujamaa—Essays on Socialism.* Dar es Salaam: Oxford Univ. Press, 1968.

Nzekwu, Onuora. *Wand of Noble Wood.* New York: New American Library, 1963. (First published 1961.)

Obiechina, Emmanuel N., ed. *Onitsha Market Literature.* London: Heinemann, 1972.

Odinga, Oginga. *Not Yet Uhuru*. London: Heinemann, 1967.

Ojike, Mbonu. *I Have Two Countries*. New York: John Day Co., 1947.

———. *My Africa*. New York: John Day Co., 1946.

———. *Portrait of a Boy in Africa*. New York: East and West Association, 1945. (Condensation of a section of *My Africa*.)

Okafor-Omali, Dilim. *A Nigerian Villager in Two Worlds*. London: Faber & Faber, 1965.

*Okike: A Nigerian Journal of New Writing*, ed. Chinua Achebe. (No. 1 [1972] includes "Three Poems" and "Vengeful Creditor, a short story" and No. 2 [also 1972] includes "Civil Peace," all by Achebe.)

Okpaku, Joseph. "Tradition, Culture and Criticism." *Présence Africaine*, NS No. 70 (2d Quarter 1969), pp. 137-46.

Olney, James. *Metaphors of Self: The Meaning of Autobiography*. Princeton: Princeton Univ. Press, 1972.

Osahon, Naiwu. *The Climate of Darkness*. Lagos: Di Nigro Press, 1971.

Ouologuem, Yambo. *Bound to Violence*, trans. Ralph Manheim. New York: Harcourt Brace Jovanovich, 1971.

———. *Le devoir de violence*. Paris: Éditions du Seuil, 1968.

———. *Lettre à la France Nègre*. Paris: Éditions Edmond Nalis, 1968.

———. "Marx et l'étrangeté d'un socialisme africain." *Présence Africaine*, NS No. 50 (2e trimestre 1964), pp. 20-37. (Signed "Yambo.")

———. *Les milles et une bibles du sexe*. Paris: Éditions du Dauphin, 1969. (Written under pseudonym of Utto Rodolph.)

———. Review of *Patron de New York* (Bernard Dadié). *Présence Africaine*, NS No. 53 (1er trimestre 1965), pp. 255-58.

————. Six poems in *Nouvelle somme de poésie du monde noir*, special number of *Présence Africaine*, NS No. 57 (1er trimestre 1966), pp. 88-95. (Poems are "Au milieu des Solitudes," "Passage humain," "Quand parlent les dents nègres," "Le Souffle du Guerrier," "Requiem pour une Négresse," and "A mon mari.")

Pageard, Robert. *Littérature négro-africaine; Le mouvement littéraire contemporain dans l'Afrique Noire d'expression française*. Paris: le livre africain, 1966.

————. "Soundiata Keita et la tradition orale." *Présence Africaine*, NS No. 35 (1er trimestre 1961), pp. 51-70.

Palmer, Eustace. *An Introduction to the African Novel*. London: Heinemann, 1972.

*Pan-Africanism Reconsidered*. Berkeley and Los Angeles: Univ. of California Press, 1962. (Papers from the Third Annual Conference of the American Society of African Culture; includes comments by Mphahlele on *négritude*.)

p'Bitek, Okot. "The Self in African Imagery." *Transition*, No. 15 (1964), pp. 32-35.

Perham, Margery, ed. *Ten Africans: A Collection of Life Stories*, 2d ed. London: Faber & Faber, 1963. (First published 1936.)

Pieterse, Cosmo and Donald Munro, eds. *Protest and Conflict in African Literature*. London: Heinemann, 1969.

Press, John, ed. *Commonwealth Literature: Unity and Diversity in a Common Culture*. London: Heinemann, 1965. (Includes Chinua Achebe's "The Novelist as Teacher," pp. 201-05.)

Pritt, D. N. *The Autobiography of D. N. Pritt*, 3 vols. London: Lawrence & Wishart, 1965-1966.

Reed, John. "Between Two Worlds: Some notes on the presentation by African novelists of the individual in modern African society." *Makerere Journal*, No. 7 (1962-1963), pp. 1-14.

Rive, Richard, ed. *Quartet: New Voices from South Africa*. London: Heinemann, 1965.

Rodolph, Utto, *see* Ouologuem, Yambo.

Saidi, Amini Bin, *see* Perham, ed., *Ten Africans*.

Sainville, Léonard. "Le roman et ses responsabilités." *Présence Africaine*, NS No. 27-28 (août-novembre 1959), pp. 37-50.

Samba, *see* Westermann, ed., *Autobiographies d'Africains*.

Sardauna of Sokoto, *see* Bello, Alhaji Sir Ahmadu.

Sartre, Jean-Paul. *Black Orpheus*, trans. S. W. Allen. Paris: Présence Africaine, n.d.

Seid, Joseph Brahim. *Un enfant du Tchad*. Paris: Sagerep L'Afrique Actuelle, 1967.

Sekoto, Gerard. "Autobiography." *Présence Africaine*, NS No. 69 (1st Quarter 1969), pp. 188-94.

Sellassie, Sahle. *Shinega's Village: Scenes of Ethiopian Life*. Berkeley and Los Angeles: Univ. of California Press, 1964.

Sellin, Eric. "Ouologuem's Blueprint for *Le devoir de violence*." *Research in African Literatures*, 2 (Fall 1971), pp. 117-20.

Selormey, Francis. *The Narrow Path*. London: Heinemann, 1967. (First published 1966.)

Senghor, Léopold Sédar. "L'esprit de la civilisation ou les lois de la culture négro-africaine." *Présence Africaine*, Nos. 8-10 (juin-novembre 1956), pp. 51-65.

———. *Liberté I: Négritude et Humanisme*. Paris: Éditions du Seuil, 1964.

———. "On Negrohood: Psychology of the African Negro." *Diogenes*, No. 37 (Spring 1962), pp. 1-15.

Shuaibu, Malam, *see* Hassan, Malam.

Simpson, Clarence L. *The Memoirs of C. L. Simpson, Former Liberian Ambassador to Washington and to the Court of St. James's*. London: Diplomatic Press & Publishing Co., 1961.

Sithole, Ndabaningi. *African Nationalism*, 2d ed. London: Oxford Univ. Press, 1968.

Siwundhla, Alice Princess (Msumba). *Alice Princess: An Autobiography*. Mountain View, Calif.: Pacific Press Publishing Assn., 1965.

Slater, Montagu. *The Trial of Jomo Kenyatta*. London: Mercury Books, 1965. (First published 1955.)

Smith, Mary F. *Baba of Karo: A Woman of the Muslim Hausa*. New York: Philosophical Library, 1955.

Smith, Venture. *A Narrative of the Life and Adventures of Venture, A Native of Africa, But Resident Above Sixty Years in the United States of America. Related by Himself*. Middletown, Conn.: J. B. Stewart, 1897. ("New London: Printed in 1798. Reprinted A.D. 1835, and Published by a Descendant of Venture. Revised and Republished with Traditions by H. M. Selden, Haddam, Conn., 1896.")

"Something *New* from Africa?" *Times Literary Supplement*, 5 May 1972, p. 525.

Soyinka, Wole. "From a Common Back Cloth: A Reassessment of the African Literary Image." *American Scholar*, 32 (Summer 1963), pp. 387-96.

————. *The Interpreters*. London: André Deutsch, 1965.

————. *The Man Died: Prison Notes of Wole Soyinka*. London: Rex Collings, 1972.

————. "The Writer in an African State." *Transition*, No. 31 (June/July 1967), pp. 11-13.

Stoneham, C. T. *Mau Mau*. London: Museum Press, 1953.

Taiwo, Oladele. *An Introduction to West African Literature*. London: Nelson, 1967.

*Tarikh el-Fettach, ou Chronique du chercheur pour servir à l'histoire des villes, des armées et des principaux personnages du Tekrour*, par Mahmoûd Kâti ben El-Hâdj El-Motaouakkel Kâti et l'un de ses petit-fils, traduction française par O. Houdas et M. Delafosse. Paris: Li-

*Tarikh el-Fettach* (*cont.*)
brairie d'Amérique et d'Orient, Adrien-Maisonneuve, 1964. (Photographic reproduction "de l'édition originale datée de 1913-1914.")

*Tarikh es-Soudan*, par Abderrahman ben Abdallah ben 'Imran ben 'Amir es-Sa'di, traduit de l'Arabe par O. Houdas. Paris: Librairie d'Amérique et d'Orient Adrien-Maisonneuve, 1964. ("Reproduction photographique de l'édition originale datée de 1898-1900.")

Tempels, Placide. *Bantu Philosophy*. Paris: Présence Africaine, 1959.

Thompson, John. "In Africa." *New York Review of Books*, 23 September 1971, pp. 3-7.

Tucker, Martin. *Africa in Modern Literature: A Survey of Contemporary Writing in English*. New York: Frederick Ungar, 1967.

Turnbull, Colin. *The Lonely African*. New York: Simon & Schuster, 1962.

Uchendu, Victor C. *The Igbo of Southeast Nigeria*. New York: Holt, Rinehart & Winston, 1966.

Umeasiegbu, Rems Nna. *The Way We Lived: Ibo Customs and Stories*. London: Heinemann, 1969.

Ushpol, Rowse. *A Select Bibliography of South African Autobiographies*. Cape Town: Univ. of Cape Town, 1958.

Waciuma, Charity. *Daughter of Mumbi*. Nairobi: East African Publishing House, 1969.

Wake, C. H. "African Literary Criticism." *Comparative Literature Studies*, 1, No. 3 (1964), pp. 197-205.

Wali, Obiajunwa. "The Individual and the Novel in Africa." *Transition*, No. 18 (1965), pp. 31-33.

Wästberg, Per, ed. *The Writer in Modern Africa*. Uppsala: The Scandinavian Institute of African Studies, 1968.

Watkins, Mel. "Interview with Yambo Ouologuem." *New York Times Book Review*, 7 March 1971, pp. 7 and 34.

Wauthier, Claude. *L'Afrique des Africains; inventaire de la négritude*. Paris: Éditions du Seuil, 1964.

Westermann, Diedrich, ed. *Autobiographies d'Africains: onze autobiographies d'indigènes originaires de diverses régions de l'Afrique et représentant des métiers et des degrés de culture différents*, traduction française de L. Homburger. Paris: Payot, 1943.

"The Writer and His World" (interview with Camara Laye conducted by J. Steven Rubin). *Africa Report*, 27, No. 5 (May 1972), pp. 20, 22, and 24.

"The Writer and His World" (interview with Chinua Achebe conducted by Ernest and Pat Emenyonu). *Africa Report*, 27, No. 5 (May 1972), pp. 21, 23, and 25-27.

Xkoou-Goa-Xob, *see* Westermann, ed., *Autobiographies d'Africains*.

Yambo, Ouologuem, *see* Ouologuem, Yambo.

Zell, Hans and Helene Silver, eds. *A Reader's Guide to African Literature*. London: Heinemann, 1972.

# Index

**Library of Congress Cataloging in Publication Data**

Olney, James.
  Tell Me Africa.

  Bibliography: p.
  1. African literature—History and criticism.
2. Africa—Social life and customs. I. Title.
II. Title: An approach to Africa literature.
PL8010.04        809′.8967        72-12111
ISBN 0-691-06254-4